THERE IS A BONNY FITBA TEAM

Ted Brack has lived most of his life in Edinburgh. He retired in 2007 after serving as a head teacher for thirty years and has written many freelance articles for Hibs fanzines and other publications. Married with four children and three grandchildren, Ted's greatest wish is to see Hibs finally win the Scottish Cup for the first time since 1902.

Robbie,

I believe that you are a football enthusiast with a 'soft spot' for Hibs.

I hope that you enjoy reading my book.

With Best Wishes

Ted Brack

THERE IS A BONNY FITBA TEAM

FIFTY YEARS ON THE HIBEE HIGHWAY

Ted Brack

BLACK & WHITE PUBLISHING

First published 2009
by Black & White Publishing Ltd
29 Ocean Drive, Edinburgh EH6 6JL

1 3 5 7 9 10 8 6 4 2   09 10 11 12 13

ISBN: 978 1 84502 255 6

Copyright © Ted Brack 2009

Typeset by Ellipsis Books Limited, Glasgow
Printed and bound by MPG Books Ltd, Bodmin

CONTENTS

ACKNOWLEDGEMENTS

When I decided to write this book, I imagined that it would be a labour of love. It was. I derived huge pleasure from recalling and recording so many Hibee memories. I also discovered that writing a memoir, enjoyable though it may be, is also rather hard work. I would like to thank a number of people who provided me with encouragement and support in equal measure as I undertook the task of chronicling more than fifty years of devotion to Hibernian Football Club.

Campbell Brown, Alison McBride and their colleagues at Black & White Publishing were always pleasant and positive, and their expertise in publishing matters helped me a great deal. My friends and extended family, almost all of whom, unsurprisingly, share my love of Easter Road's finest, took an interest in all that I was doing and spurred me on by telling me how much they were enjoying the early drafts of the book. My close family helped jog my memory and put me right when my recollections were not always fully accurate. They made me feel that I was achieving something worthwhile and I greatly appreciated the positive reinforcement which they supplied. Thanks then to Patrick, Lisa, Dominic and Kevin.

My wife Margaret does not give praise lightly. When she told me that the book was a great read, I knew that I was doing something right. I thank Margaret for all her support with *There is a Bonny Fitba Team* and for forty magnificent years of married life.

I am indebted to the great Pat Stanton for a kind and generous foreword. I also owe a vote of thanks to those other Hibee legends, Lawrie Reilly and Keith Wright, as well as former Chairman Tom O'Malley for their comments for the cover of the book. Tom also helped me in my quest to find the right publisher. Thanks too to Lawrie, Pat and Keith for joining me for the back cover photograph. My brother-in-law Brian Dishon took that photograph and I am grateful to him for doing so.

I also owe a thank you to Rod Petrie and all at Easter Road for their co-operation in allowing me to use our beloved ground for photographs and events to launch the book's publication.

Finally, may I thank all of you, my fellow Hibees, who have bought this book. I hope you enjoy reading it as much as I enjoyed writing it. I promise you that if Hibs do eventually win the Scottish Cup, I will begin writing the story of how they did it the very next day.

Sadly, one true Hibs fan who won't read this book is my friend Russell Mould who shared the journey to League Cup triumph with me in 1991. Russell died tragically at the age of forty-two, just days before Christmas 2008. His widow Heather and children Stuart and Catriona will read this book on his behalf. They will do so knowing that a little of Russell the Hibee lives on in my reminiscences.

Ted Brack

FOREWORD
BY PAT STANTON

Things happened during my football days, some good, some not so good, but to be invited to write the foreword for this book by Ted Brack is a wee bit special. I have known Ted for a long time, so when asked, I had no hesitation.

It helps to be a bit of a romantic when you follow the Hibs but Ted is a clever, hard-headed romantic with a great love of the club and its history. He also has a great knowledge of games and players and is able to recall events from the past which I had long forgotten.

Not many supporters get the chance to publish a book about their favourite football team and some may think that Ted would have written his story through green-tinted spectacles. This is certainly not the case. Ted Brack is totally honest in his appraisal of all things Hibernian and can be a hard critic of the club when he does not agree with its actions.

Being a fan of Hibs, or any other team for that matter, can be hard at times. When the team is doing well though that faithful support becomes worthwhile as you will gather from Ted's book, which makes great reading.

When a Hibs supporter gets a ticket for a game, he buys it. You don't sell it to him. There is a world of difference between the two. Ted Brack knows that difference and this comes through strongly in his excellent book, which is a must for all Hibs fans.

INTRODUCTION

Around two o'clock on Sunday, 18 March 2007, I walked through the swirling West of Scotland spring snow showers along the road leading to Scotland's national stadium at Hampden. There were six of us: my wife, my three sons, my daughter and myself, the Hibee-in-chief.

We were heading for the 2007 CIS Cup Final and we were united in obsession. That obsession was a lifelong commitment to the cause of Hibernian Football Club. It was an obsession which had brought some glorious highs but many more shattering disappointments. It was also an incurable condition. 'Once a Hibee always a Hibee' sums up the hold that Scotland's most romantic, but also most frustrating of clubs, has on those of us who were born to follow their fortunes.

My wife and I met on a Hibs supporters' bus. My children were brought up in the Hibee faith. They have young children of their own now and, no doubt, the latest generation of the Brack clan will also be hopelessly hooked on the fortunes of Leith's finest.

Robert Louis Stevenson once said that it is better to travel with hope than to arrive. This dictum has never rung truer than when applied to Hibs and Hampden.

I travelled with my late father to the Scottish Cup Final of 1958 to see Hibs take on Clyde. Clyde were a more powerful force in Scottish football then than they are now but I, like the many thousands of Hibs fans who made the pilgrimage west that day, did so with no lack of confidence. We had knocked the league champions Hearts out of the cup at Tynecastle with an epic 4–3 victory that featured four goals from a teenage scoring sensation called Joe Baker, and an unforgettable display of goalkeeping from Lawrie Leslie. We had then come from 2–1 down with minutes to go to beat Third Lanark 3–2 in the quarter-finals, and had capped it all by beating Rangers after a replay in the semi-final.

Surely at last the name of Hibernian was on the Scottish Cup? It wasn't of course. Clyde won 1–0 with a deflected goal in front of 97,000 supporters and all we Hibees dragged ourselves back to Edinburgh in a state of dismay and dis-belief. As we left the ground, my dad said to me 'Don't worry son, they'll win it next year.' They didn't win it the next year and fifty years on they still haven't won it.

Many times we Hibbies have trekked to Hampden for finals and semi-finals. There have been glorious exceptions, but usually we have returned defeated and disillusioned. Our opponents on this cold, grey afternoon in 2007 were Jim Jefferies' Kilmarnock, a team capable of beating anyone on their day. None of us were taking anything for granted. I am sure that while we knew we were more than capable of winning the match and the trophy, we also felt foreboding because we knew that no team was more liable to provide its supporters with a deflating anticlimax than our beloved Hibernian FC.

We needn't have worried. Sunday, 18 March 2007 was destined to be one of the rare, but unforgettable glory days, which Hibs serve up to their fans on a strictly limited basis. Our team won 5–1 and did so in style. All across the pitch we displayed class and commitment in equal measure and the result was a notable occasion in Hibernian history.

As we left the ground, eagerly anticipating the victory

celebrations back in Edinburgh and the party to follow, I couldn't have been happier if I had won the lottery and seen Hearts relegated on the same day. Walking through the delirious green and white hordes back to our coach, it dawned on me that this was what made supporting Hibs so special.

We could always snatch defeat from the jaws of victory, we would never be able to compete with the monolithic power and wealth of the Old Firm and we would continue to sell our best players. This was more than counterbalanced though by the fact that we would always attempt to play football in an exciting, attractive, attacking manner which, when it came off, gave us fans an unimaginable combination of pride and pleasure.

By the time our coach had reached the outskirts of Edinburgh, I had decided to write this book. I wanted to record what it was like to follow the same club for fifty years, knowing that your Saturday evening would be made or marred by the performance which preceded it on the Saturday afternoon.

This book gives me an opportunity to recall great victories against Barcelona and Real Madrid, share memories of classic derby day victories including, of course, the seven goal slaughter at Tynecastle which brought in the year of 1973, and reflect upon five cup-winning journeys to Hampden finals if I include the back-to-back Drybrough Cup wins over Celtic in 1972 and 1973.

I can also bring back to life the achievements of some of the greatest players who have graced the Scottish game. When I started to watch Hibs, four of the Famous Five were still with the club. Shortly afterwards the striking phenomenon that was Joe Baker arrived on the scene. I have never seen a better centre forward. The king of the 1960s was the incomparable Willie Hamilton. This mesmeric magician of an inside forward lost his battle with the bottle, but he rarely lost a duel on the football field.

The 1970s, of course, was the era of Turnbull's Tornadoes. This team was a delight on the eye and should definitely have won more than it did. It contained an awesome midfield in the shape of the classy, but fiery, playmaker Alex Edwards, the flint hard, but silkily skilful, Alex Cropley and the peerless prince of pure football, Pat Stanton.

Our decline as the '70s gave way to the '80s was softened by the cameo appearances of George Best, who was as brilliantly talented as he was self-destructive. The late 1990s saw the Alex McLeish era when Hibs supporters were again able to witness footballing skill of the highest class through the tantalising talents of Franck Sauzée and Russell Latapy.

A conveyor belt of young talent has ushered in the twenty-first century by securing a trophy and then being sold off to make the club a fortune. The future on the field is uncertain but that is usually the way of it at Easter Road.

Recording my memories allows me to share with you half a century of being a Hibee. I will tell you my tales of players, matches and events, on and off the field. I won't miss out the disappointments but I will concentrate mainly on the greatness and the glories.

I can still remember walking up the steps into the old Easter Road Stadium for the first time in the 1950s. I hope that when my time comes, my ashes will be sprinkled on the emerald green swards of our beloved home.

In the meantime, join me on a journey through five decades of pain and pleasure and share with me the unique and incomparable experience of being a lifelong Hibee.

1

FAREWELL TO THE FIVE

I was nine years old before Hibs came into my life. Between my birth and my fifth birthday, Hibs won the league three times. Sadly, I was too young to be aware of these momentous events and, even more sadly, we have never been Scottish champions since that time. Although I lived in Leith until I was eight years old, my dad was a Londoner who supported Fulham and my mum had no interest in football, so Hibs didn't play a big part in my early years.

The discovery, which was to change my life, came in 1957. Early that year, I started to go home from school for lunch. I walked from school and back with a boy in one of the older classes called Alex Burgess. Alex was a Hibs fan and talked about little else. Not only that but he also actually went to the games and every Monday gave me a complete rundown on the previous Saturday's match. In those days, of course, all teams played their league games on a Saturday. Alex was a natural raconteur and in no time at all his match reports and descriptions of Hibs players had me completely hooked.

I started off as a second-hand Hibee as initially my parents wouldn't let me go to matches on my own. I solved that problem by telling my friends all about Hibs and soon they too were fans by proxy. The next logical step was for us to start going to matches. Since we were all planning to go in a group, our mums relented and let us go. My first match was a friendly against Leicester City which Hibs lost 3–2. The result didn't put me off. I was overwhelmed by the ground with its high terracing and by the sloping pitch with its striking green turf. The player who impressed me most on my first visit to Easter Road was our goalkeeper Lawrie Leslie. Lawrie exuded style and confidence and was an excellent keeper. In true Hibs fashion we were stupid enough to let him go to Airdrie a couple of years later. From there he moved to West Ham and became the Scotland goalkeeper.

After my debut against Leicester, my pals and I started going to all the home matches. In those days children entered through what, in those politically incorrect days, was called 'the boys' gate'. Admission was nine pence in old money, which would be about four pence today. However, that was more than I could afford some weeks, especially since I also needed money for bus fares to and from the game. But shortage of funds never stopped us getting in. We simply asked the men who were heading towards the gate if they would give us a 'liftover'. This was the name we gave to being lifted over the turnstile and getting in for free. Somebody always agreed to our request and in no time at all we were into the ground and racing up the steps full of anticipation and excitement.

Although by this time Hibs were a shadow of the all-conquering side of the late 1940s and early 1950s which had dominated Scottish football by playing classy, free-flowing attacking football, there was still a lot to be excited about.

By then, Bobby Johnstone had been sold to Manchester City but four of the Famous Five were still with Hibs. Lawrie Reilly was fighting a losing battle with injury but when he played he usually scored. Eddie Turnbull was a powerhouse who could play and packed a shot of high velocity. Willie

Ormond continued to patrol the left flank and was still good enough to be picked by Scotland for their 1959 trip to play England at Wembley on the occasion of Billy Wright's 100th cap. Then there was Gordon Smith. Of all the Hibs heroes, he was the one I had heard the most about. If the descriptions of his prowess that I had heard were only half true, then Gordon had to be a very special player indeed. All Hibs fans put him on a pedestal and, when I first saw him play, it wasn't difficult to know why.

My first sight of Smith was when he returned from a long-term injury to play against Falkirk at home. The game, mainly due to Hibs defensive deficiencies of that time, ended 3–3. Gordon scored Hibs second goal direct from a corner and I knew that I was in the presence of greatness. Looking back, for all I know that goal may have been a complete fluke but no one around me doubted for a moment that Gordon had planned and executed his scoring corner completely intentionally. I certainly wasn't going to argue. I was too busy marvelling at a masterclass in wing play.

Gordon continued to be plagued by injury problems and, to the amazement and dismay of all Hibs fans, the club decided to release him. He may not have been the player he had once been but he was still a mighty performer and Hibs decision to terminate his contract was as ludicrous as it was costly.

Gordon left Hibs after a great career and with no little sadness. He moved to Hearts and helped them to win the league. He then led them into their European Cup campaign. When Hearts decided that they didn't want him any more, he moved to Dundee, played a significant part in their winning of the championship and played for them in a famous European Cup defeat of the German champions Cologne. Incredibly, Dundee demolished their opponents 8–1 at Dens Park. Unsurprisingly, the player deemed surplus to requirements by

Hibs three years previously played a leading role in that historic victory.

Shortly before Gordon's departure, Hibs fans' spirits were lifted by the arrival on the scene of a player who, like Smith, was genuinely world-class. Joe Baker made his home debut against Queen's Park at the age of seventeen early in season 1957–58, and I was lucky enough to be there to see it. Hibs won 2–0 and the teenage Baker notched both goals. I had witnessed the beginning of a meteoric career. Barely two days later, I was back at Easter Road on a Monday night to watch Hibs drub mighty Tottenham Hotspur 5–2. The teenage tyro Baker weighed in with a brilliant hat-trick.

When the Scottish Cup came round things really began to happen. We kicked off our campaign by beating Dundee United 2–0 after a replay at Easter Road. Baker was again on the scoresheet with a twenty-yard power drive. The draw for the next round produced an Edinburgh derby at Tynecastle. Hearts were top dogs in the Scottish game at that time. They had players of the class of Dave Mackay and Alex Young, as well as the 'Terrible Trio' of Conn, Bauld and Wardhaugh in their ranks, and were on their way to winning that season's league championship. They must have fancied their chances of winning the Scottish Cup as well, but they hadn't reckoned with the mighty Hibees. Our seventeen-year-old centre forward played the game of his young life. He gave Hearts centre half Jimmy Milne the most torrid of times. He outpaced him, outjumped him and generally led him a merry dance. He scored four superb goals into the bargain.

Four goals should be enough to win any match, but the Hibs defence of that time was less than watertight. Enter hero number two. Lawrie Leslie, the Hibs goalkeeper, was a local lad from Niddrie. He made his fair share of errors but he was also capable of brilliance. On this day, he was at his magnificent best and denied Hearts continually by producing a string of brave and inspired saves. Hearts beat him three times and pressed for an equaliser as the clock ran down. As a ten-year-old schoolboy I watched all this from high up on what was then the main terracing at Tynecastle. I thought that the last five minutes would never pass but pass they did. Hibs had achieved one of their most momentous victories and the Baker Boy as he was now known had written himself into the history books. The Hibs fans invaded the pitch and carried Baker and Leslie shoulder high. I didn't need carrying because I was walking on air. When I got home, having treated myself to a 'Hibs for the Cup' rosette on the way home, my mother said, 'Aw son, yon rosette's bigger than your wee face!' My dad looked up from his newspaper and asked, 'Were Hibs playing today?'

Third Lanark at Easter Road was the draw for the quarter-finals. The Hi Hi's, as they were known, were a strong side back then and Hibs expected a hard game. They got one too. Joe continued his personal crusade to bring the Scottish Cup to Easter Road by opening the scoring with an outstanding goal. With quicksilver feet, he left two defenders in his wake and fired the ball home from twenty-five yards. With two minutes left, however, the tide had turned and Hibs were 2–1 down and heading out of the Cup. Then, miraculously, or at least that's how it seemed to me at the time, Baker and John Fraser struck in the closing moments to snatch a dramatic win.

Our cup run was now the talk of Leith and everywhere you went, you heard the same phrase being uttered: 'Our name must be on the cup.' It was on to Hampden to face the mighty Rangers in the semi-final. Hibs, inspired by a young, recently introduced inside forward called Andy Aitken, were excellent in the first game but had to settle for a 2–2 draw.

We again played well in the replay and were leading 2–1 with seconds left. At that point, Lawrie Leslie went up for a cross with Rangers' Ralph Brand. The ball escaped from Leslie's grasp and Brand's colleague Max Murray drove in what appeared to be the equalising goal. However, the referee Bobby Davidson, who proved to be no friend of Hibs in future years (he even abandoned a game at Parkhead because of fog when Hibs were winning 2–0 with only ten minutes to go), stepped in to disallow the goal because Brand had punched the ball out of Leslie's hands. Press photographs the next day proved Davidson right. Hibs were in the Scottish Cup Final and overnight 'Ralph Brands' became rhyming slang for hands in the Leith area.

My non-footballing dad had promised me that if Hibs got to the Cup Final he would take me. He kept his promise, although he admitted to me years later that he had never seriously expected to have to do so, as he had been sure that Rangers would beat Hibs at Hampden at the second time of asking. We travelled through on a coach from my dad's work in Leith. The mood was confident. Again that phrase 'our name must be on the cup' did the rounds and there was a strong feeling that what was then a fifty-six-year-old hoodoo was about to be broken.

Our opponents were Clyde, a top six team at that time, but we felt that we could beat them and we were sure that the Baker Boy would lead the way. In the late 1980s, I was privileged to collaborate with Joe Baker in writing his life story. Joe's story was shared with fans through serialisation in the *Hibs Monthly* fanzine. It was a delight to meet Joe who was as wonderful a man as he was a football player. His thoughts on that fateful Cup Final day against Clyde surprised me at the time and still surprise me now. Joe told me:

In all honesty, I should never have played in that final. I had shaded by the time of the Rangers matches. My hectic debut season had begun to catch me up and the spring had gone from my legs. I had sailed through previous games unaffected but now I was beginning to realise what big game pressure really was. I toyed with the idea of telling Hugh Shaw our manager all this. On the Monday before the final, we beat Rangers 3–1 at Easter Road in Lawrie Reilly's last game. Both Lawrie and I scored. Lawrie was clearly not fully fit at that time but the thought did occur to me that it should be him and not me who played in the final. In the event, I said nothing, played and contributed little.

The final proved to be a disaster for Hibs whose good fortune in the earlier rounds was more than balanced by a catalogue of ill luck on Cup Final Day. Semi-final hero Andy Aitken was injured early on and spent most of the rest of the match, in those pre-substitute days, hirpling on the right wing. John Baxter deflected a Johnny Coyle shot into his own net, Baker punched the ball past the Clyde goalkeeper when he might have headed it and then a net-bound thunderbolt from left back Joe McLelland struck Clyde's Mike Clinton in the face, knocking him out cold but crucially diverting the ball wide of the goal.

The crowd at the match was over 97,000 and I am certain that at least two thirds of those present were Hibs supporters. We were a demoralised bunch as we headed for the exits with our heads and banners drooping. I'll never forget the scene when we returned to Edinburgh a couple of hours later. The coach dropped us off at the West End. All the way along Princes Street I could see a dejected stream of Hibs fans making their misery-laden way home; a sad and silent cast of thousands that had seen their cup-winning dreams come to nought.

Thus ended my first full season of supporting the Hibees. After his cameo appearance at the Cup Final my dad never went back. As for me, I have never stopped going back since.

2

GOAL MACHINES IN GREEN

Hibs were in transition. The Famous Five were coming to the end of their time with the club. Bobby Johnstone was now playing in England and Lawrie Reilly had retired. Season 1958–59 would prove to be Gordon Smith's last with the club. Eddie Turnbull and Willie Ormond would last a little longer, but to all intents and purposes the great team of the late 1940s and early 1950s had passed its sell-by date, and Hugh Shaw who remained at the managerial helm was building a new team.

Lawrie Leslie was still in goal and the full backs were John Grant and Joe McLelland. Grant was a seriously underrated attacking right back who was good enough to be capped by Scotland. McLelland was the proverbial old-fashioned full back. He kicked everything that moved, including the ball. No one would ever have described his playing style as cultured. Eddie Turnbull had stepped back to right half by this time. He was accompanied at halfback by a promising young centre half in Jackie Plenderleith and the inimitable John Baxter. Baxter, who was nicknamed 'Stanley' because there was a Scottish comedian of the same name and 'Chinny' due to his jutting jaw, was a left-sided powerhouse with a rocket shot, a totally committed approach to every match and an eccentric manner. He once played with stitches in a head wound wearing a rugby skullcap and managed to score a diving header. In a reserve game against Hearts, he injured himself early on and spent the rest of the game limping heavily and ostentatiously, except when the ball came anywhere near him. When he got the ball, he went into overdrive. As soon as he lost possession, the limp returned. In a game against Dundee, he scored two outstanding second-half goals with long shots. In the last minute, Hibs were awarded a penalty down the slope. Chinny was given the chance to notch his first ever hat-trick. Having scored two goals from thirty yards, he managed, in his own unique way, to hit his penalty shot from twelve yards over the bar and out of the ground.

An exciting young winger called Johnny McLeod was on the right wing by this time. Johnny was fast and tricky, crossed the ball well and although naturally left-footed could also use his right foot to good effect. Willie Ormond continued to patrol the left wing and was the best in his position in Scotland. The brilliant Baker continued to torment every defence in the country from centre forward. Stewart Brown of the *Evening News* summed up Joe thus: 'he is a one man goal machine, with two good feet, great pace and excellent ability in the air, a combination rarely seen in modern football.' Joe's inside forward partners came from Andy Aitken, Des Fox, Davie Gibson and Tommy Preston. All of these players had great creative talent and were also capable of scoring goals. So Hibs were a team in transition who were exciting and incisive going forward, but less than secure at the back.

By this stage, my support for Hibs was becoming ever more intense. What had begun as an interest was now a fully developed passion. I had begun to live and breathe everything Hibernian. I was at every home game and I attended as many away matches as I possibly could.

The camaraderie on the supporters' club coach on which

I travelled was wonderful. There were quite a few of us youngsters and we were really well looked after by the older supporters on the bus. The only complaint we had was that the men on the bus (and there were a couple of women too!) always wanted to make a pub stop en route to the game. Sometimes these stops became so extended that we were late for kick-off. The old 'uns never seemed too bothered by this but we youngsters were inevitably furious since our priority was always getting to the game. It may have been a bit of a social outing for the older supporters but for us it was a very serious matter indeed.

The journey home was never dull. A victory would see us sing ourselves hoarse all the way back to the supporters' club base in Easter Road. We still sang to cheer ourselves up if we lost, but that was never quite the same. The coach also stopped on the way back. Again the older supporters all piled into the pub whereas the younger ones headed for the nearest chip shop. We usually ended up flushing the drinking squad out of the pub to allow us to continue our journey home. They wanted to postpone the return to their domestic routine. We couldn't wait to get home to enjoy our Saturday night.

If you were under sixteen you could travel on the bus for half price. It's fair to say that some of the teenage members of the travel club abused that ruling ever so slightly. George and Keith Gillan were two brothers who knew how to save money, but were less well versed in the facts of life. George was seventeen and Keith was fifteen. They both claimed to be under sixteen. One day, the bus convenor looked them both up and down and said, 'Are you two twins then?' George's answer went down in the annals of Eastern Branch history when he replied 'No. There's four months between us!'

Season 1958–59 was not one of great achievement for Hibs but there were highlights. Celtic came to Easter Road on

29 November 1958, which just happened to be my eleventh birthday. What a present the Hibees gave me by beating the Parkhead team 3–2. The star of the show was the Baker Boy with the perfect hat-trick consisting of a right foot shot, a left foot shot and a diving header. Billy McNeill was Celtic's centre half that day. Prior to the game, the press had been touting him for a call-up to the Scotland team. After the match, one journalist wrote, 'Baker gave McNeill the complete runaround and left his international prospects in tatters.'

Baker scored seventeen goals in one eight-game spell that season, and netted thirty goals in total despite missing three months of the campaign through injury. He played in the Scottish Cup quarter-final against Third Lanark at Cathkin when less than fully fit and only succeeded in aggravating his injury. Hibs went out of the cup 2–1 that day but it was sad day for much more significant reasons. The great Gordon Smith also sustained an injury and was never to play for Hibs again.

Gordon Smith was probably Hibs' greatest ever player. He was renowned throughout the football world as a player of the highest class. He opened his Hibs career by scoring three goals against Hearts. In his testimonial match against the mighty Manchester United, he led Hibs to a 7–3 victory. He personified dedication and was an example to all other players. He was so good that in Scotland the legendary Stanley Matthews was known as the 'English Gordon Smith'.

Gordon served Hibs admirably. In return the club treated him shabbily. His injury against Third Lanark was the latest in a series of problems and he was told he would need another ankle operation. Hibs refused to fund this surgery and told him that he was no longer required at Easter Road. Eighteen years of outstanding service to Hibs were disgracefully dispensed with at a stroke. In terms of ineptitude this decision by Hibs ranked with that of the Decca Records executive who told the Beatles that they would never make it, as guitar groups were a thing of the past.

Gordon unsurprisingly was hurt to the core. Hibs fans were dumbfounded and distressed in equal measure. I remember spending a whole week in my Primary 7 class in a state of shock, hardly able to believe the club's insensitivity and poor judgement. At the end of that week, my teacher asked me, 'Edward, you're not yourself – what is wrong with you? Has there been a death in your family?'

I simply replied, 'No Miss. It's much worse than that.'

Gordon Smith was arguably the finest player ever to wear the green jersey of Hibs. He was certainly one of the outstanding players of his era. When he sadly passed away in 2004, tributes were paid from all corners of the footballing world. Two of the most eloquent came from former Hibs team mates of Gordon.

Lawrie Reilly said: 'Gordon could make the ball speak. He was the best player I have seen at Hibs.'

Jimmy Thomson added: 'Gordon was a wonder. One of the greatest players who ever lived.'

Gordon Smith had five years of good quality football left in him when he was released by Hibs. Only those in power at the club at the time knew why they took their fateful decision. Whatever reasons they had, they were wrong and even I, as an eleven-year-old schoolboy supporter, could see that very clearly.

However, as we lost one Hibernian great in the peerless Smith, we regained another in the shape of Bobby Johnstone. Bobby was brought back from Oldham and several thousand fans turned up to welcome him home in a reserve fixture against Hearts. Johnstone was known as 'Nicker' because he came from Selkirk and there was a Border collie of that name in a *Sunday Post* comic strip. When he ran out for his first match back, he drew gasps of amazement from the crowd. There was no doubt that Nicker was considerably thicker. Wee Bobby's waistline had spread alarmingly since he had left Hibs. However, his football brain remained razor-sharp and his silky skills were undiminished. Johnstone could pick out a pass with unerring foresight and accuracy and was also an accomplished finisher. As his fitness improved, which it did rapidly, he added an extra dimension to what had already been a formidable Hibs attack. In those days, defences were square and more easily pierced. Throughout season 1959–60, Johnstone continually threaded exquisite passes through to his fellow forwards Joe Baker, Johnny McLeod, Tommy Preston and Willie Ormond. The result was an avalanche of goals and an unforgettable season of attacking football.

Hibs scored 104 league goals and achieved some remarkable results. At home, Dunfermline were drubbed 7–4 and Third Lanark were thrashed 8–4 at Christmas. The goals flowed even more freely in away games. Airdrie were annihilated 11–1 at Broomfield and Partick Thistle were decimated 10–2 at Firhill. A certain Joseph Baker scored a total of sixteen goals in these four games. He wasn't Hibs' only prolific scorer though, as his other attacking colleagues – in particular, Tommy Preston – also made significant contributions.

The two massive away wins have a strange Hearts connection for me. By that time, I had just started secondary school at Holy Cross Academy and tried to get to most away games. When I wasn't able to travel, my Uncle Jack, who was a Hearts fan, would take me to see the Maroons. On the day of the game at Airdrie, Uncle Jack took me to Hampden to see Hearts play Third Lanark in the League Cup Final. Hearts won 2–1 and coming back on the train, a passenger in our compartment mistaking us both for Jambos said, 'You two will be happy men then.'

My uncle replied, 'Well, I am but he's not because he's a Hibee.'

Our fellow passenger's reply sticks in my mind to this day. He said, 'He'll be even happier than you because his team won 11–1 at Airdrie today.'

Coincidentally, on the day of the 10–2 victory at Firhill I was watching Hearts playing Motherwell. In those days the half-time scores were not announced. To encourage fans to buy match programmes the day's fixtures were listed in the programme and each fixture was allocated a letter. At Tynecastle, the scores were displayed by placing letters and numbers along the perimeter wall. That day the sequence of numbers around the Hibs half-time result read 0–5–0. The Hearts crowd let out a huge roar thinking that Partick were leading Hibs 5–0. The groan that followed was twice as loud when they realised that it was in fact Hibs who were five up – five up with five more to come in the second half.

Joe Baker's form was such that by this time he was catching the attention of the England selectors. Joe had been born in Liverpool but considered himself very much a Scot. In those days, however, you could only play for the country of your birth. The fact that a 'Scottish player' was being considered for the mighty England caused a sensation at the time. Joe's rival for an England place was none other than Brian Clough – old Big 'Ead himself. As well as being one of the all time great football managers, Clough was an outstanding goalscorer as a player until injury cut short his career.

Clough played for Middlesbrough and Hibs arranged a friendly match against them. Inevitably the match was billed as the battle of the centre forwards. During the pre-match warm-up, the photographers asked Baker and Clough to pose together for a photograph. Joe was happy to do so. According to Joe, Clough, bombastic as ever, didn't want to know. He snapped at the photographers in that inimitable voice of his, 'No way! I'm not having my picture taken with the like of him.' Typically for that goal-crazed season, the match finished 6–6. Clough scored for Middlesbrough but Baker got three for Hibs.

Joe's reward was to be chosen for England. He almost didn't reach Wembley as the taxi driver taking him there from the airport thought he was a hoaxer when he heard his Scottish accent and called the police. England won 2–1 against Northern Ireland and Joe scored a superb debut goal. He went on to win eight caps for England and was in Alf Ramsey's original list of forty players for the 1966 World Cup Finals. He finished season 1959–60 with a club record total of fifty-one goals.

As the scores mentioned above suggest, Hibs were unstoppable going forward but porous at the back. This led to a mid-table finish to the season when there could have been real success if a couple of top defenders had been signed. It could have been done too because good players came cheap in those days. However, when was it ever the Hibernian way to speculate to accumulate?

If season 1959–60 had been full of incident, the season that followed would surpass it in every way, as Hibs set out on one their greatest ever European adventures.

3

EVENTFUL EVENINGS IN EUROPE

Season 1960–61 got off to a disastrous start for Hibs. We lost our first eight league games and sat bottom of what was then an eighteen-team top league. Of course, this didn't please us Hibs fans. We had always had high expectations and we were most unhappy with the team's performances. We were even more unhappy when the club sold Bobby Johnstone back to Oldham. The supporters loved Nicker and couldn't understand why he had been allowed to go for such a nominal fee, particularly after the magnificent form he had displayed in the previous campaign. His departure did not go down at all well and no reason was given for it.

Johnstone was a magnificent all-round player. When describing him, words like 'exquisite' and 'artistry' come to mind. Joe Baker considered him 'the best goal maker I ever played with.'

Hugh Shaw took steps to stop the rot. He signed Sammy Baird from Rangers and Ronnie Simpson from Newcastle United. Not long after they were signed, Hibs lost 6–0 at home to Celtic. After this less than auspicious start, both Ronnie and Sammy proved to be excellent acquisitions and became big fans' favourites. Baird was no Bobby Johnstone but he read the game well, distributed the ball skilfully and brought much needed composure to the team. He played brilliantly

17

for Hibs in major European matches. Simpson was a marvellous goalkeeper. He served Hibs superbly until he was dropped surprisingly and sold to Celtic by Jock Stein during the Big Man's time at Easter Road. Even more surprisingly, and not a little suspiciously, when Stein left Hibs for Celtic, he made Ronnie his first choice goalkeeper and Simpson went on to win a European Cup Winners Medal and Scottish international caps.

However, in November 1960, Ronnie and Sammy were setting their sights on nothing more ambitious than helping Hibs climb out of the relegation zone. I was in early secondary school at this point and was experiencing for the first time just how hard Hibs supporters can be on their own players. The fans gave the team a torrid time during its early season problem period. I just couldn't understand this as I was desperate for the team to do well and only wanted to cheer the Hibees on. I think that it's fair to say that nearly fifty years on, Hibs fans are still among the most passionate, but critical, of supporters' groups.

We eventually managed to beat St Mirren 4–3 at Easter Road in our ninth league fixture. We followed this by going on a good run in the league and ended the season in a respectable mid-table position. Ronnie Simpson created a reputation as a master of the art of saving penalty kicks. At one stage in the season he had saved six spot kicks in a row. His secret was to leave a slightly larger gap to one side of his goal than to the other. The penalty taker, thinking that Ronnie didn't realise that he had left this inviting space, would inevitably shoot to that side. Simpson would know that the ball was going there, of course, and would throw himself swiftly to that side of the goal and pull off a save. He did this most notably against Hearts in the New Year's Day derby at Tynecastle. Ronnie's brilliant save from Ian Crawford enabled

Hibs to win the match 2–1 and gave us fans the happiest of starts to 1961.

The players called Ronnie Simpson 'the India Rubber Man' and it wasn't difficult to see why. He was blessed with outstanding natural agility and elasticity. He was eventually beaten from the penalty spot at the seventh time of asking by St Johnstone's Joe Carr. Carr had worked out Simpson's strategy and calmly slotted the ball into the opposite corner to that which Ronnie expected. As our ace goalkeeper dived the wrong way and the ball rolled into the unguarded corner of his net, I remember turning disbelievingly to my friends and saying, 'That's the first penalty I have ever seen Ronnie Simpson let in.' A man standing behind us replied, 'Aye and it'll be the last one you'll ever see him let in as well.' It wasn't but he did save a few more spot kicks during his Hibs career.

It wasn't the league that caused the excitement though that season. It was Europe. We were competing in the Inter-Cities Fairs Cup, the forerunner of the UEFA Cup of today. We were originally drawn against Lausanne of Switzerland but they withdrew from the competition. This gave us automatic entry to the next stage of the draw where we were paired with Barcelona. Barca were just as big a name then as they are now. The mighty Catalans had just won the Spanish League and had knocked Real Madrid out of the current season's European Cup. You'll appreciate the magnitude of this achievement when I point out that this was the great Real Madrid team of Di Stéfano, Puskás and Gento, which had just enthralled Hampden by beating Eintracht Frankfurt 7–3 in the previous season's European Cup Final. Prior to losing to Barcelona in the current season's competition, Real had won the first five European Cups. Barca were operating on two European fronts in season 1960–61, which was allowed at that time, and Hibs had been given the formidable task of taking them on.

Hibs headed for the Nou Camp on Boxing Day 1960 and met Barcelona the next night. The Catalan team contained all-time great players like Luis Suárez of Spain and the world-famous Hungarians, Koscis and Kubala. There wasn't anything like the level of media coverage of football then that there is now so the game wasn't broadcast. There was no Scottish news programme on television or radio after ten o'clock either, but my friends and I just couldn't wait till morning to discover the result. So we made our way to the local telephone box at around 10.30p.m., gathered all our loose change together and made a phone call to the *Daily Record*. We asked to be put through to the sports desk but the girl on the switchboard asked why we were calling. We told her that we were trying to find out the score between Hibs and Barcelona.

'Have you not heard?' she said. 'It was 4–4.' We honestly thought that she was joking. We only believed her when she did actually put us through to the sports desk and the reporter there confirmed it. We couldn't believe it. We raced into the cold night chanting 'Hibees Hibees.' We got a few funny looks as we sprinted home, beside ourselves with excitement. When we got back to our own street, we knocked on the doors of the Hibs supporting families to tell them the good news. In no time at all, the street was full of people discussing this sensational event. We were all agreed that we couldn't wait to read the next day's papers.

The *Daily Record* headline summed it up. The sports pages proclaimed 'HURRAH FOR HIBS – THE MIRACLE MEN SHOCK BARCELONA'. We were shocked too when we read the match reports. Hibs had twice led by two goals and had in fact been 4–2 ahead with only six minutes to go. Joe Baker had, of course, led the way with two brilliant strikes and Tommy Preston and Johnny McLeod had chipped in with the other two goals. Hibs had stunned 50,000 Barcelona fans and to be honest they had also stunned their own supporters. We were amazed but deliriously happy. To say the second leg at Easter Road, which was scheduled for February 1961, was keenly anticipated would be a huge understatement. We just could not wait.

However, we had no option but to wait and in the meantime, Hibs had some Scottish Cup business to take care of. The East of Scotland side Peebles Rovers had fought their way through to the later stages of the competition and had been drawn to face Hibs at Easter Road. Their centre half Willie Moles had once played for Rangers and was very confident about facing Hibs great centre forward. He was quoted in the press as saying, 'Baker won't get a kick of the ball.' Joe Baker was a modest man and he didn't like immodesty in others. He told me many years after the Peebles Rovers game: 'Moles' comments were a spur to me. I was determined to play out of my skin.'

There is no doubt that Joe made good his promise. By halftime he had scored five goals. Hugh Shaw told him at half-time that he had made his point and should consider easing off. Joe had absolutely no intention of doing so. With twenty-five minutes still to play, Joe had notched up nine goals and was on the trail of a tenth.

His brother Gerry had once scored ten goals against Glasgow University in a Scottish Cup match and Joe was determined to take the family honours. The Peebles goalkeeper Willie Lucas had other ideas. He defied Baker on a number of occasions and even saved a penalty from the great man. The match ended 15–1 and Gerry's record stayed unbroken. I remember two things from this amazing match. One is a goal which Joe Baker scored in the first half. I was standing directly behind the goal at the foot of the slope when Willie Ormond shot from an acute angle. He hit the ball like a rocket and as it flew across the goal, the horizontal figure of the Baker Boy catapulted through the air to crash it into the roof of the net with his head. I think that was the most incredible demonstration of the striker's instincts that I have ever witnessed. My second recollection is that everyone went home feeling really downhearted that Joe hadn't beaten his brother's record. It must be the only time in football history that a group of supporters have gone home disappointed after watching their team win by fourteen goals.

Hibs cup run came to an end at the quarter-final stage. We met Celtic at Parkhead, played well and led through a Bobby Kinloch goal until the last few minutes when Bobby Lennox equalised. The replay was at Easter Road the following Wednesday. At this stage of my life, I had never been in the Easter Road stand. The stand, especially the centre stand, was much too posh and much too expensive for a teenager from Leith to contemplate. I was a terracing regular. We used to stand behind the goals which Hibs were attacking in the first half and then change round at half-time and do the same at the other end in the second half. This was a regular routine for a lot of fans in those days. However, I was about to move up in the world on a one-off basis. A police sergeant friend of my parents had been given three tickets for the centre stand and he took his son and me. The policeman was a lovely Highlander called Pax McDonald. *Pax* is the Latin word for peace and his name had been carefully chosen by his parents who were firmly in favour of the pacifist way of life.

There wasn't too much peace in evidence at Easter Road on the night of the quarter-final replay. There was a huge crowd and the gates were closed just before kick-off time. A large number of Celtic fans, who had arrived late, climbed into the graveyard adjacent to the ground in the hope of being able to see the match from there. Some of the gravestones were disturbed and this incident was not well received in the Leith area.

On the pitch, Hibs played excellently. We now had a brilliant young centre half in Jim Easton. Easton had turned the sliding tackle into an art form. Time and again, he would launch himself into a challenge from five yards away and emerge with the ball having won it cleanly. Easton was outstanding in this replay as were his colleagues. With Hibs creating and missing many chances, Celtic won the game with a goal from John Clark in extra time. I have rarely known a Hibs team to play so well and lose as they did that night.

Everyone's thoughts now turned to the Fairs Cup second leg match with Barcelona. The game attracted massive attention and 47,000 people crowded into Easter Road to see it. I was in bright and early behind the goal at the Dunbar end. In my group was Jimmy O'Rourke who was in the year above me at school, and who was to go on to be a great Hibee himself of course. It was a cold night but we were all warm because the crowd was so closely packed that the cold air had no chance to circulate.

One person who did not arrive bright and early was Joe Baker. Joe had travelled through from the west by train as usual. When he came out of the station he couldn't believe the crowds that were heading for Easter Road. He knew that there was no point in taking a bus as the bus would never have got through the crowds so he decided to walk. I will let Joe take up the story from here:

By the time I reached the dressing room, it was un-comfortably close to kick-off time. Hughie Shaw was tearing his hair out.

'Where in God's name have you been Joe?' he said.

'Don't worry Hughie,' I replied. 'You know what they say. Late arrival, early goal.'

Joe's words proved prophetic. In seven minutes, Hibs were awarded a free kick. Johnny McLeod glanced up and saw Joe already on the move. He chipped the ball goalwards and the Baker Boy's head did the rest. However, Barcelona were a great side and didn't take kindly to this early reverse. By half-time, they were 2–1 ahead and well in command of the game. I am sure that they went in at half-time thinking that they had the game well in hand.

What they hadn't taken into account was the Easter Road slope factor. Hibs attacked down the hill relentlessly and the crowd roared them on. The inside of Easter Road was a cauldron of noise and the sound reached new levels when Hibs equalised with seventeen minutes left. Willie Ormond swung in a corner from the left, Sammy Baird headed it on and Tommy Preston dived through the packed goalmouth to head the ball into the net.

Hibs intensified the pressure even further with Sammy Baird to the fore. The skipper was inspirational and his efforts were described thus in the next day's press: 'No man played a better part in Hibs victory than Sammy Baird. He put in a power of work and was the dominating personality on the field.' As the Hibs pressure increased, Barcelona's composure reduced. Twice Baker was fouled in the box and twice the German referee Johannes Malka looked the other way. Then, with five minutes to go, Easter Road erupted. Johnny McLeod was downed in the box and this time the referee awarded a penalty. The Barcelona players completely lost the place. They surrounded the referee, pushing and pulling at him. It took all the efforts of the police to restore calm and allow the penalty kick to be taken.

Bobby Kinloch stepped forward to take the kick and, showing remarkable coolness in a tinderbox situation, he drove the ball past goalkeeper Medrano's right hand to give Hibs the lead. This sparked off another riot, with the Barcelona players chasing the referee to the halfway line where one of them sent Mr Malka spinning onto the track. Again Lothian and Borders finest were charged with the task of restoring order, which they eventually managed to do. While all this was going on, the Hibs players calmly sat themselves down on the pitch and had a chat.

When the game eventually restarted, the referee positioned himself close to the players' tunnel and didn't move more than five yards from his chosen spot for the time that remained. Barcelona threw themselves into a frenzied attempt to equalise. Every Hibs fan in the ground knew that we were on the verge of a momentous victory. We also knew that it could still be snatched away from us and we held our breath as the clock moved with the speed of a calendar. Our defence was heroic and Ronnie Simpson in goal was calmness personified. You would have thought that the referee would have been desperate to get off the field but he didn't seem in a hurry to blow the final whistle. Eventually he did and raced down the tunnel to the sanctuary of his dressing room.

The Hibs players went to the fans to celebrate but Barcelona had only one thing on their mind and they headed straight for the referee's room. He had locked his door but the Barcelona players tried to kick it in. Yet again the police had to intervene and the damage that might have befallen the referee if they hadn't done so is too frightening to consider.

When Joe Baker recalled this historic match to me many years later, he had two amusing stories to tell. The first concerned Bobby Kinloch who took the penalty:

Bobby had come late to a career in professional football because he had served in the RAF for several years. On the day of the Barcelona game, he had spent part of the afternoon practising penalties. He hadn't scored with very many of them but when the referee pointed to the spot Bobby was the first to step forward. Completely unfazed by the furore which had preceded his kick, he drove the ball perfectly into the right-hand corner of the Barcelona goal. He never lacked confidence although his deeds on the park did not always match his high level of self-belief. On this occasion, however, his confidence was fully justified.

Joe's second story related to Barcelona's centre half, the Spanish international Jesus Garay.

When we came in after the match we passed the referee's dressing room. Garay was hammering on the referee's door with his boots. We could hear the ref wailing, 'Oh Jesus, Jesus, please help me.' However, I don't think that he was trying to initiate a conversation with the Barcelona centre half.

The Barcelona players' behaviour on that faraway night was reprehensible. They had come to Easter Road expecting a comfortable victory and when things turned out differently, they just couldn't take it. Today, if they had behaved the way they did, a number of their players would have been arrested, would have received a massive fine and would have been suspended from European football for a lengthy period.

Back in 1961, they simply apologised and promised to come back to Easter Road the following season to play a goodwill friendly. As far as I know, no further action was taken against them. The incredibly tolerant referee Malka's post-match comment was: 'Perhaps I should have ordered some of the Spanish players off during those hectic minutes. I thought that it was better to complete the game with both sides at full strength.'

As a Hibs supporter I have never felt prouder of my team than I did that night. We had outplayed and defeated the best team in Europe and given them a lesson in sportsmanship as well. Hibs Chairman Harry Swan said at the time, 'I have nothing but the greatest admiration for the behaviour of our players.'

Hibs were now in a European semi-final for the second time in five years and I, for one, was starting to believe that we could win the trophy. Our next match was against the crack Italian side Roma. The first leg was at Easter Road and on a warm April night, 40,000 Hibees were inside the ground. Roma had some high-class players, most notably the two Uruguayans, Lojacano and Schiaffino, and Italy's top striker, Manfredini. The Italian team put on a great display against Hibs but marred their performance by a cynical and crude approach. The game ended 2–2. Joe Baker and Johnny McLeod scored excellent goals for Hibs and Lojacano notched both goals for Roma.

The next day's *Daily Record* report summed up Roma's tactics perfectly when it said: 'Once again a continental team blotted its copybook at Easter Road with a display of bad temper and vicious fouling when things were going against them.' The paper also reported that: 'Baker boosted his prestige with a glorious goal and many flashes of his brilliant best despite the fact that two defenders had been specially briefed to mark him.'

So Hibs were still in with a fighting chance and there is no doubt that fighting was the operative word. In two short months, I had been privileged to watch two of Europe's best teams in action at Easter Road. On each occasion, I had been impressed by their skill and disgusted by their behaviour.

The return match with Roma took place in the Italian capital exactly a week after the original bruising encounter at Easter Road. On the same night, Dunfermline shocked Celtic by winning a Scottish Cup Final replay at Hampden 2–0. Managing the Fifers that night was none other than a certain Jock Stein, who in less than three years time would become manager of Hibs.

Hibs current manager though was still Hugh Shaw. By this time, Shaw was leaving a lot of the team tactics to his trainer. The title of trainer in the 1960s was equivalent to that of coach today. Hibs had installed Eddie Turnbull in that key position and he came up with a tactical masterstroke for the second-leg match in Rome. Bobby Kinloch wore the number nine jersey and Joe Baker wore Kinloch's number eight shirt. You would have thought that the Italian players would have been able to recognise the Hibs centre forward but apparently not. The *Daily Record* reported next day: 'Hibs numbering strategy baffled the 30,000 crowd and seemed to mystify the Roma defence.'

The Italians' man marked and hacked Kinloch and allowed Baker unaccustomed space. With three quarters of the game gone Hibs were 3–1 up and in sight of a famous victory. Kinloch had notched a goal and Baker had scored two beauties. Sadly, the Italians scored two late goals and the match finished 3–3. Nowadays, of course, Hibs would have gone through on away goals. That rule wasn't in existence then, so a third match was arranged and it would again take place in Rome.

It was reported that Roma had won a toss for the choice of venue. Joe Baker remembered it differently: 'We were sold down the river by Harry Swan and the board. The board wanted to make more money out of getting half the gate receipts from a match in Rome.'

The third match didn't take place until the end of the Italian season and by that time the Scottish season had been finished for a few weeks. Inexplicably, Hibs had done minimal training and arranged no games to provide match practice. It was almost as if they had written off this play-off game, which was totally wrong since Hibs had every chance of winning and qualifying for a European final.

The original game in a Rome had been played in a spectacular thunderstorm but the play-off took place in blazing heat. Predictably and tragically Hibs lost 6–0. They were out of condition, outplayed and out of the tournament. As a young Hibs fan – no, make that fanatic – at the time, I just could not understand why Hibs put money before the chance of European glory. Nearly half a century later, I am no nearer understanding the club's attitude at that time.

More disaster was to follow. In the close season of 1961, Hibs sold Joe Baker to Torino for £65,000 which was a veritable fortune then. The sad thing was that Joe did not want to go. He recounted the events of that summer to me many years later:

At the end of each season Hugh Shaw would call me to his office and say 'Right Joe, put your name on that and that'll be us for another season.' I would dutifully sign up for another year at £12 a week and go back to my training. This time it was different. The rest of the players, led by wee Willie Ormond, had urged me to ask for a rise. They said that I deserved it and promised to back me up.

When I entered Hughie's office, he was sitting there with the Chairman Harry Swan. He started the annual ritual but I interrupted him to say that I wanted a rise. Harry Swan looked up and asked, 'How much did you have in mind Joe?' I hadn't really thought but blurted out £5 per week. The Chairman retorted, 'This is serious Joe. We'll have to give it some thought.'

He couldn't have given it too much thought because the next morning's newspapers announced that Hibs had reluctantly decided to sell Joe Baker because he was making unreasonable demands on the club. I can truthfully say that I did not want to leave Hibs. If Harry Swan had offered me a ten-year contract at £30 a week I would have signed it.

Hibs fans were devastated. We couldn't believe that our club would sell a truly world-class player when it didn't have to. Harry Swan tried to make it look like the club was being held to ransom by its centre forward and therefore had no option but to sell him. The supporters knew better. We knew that Harry Swan was far more interested in putting money in the bank than he was in putting goals in the opposition net.

So a centre forward, who loved Hibs and had scored the scarcely believable total of 159 goals in four seasons before he had even reached the age of twenty-one, was sold to Torino for the sake of £5 a week. To make matters worse, Hibs also sold Joe's brilliant colleague, the tricky, pacy winger Johnny McLeod to Arsenal for £45,000. We fans couldn't believe it. Surely after selling Baker, the club didn't need any more money? Harry Swan never offered an explanation. He simply reminded the supporters that season tickets for season 1961–62 were available.

These days, there would be an outcry and the fans would demand explanations. Back then, we simply accepted it with heavy hearts and wondered what the new season would bring.

4

GOING FOR GALBRAITH

I thought that the world had ended when Hibs sold Joe Baker to Torino in 1961. Johnny McLeod had also gone, of course, and Willie Ormond – the last member of the Famous Five – had signed for Falkirk in August 1961. Davie Gibson, an outstanding inside forward, was sold to Leicester City and this followed the sale of Andy Aitken to West Bromwich Albion and Jackie Plenderleith to Manchester City. Clearly Hibs were as much of a selling club then as they are now. The difference then was that the maximum wage was still in place and players had nothing to gain financially by moving to the Old Firm or going down south. Round about this time, Prime Minister Harold MacMillan was telling the country, 'You've never had it so good.' We Hibs fans thought that we had never had it so bad.

Another seismic change occurred at Easter Road in 1961 when Hugh Shaw resigned as manager. Hughie had played for Hibs from shortly after the First World War and had taken over as manager after the tragic death of the legendary Willie McCartney in January 1948. He had overseen the development of the Famous Five (although all five players had been signed by McCartney) and had led Hibs to three league titles in five years. He was growing old now and felt it was time to give someone else the chance to take the Hibee helm.

This was a time of real depression for Hibs fans, especially the older ones who had known the great days of the '40s and early '50s. They had put up with the break-up of that team because, even though the new team had its weaknesses in defence, it was an exciting attacking force. Now the great forwards were gone and the supporters knew that the team that they were now watching was simply not good enough. As I moved from boyhood to adolescence, Hibs took over my life. I was too old now to play children's games and too young for drinking and chasing girls, so it was Hibs all the way. When we weren't at school, my pals and I were talking about Hibs, reading about Hibs, watching Hibs or playing football ourselves and pretending we were Hibs. We were not the most critical of supporters but even we knew that things were not good at Easter Road.

The Hibs board decided to replace Hugh Shaw with Walter Galbraith. Galbraith came from the dizzy heights of Accrington Stanley having previously played for Queen's Park, Clyde and Grimsby, and having managed Bradford Park Avenue and Tranmere Rovers. It wasn't a CV to set the pulse racing and it wasn't an appointment which displayed ambition. Galbraith looked like a 1930s film star with his pencil moustache and slicked back hair. He was much more at home in a lounge suit than a tracksuit and he was not a roaring success. He started his career at Easter Road by signing a procession of lower league players from England and following the team swiftly became an exercise in masochism.

Apparently every time Galbraith came into the dressing room, which was not all that often, he would ask the players, 'Everything all right boys?' before checking his appearance in the mirror and leaving again. Yet he had some good players to work with. The young Jimmy O'Rourke, Eric Stevenson and Jim Scott were all at the club and were all extremely talented footballers. The club had also signed Joe Baker's brother Gerry from Manchester City. Gerry was an excellent goalscorer with frightening pace and did well for Hibs. He wasn't anything like as good as his younger brother of course (no one was) and in my opinion was always compared unfavourably, and unfairly, with Joe during his time at Easter Road.

I attended Holy Cross Secondary School at this time and played for the school team. When our Saturday morning school match finished, we always changed quickly and raced back out to watch the 'Firsts,' as we called the school's top team, play their match. These games were huge occasions, often watched by large crowds. In the Holy Cross team were three players who would play for Hibs – Davie Hogg, Jimmy O'Rourke and Pat Stanton. Pat was quiet then as now, Davie was a tricky winger who was handicapped by short-sightedness and Jimmy was just Jimmy – a tremendous character. He used to regale us youngsters with outrageous stories about his times with the Scotland schoolboy team and his training sessions at Hibs. He also devised, and carried out, many a practical joke although he always made sure that he was the instigator and not the victim!

I remember a weekend school trip to Middleton Camp in Gorebridge one freezing February. We had to sleep in bunk beds. I was amazed when Jimmy showed unusual magnanimity and offered the boy who was sharing his bunk the opportunity to take the top bed. He gratefully accepted only to wake up in the middle of the night shivering with the cold. Jimmy had waited until he was asleep and then pinched his bedcovers. While Jimmy slept soundly wrapped in two lots of blankets his friend lay awake most of the night chittering.

The biggest Holy Cross matches were against Tynecastle High School and St Anthony's. The Tynecastle games were seen as mini Hibs-Hearts games and were taken very seriously. Holy Cross usually came out on top. I remember one game when Jimmy O'Rourke scored with a rocket drive. The nets were not completely secured and Jimmy's shot went straight through the bottom of the net and crashed into the front wheel of a bike belonging to a boy behind the goals with such force that it broke the spokes. The boy with the bike was an American who was on holiday and was flabbergasted at the damage that the O'Rourke thunderbolt had wrought on his machine. When he regained his composure, he exclaimed, 'Hey, that guy's a human cannonball!'

The matches with St Anthony's were also keenly fought. I remember in particular a Colonel Clark Cup Final, which was played at Easter Road. The schools drew 2–2 and shared the cup. O'Rourke netted a beauty for Holy Cross and the St Anthony's goalkeeper, who produced an outstanding performance, was none other than Alan Lugton who went on to write the magnificent *Making of Hibernian* trilogy.

Jimmy made his debut for Hibs in December 1962 at the age of sixteen, in a Fairs Cup match against the Dutch team Utrecht. Hibs won 2–1. Gerry Baker scored a goal described in the press as 'a goal in a thousand' and Jimmy O'Rourke was the star of the show. The *Daily Record* noted: 'A youngster with an Irish name – Jim O'Rourke – played a notable part in Hibernian's victory.' Next day at school, Jimmy was surrounded by adoring acolytes wherever he went. As always, he took the adoration in his stride and took great pleasure in recounting his every move from the previous night's game.

1962–63 was the season of the 'Big Freeze' when hardly any football was played during January and February due to Arctic conditions. Hibs looked doomed to relegation under Galbraith but stayed up by virtue of a late rally which culminated in a victory over Raith Rovers at Starks Park on the last day of the season. The team not only won that day but also scored four goals, so we saved ourselves in style.

The next season saw Harry Swan hand over the reins to a new chairman in William Harrower. Swan had presided over years of success and innovation. He had pioneered floodlit football, led Hibs into the first ever European Cup and taken the club on tour to countries such as Brazil when other teams were content to stay much closer to home. He was never one to refuse a good offer for a player though. Hibs drew huge crowds in the late 1940s and early 1950s and their outlay in wages was not large. Still, Swan chose to sell Bobby Johnstone to Manchester City when he could easily have kept him. Later, as we have seen, his response to Joe Baker asking for a wage increase of £5 per week was to sell him to Torino for £65,000, which was a massive amount in those days. However as we have also seen, it wasn't massive enough to stop Swan selling Johnny McLeod to Arsenal for £45,000 a few weeks later.

Swan made Rod Petrie look like a spendthrift. As Hibs fought desperately to retain their top league status in 1962–63, we fans were delighted one day to see a billboard proclaiming 'HIBS SWOOP FOR SCOTLAND STAR'. On buying the paper, I found out that the aforementioned 'Scotland star' was Kilmarnock's veteran centre half Willie Toner whose Scotland days were well behind him. The report also revealed that Kilmarnock had wanted £1,000 for Toner but Swan had beaten them down to £750! Hibs fans were severely disillusioned at this time. The crowd at the Utrecht match in which O'Rourke made his debut was 5,000. When Hibs met Valencia in April 1963, only 4,000 turned up. Only two years earlier, 47,000 had crammed into Easter Road for the match with Barcelona and another 40,000 had made the return journey for the tie with Roma

It was not difficult to see why the fans had lost faith.

Galbraith had replaced the outstanding players, which Harry Swan had sold, with lower league non-entities from England. Most prominent among this group was a centre forward called Harvey McCreadie. Harvey was a wholehearted but extremely limited player. He was good in the air but his efforts on the ground were generally lamentable. In one match, he had struggled even more than usual, displaying poor ball control and wayward shooting. Near the end of the game, Hibs got a free kick on the edge of the opposition penalty area. To the amazement of the crowd, McCreadie lined up to take it. At that time, there was a fan called Big Walter who stood near us. He had a repertoire of what he considered to be pithy comments. Sometimes he found his comments to be more amusing than did those about him. On this day, however, he found exactly the right phrase. As McCreadie placed the ball for the free kick, Walter shouted, 'Take it wi' your heid, Harvey.'

The Fairs Cup match against Valencia at Easter Road was the second-leg match. Hibs won 2–1 but sadly this mattered little as they had lost the first leg 5–0. Gerry Baker was again on target that night. Like his brother, he thrived on European competition. The newly signed Willie Toner also excelled at centre half in this match. Toner, in fact, proved to be a good signing as his experience when allied with the skills of players like O'Rourke, Scott, Baker and Stevenson proved enough to keep Hibs up, even if it was a close-run thing. Hibs fans are passionate, can also be short on patience and critical, but above all they are knowledgeable. We all knew that we had some good players, but we also knew that we had even more poor players and our struggling team was only a shadow of its forerunners and not nearly good enough. The change of chairman had come at exactly the right time.

The new chairman was a successful Edinburgh bookmaker and he bucked the trend set by his predecessor by giving his manager money to spend on players. Galbraith, to his credit, used the money wisely. Able now to operate in a higher market, he made some outstanding signings. From Queen of the South, he brought in Neil Martin, a prolific goalscorer who was particularly good in the air. Willie Hamilton, a flawed genius who had outstayed his welcome at Hearts, was bought for the scarcely credible sum of £6,000 and went on to become a Hibernian legend. Pat Quinn, who was what used to be known as a midfield general, had made his name at Motherwell alongside great players like Ian St John and Bert McCann. Pat had moved to Blackpool, who were then in the top flight of English football, for £34,000. A year later, Walter Galbraith signed him for Hibs for £26,000. The last of Galbraith's signings was John Parke, a classy, footballing left back from Linfield whom he had watched starring in a home international match for Northern Ireland against Scotland. Around this time Galbraith also introduced a promising local teenager called Patrick Gordon Stanton to the Hibs first team. Pat scored against Motherwell on his debut but the team lost 4–3. The team now contained much better players and had become fun to watch again, but we continued to be unpredictable and results, although better, were still disappointing. It wasn't clear what the future held for Hibs under the guidance of Walter Galbraith. However, things were about to change and to change in a big way. In March 1964, Walter Galbraith resigned and was replaced by Jock Stein.

Stein was only with Hibs for a year but what a year it was to prove to be. He added John MacNamee's commanding physical presence at centre half to the gifted set of players he had inherited from Galbraith. He organised them and motivated them, and the good times began to roll.

5

JOCK STEIN AND THE SHORT-LIVED DREAM

When Jock Stein was named as Hibs manager to replace Walter Galbraith, every Hibs fan welcomed his appointment. Stein had transformed Dunfermline in his three years in charge of the Fife club. He had saved them from what had seemed like certain relegation when he took over, had won the Scottish Cup beating his old team Celtic in the final and had achieved memorable victories in Europe, most notably over Everton and Valencia. Now the Big Man was at Easter Road. He inherited some excellent players and quickly did what his predecessor had failed to do, turning a collection of talented individual players into a successful team.

He had Ronnie Simpson in goal when he first came but for some reason he left Ronnie out, then sold him to Celtic. Simpson, of course, went on to have a great end to his career at Celtic and the conspiracy theorists were convinced that Stein had let Simpson go to Celtic because he knew that he himself would be going back there in due course. We'll never know the truth of it but it did seem a strange decision to let such a talented goalkeeper go for next to nothing. After Simpson's departure, Stein used Willie Wilson as his first-choice goalkeeper. Willie was a naturally gifted goalkeeper who could play brilliantly on some occasions and make costly errors at other times. He also tended to carry a little too much weight, which was surprising in a goalkeeper as young as he was when Stein was manager. I got to know Willie many years later when my son played for a juvenile team in East Lothian and Willie, who came from Wallyford, was the goal-keeping coach. After he had put his teenage goalkeepers through their paces in training, Willie would come and join the parents for a blether. He was a lovely man and liked nothing better than recalling his days with Hibs. It often occurred to me that it may well have been his easy-going nature which had stopped him being sufficiently driven to reach the top as a player. He had certainly had the ability.

Stein's full backs were John Fraser and John Parke. Fraser had started his career as a forward and liked nothing better than attacking down the right wing. He was also sound defensively, which is why he earned the nickname 'Safety Razor'. Parke was a cultured footballer who tackled expertly and used the ball skilfully. When Stein received an offer of £40,000 from Sunderland for Parke, he quietly accepted it then went out and bought Joe Davis from Third Lanark for £14,000 before he made both deals public. This was an excellent piece of business as Davis went on to become club captain, recorded 273 consecutive appearances at one stage and scored forty-three goals from full back, mostly from the penalty spot.

Stein bought John MacNamee from Celtic when he first came to Easter Road. Big John was a magnificent centre half. He used his formidable physique to intimidate opposing forwards and was a menacing presence in the opposition penalty box at free kicks and corners. He often fell foul of referees and claimed to be a marked man. Some of the centre forwards he played against were also marked men – literally! Pat Stanton tells the story of how MacNamee almost surpassed himself before a Scottish Cup match against Rangers.

John was always even more motivated than usual when we played Rangers. He had an intense dislike of Jim Forrest who was Rangers' main goalscorer at the time. This day the two teams were waiting side by side in the tunnel before the game. John was standing next to Forrest and was telling him in no uncertain terms what he intended doing to him when the game started. At that point the referee Tiny Wharton materialised. He had clearly heard every word that big MacNamee had uttered. 'Mr MacNamee,' said Wharton. 'You are in grave danger of being the first man in football history to be sent off before the game has started.'

Pat Stanton was MacNamee's defensive partner in Stein's time at Hibs. Although he was only twenty years old at this stage of his career, Pat was a consummate sweeper. He read the game astutely, made tackles and interceptions on a regular basis and used his footballing ability to start many moves from the back. Time and again, he would stride forward to link with his midfield and set yet another free-flowing attack in motion.

Stein had an embarrassment of riches in midfield, with Pat Quinn and Willie Hamilton as playmakers. Pat was a superb little player. In those days, the men who controlled the centre of the park were known as 'midfield generals.' Pat was the ultimate midfield general. Years later when I was managing the Edinburgh Primary Schools football team, I worked on a summer coaching course with Pat. He told me how he had gone home one night during his early career at Motherwell to be met by his mother who was clearly distressed.

'Oh son, you never told me,' she said.

'Never told you what, ma?' asked Pat.

'That you had joined the army,' wailed Mrs Quinn.

'What are you talking about?' replied her son.

She handed Pat a copy of that day's newspaper which had a photograph of Pat underneath the caption 'The Little General.'

Pat Quinn could thread a pass through the eye of a needle and he was the perfect complement for the one and only Willie Hamilton. Willie joined Hibs in 1963 at the age of twenty-five. He looked much older. Indeed he looked like he had had a hard life! He had begun his career in England playing for Middlesbrough and Sheffield United. At Sheffield his manager the late, great Joe Mercer hailed him as an outstanding talent. However, Willie was a man of wayward temperament and, in 1961, he was allowed to move back to Scotland to Hearts. He made a magnificent start to his career at Tynecastle. In 1962, he almost single-handedly inspired a League Cup Final victory over Kilmarnock. Willie laid on the winning goal for Norrie Davidson that day. Davidson was not only Hamilton's playing partner, he was his drinking partner off the field as well. Soon Hearts' strait-laced manager Tommy Walker decided that he had had enough of Willie's over-enthusiasm for socialising and his unquenchable thirst and sold him to Hibs for the incredibly low sum of £6,000.

It was Walter Galbraith who signed Willie Hamilton for Hibs but he never got the best out of him. Willie did brilliant things. I remember one game he played against Celtic at Easter Road not long after he had been signed. It was a freezing cold day but Willie was perspiring heavily, almost certainly due to the extra weight he was carrying and the amount of alcohol he had consumed the previous night. Halfway through the second half, he collected a ball on the edge of the Celtic penalty box while surrounded by defenders. He feinted to go one way but instead went the other, totally wrong-footing the Celtic players. He then instantly dispatched a low shot into the corner of the Celtic net. My friends and I looked at each other with delighted disbelief. We knew then that the Hibees had signed a genius. However, under Galbraith his performances were erratic. Jock Stein soon changed that. Stein got Hamilton fit and focused, and his midfield partnership with Quinn was a combination made in heaven.

The third member of Stein's midfield trio was John Baxter. Big Chinny had now added experience to his exuberance and under Stein was playing the best football of his career, displaying a new-found maturity.

Up front, our new manager had an array of options. Jim Scott normally led the line. Scott was a lavishly gifted footballer whose main asset was his silky dribbling. He would weave past two or three defenders with ease. He was also a regular marksman, although he tended to be more of a scorer of great goals than a great goalscorer. Out wide Stein had Peter Cormack on the right and Neil Martin on the left. Both of these players were natural strikers and tended to drift into a central position to support Scott. Cormack, who was only seventeen at this time, was a regular goalscorer and Martin was also a prolific finder of the net.

Providing backup for the forwards were Jimmy O'Rourke, Stan Vincent and Eric Stevenson. Jimmy, although still only eighteen, was a versatile powerhouse. Vincent, although awkward in style – his nickname was 'The Penguin' due to his running style – was a natural finisher and when he did play he could be relied upon to bag a goal. Stevenson was a highly-skilled left winger. He could dribble, pass, cross and shoot equally well. He was very similar in style to the late Davie Cooper, although in my opinion Stevenson was even better than that gifted performer. Stevenson had endeared himself to Hibs fans by extracting himself from Hearts and signing with Hibs. Hearts had illegally registered Eric as one of their players. He objected to this and walked out. Hearts were fined by the SFA and Stevenson was welcomed into the Easter Road fold and given the nickname 'The Rebel', a soubriquet which was to stay with him during his entire Easter Road career.

These were the players upon whom Jock Stein began to weave his magic. When the Big Man arrived in March 1964, Hibs were close to the relegation area. He soon took care of that and then set to work on winning a trophy. At the end of season 1963–64, the SFA introduced a new competition called the Summer Cup. All the top teams entered with the exception of Celtic and Rangers. Despite the absence of the Old Firm, the tournament was a great success. For once, all the other teams could compete on an even playing field and talent, rather than money or refereeing bias, was what counted.

The matches were exciting and well attended and Hibs fought their way to the final by beating Dunfermline and Kilmarnock, who were both very strong teams at that time, along the way. In the final, we were paired with Aberdeen. Unfortunately, there was an outbreak of typhoid in Aberdeen and the medical authorities ruled that the two-legged final would have to be held over until the start of the new season. The two matches were played only four days apart with the first match at Aberdeen. My Hibs-supporting friends and I were broken-hearted to miss these games. We had booked for our first teenage holiday away from the bosom of our families. Feeling really grown-up and daring, we had arranged to go to Blackpool for a week (this was before foreign holidays were commonplace) and we had paid in advance. Imagine our chagrin when we discovered that the Summer Cup Final had been postponed. We tried to get our money back but weren't able to do so and had no option but to head for what was then Britain's most popular holiday resort.

We played football on the beach, listened to the Dave

Clark Five perform their number one hit, 'Glad All Over', in the Winter Gardens, sampled the delights of the local hostelries and made the young ladies that we met aware of the fact that they were incredibly fortunate to be able to spend time with such a group of handsome and talented young men from North of the Border – but all of the time our thoughts were on Hibs and the Summer Cup Final.

The second leg of the final was on a Wednesday evening and while Hibs and Aberdeen were doing battle at Easter Road, we were on Blackpool beach at the Radio One Roadshow listening to Lulu and the Luvvers. Jimmy Savile was the DJ in charge and at one point when there was a lull in the music, one of my friends called out: 'Hey Jimmy, do ye ken the score wi' the Hibs?'

The ever-friendly Savile called back, 'Sorry mate, I can't help you there.'

As it turned out, an Eric Stevenson goal in extra time had put Hibs on the verge of winning the trophy. However, with seconds remaining, the brilliant Charlie Cooke, who was to go on to become a Chelsea legend, equalised for the Dons. When we found out next morning how close our beloved Hibees had been to winning the cup, we were devastated. Then we realised that we would be home by the time the play-off took place and we perked up no end.

The Summer Cup Final play-off took place at Pittodrie after Aberdeen had won the toss for the choice of venue, and I am delighted to say that I was there. There was huge backing for Aberdeen and a significant travelling support from Edinburgh. It was to be the green army who made all the noise. Hibs were brilliant and no one was better than Willie Hamilton. 'The Duke' as he was known to the fans (as in Duke of Hamilton) controlled the game, weaving his magic all over the field. Really though Hibs were superb in every position that night and such was their dominance that despite a missed Pat Stanton penalty, they still ran out as comfortable 3–1 winners. The fans travelled home on a high. We had great players, we had just won a national trophy (albeit of the minor variety), we definitely had the best manager in the country and it seemed like the sky was the limit.

As the season progressed, it seemed like our high hopes were more than justified. We played great football and won games and then came a historic week in October. It started badly. On the Saturday, we lost 2–1 at home to Kilmarnock. Killie were a top side at that time and managed by ex-Rangers great Willie Waddell. Hibs played superbly but missed chances galore, were defied over and over again by Kilmarnock's flamboyant goalkeeper Jimmy Brown and, in the end, were deprived of a point by the referee. With minutes to go, Jim Scott crashed a shot off the underside of the bar and over the line. It was a clear goal but the referee refused to award it and two important league points were dropped.

For once we Hibees were not overly depressed. This was because of an outstanding occasion coming up the following Wednesday. Jock Stein had arranged a challenge match against Real Madrid at Easter Road. Then, as now, the Spaniards were considered the best club team in the world. Their team of the early 1960s was their greatest ever line-up including all-time great players like Puskás, Di Stéfano and Gento. Hibs had to pay Real a massive guarantee and needed at least a 30,000 crowd to be able to meet the cost of this. Stein talked the match up relentlessly in the press and although the day of the game was one of non-stop torrential rain, 33,000 Hibees turned up to watch their heroes, wearing green shorts specially for the occasion, take on the mighty maestros of Madrid.

It was my privilege to be there to see one of Hibs' greatest ever performances. They were magnificent and won the game with a classic left-foot volley from Peter Cormack and an own goal from Zoco. Every Hibs player was outstanding but Willie Hamilton stole the show. John Rafferty, the doyen of Scottish football reporters, wrote in *The Scotsman* that Hamilton had 'out-Puskásed Puskás.' Willie was, however, his usual eccentric self. As Hibs defended a corner near the end with a famous victory on the horizon, Hamilton ran back to join his defence. This was a rare and almost unique occurrence. He beckoned the young Pat Stanton over to him. Pat came across expecting a pearl of tactical wisdom. Instead the Duke said to him, 'Hey Pat, is it true you get a watch for playing these boys?'

It was indeed true and Pat still has that watch to this day and the last time I spoke to him it was still keeping good time. Stanton came of age that night with an accomplished performance. He recalled, 'I knew that I had made it when Puskás went over the top on me. Fancy a great player like him kicking a wee laddie from Niddrie.' The Hibs team ran a lap of honour at the end of the game and they thoroughly deserved it. There was no time though for resting on their laurels because three days after beating the great Real, they were running out at Ibrox to face Rangers.

This was a top Rangers team with players like Ralph Brand and Jimmy Millar, Willie Henderson and Davie Wilson, as well as the inimitable Jim Baxter. As always that day Hibs had to face the intimidating atmosphere of the old Ibrox with 50,000 Rangers fans in it, and the certainty that the benefit of any refereeing doubt would be given to Rangers every time. Despite this and despite twice going behind, Hibs won 4–2 and played magnificently. Hibs' goals came from Cormack (with two), Quinn and Hamilton. Our attacking play was bewildering as the players constantly changed positions and displayed movement that left the Rangers international defenders floundering. Hamilton again provided the highlight of the match. Before the game, he had proclaimed that having taken care of Puskás on the Wednesday, he would 'sort out Baxter on the Saturday.' This he did in some style.

Leading 3–2 close to the end of the match, Hibs won a corner. The Duke raced across to receive the ball short. Baxter went with him with the air of a man who was thinking, 'Just leave this to me.' Hamilton took the ball, dummied to go one way and went the other. In the process he left Baxter sitting on the seat of his pants. Willie cut the ball back and Pat Quinn crashed in Hibs' fourth goal and sealed the victory. Baxter with typical chutzpah carefully tied his lace to give the impression that Hamilton hadn't actually deceived him and he had tripped over an untied lace.

He knew the truth was different though and so did we Hibees. As we left the ground we were sworn at and spat upon by Rangers fans who were unused to losing at Ibrox and were not responding well to this rare event. When we got back to our coach, they threw stones at the windows but none of this diluted our joy. We had beaten Real Madrid and Rangers in the same week and Big Jock was surely leading us to glory.

I had now taken my support to new levels of fanaticism. In those days, if Christmas Day fell on a Saturday, a full set of fixtures would be played in Scotland. On Christmas Day 1964, Hibs played Aberdeen at Pittodrie. The weather was icy and there were no underground heating systems for football pitches in those days. However, undaunted, my friends and I boarded the Eastern Branch supporters' coach at 9a.m. on that cold and frosty festive morning and headed for the Northern Lights.

We were seventeen years old and ready for a big adventure. We certainly got one. On a treacherous surface, which almost certainly wouldn't have been played on these days, Willie Hamilton put Hibs ahead and Aberdeen equalised through Don Kerrigan. Kerrigan subsequently moved to Hearts and become a bit of a thorn in Hibs flesh in derby matches. The game finished in a draw but the excitement was only just beginning.

In those days when the supporters club travelled to the more distant away games, the coach stayed on until around ten o'clock to let us fans sample the local nightlife after the game. Such were the vagaries of the roads at that time that even Perth was considered to be a distant destination!

Our intrepid group set out for the centre of Aberdeen. The pre-Christmas shopping and socialising had taken its toll. We had enough money for a good meal and a couple of drinks, or a fish supper and a major booze-up. Not surprisingly we chose the latter. Having left home at the crack of dawn, we were now ravenously hungry and our fish suppers, unhealthily delicious though they were, didn't really fill us up. We stood outside what seemed to us like a very posh restaurant and gazed enviously through the window at some of the members of the St Giles branch of the supporters club as they tucked into a slap-up meal. They compounded our agony by waving chicken legs and pork chops in front of us. The appetising aroma emanating from the restaurant tortured us further so, still hungry or not, we headed for the exotic delights of the East Neuk Pub and the Beach Ballroom. We drank, sang Christmas carols and the hits of the day and toasted our beloved Hibees until we realised that we had only had ten minutes to get back to the bus and we couldn't afford a taxi.

We were sober(ish) but had forgotten about the frosty pavements and one of our number slipped and broke his ankle. He claims to this day that his fall had nothing to do with the amount of alcohol he had consumed. We're not sure if we totally believe him. We carried him back to the bus. Two of us took his legs and two of us took his arms. As we ran through the cold night air acting as a human stretcher, we sang 'Glory Glory to the Hibees' at the top of our voices. Anyone seeing us would have thought we were mad but we didn't care because we were happy Christmas Hibees.

We made the bus and we made it home. I returned to my family home at around 2a.m. My presents were there to be opened and some cold chicken and stuffing had been left out for me (turkey was only for rich people in those days). I sat and reflected upon an eventful day. It hadn't been a traditional Christmas but it had been a special one – just another chapter in a life dedicated to supporting Hibernian FC.

Our next big challenge was the New Year derby against Hearts at Tynecastle. Again Willie Hamilton was to the fore. Halfway through the second half with the match goalless, Hamilton took a short free kick, received a return pass from Pat Quinn and hit the goal line. Everyone in the ground, including Hearts goalkeeper Jim Cruickshank, expected a cross. Instead, Hamilton swerved a glorious shot into the roof of the net with the outside of his left foot. It was a goal fit to win any game and it certainly won this one.

We received a temporary setback early in 1965 with a 4–3 defeat at Kilmarnock. We didn't deserve to lose but Willie Wilson did not have his best night between the posts and the referee did Hibs no favours. The race for the league title was now between Hibs, Hearts and Kilmarnock with the Old Firm, for once, not in contention. Stein was determined to get Hibs' challenge back on track. The return match with Rangers at Easter Road was in doubt because of snow. The Big Man pulled out all the stops to get the snow cleared and the pitch playable and the game went ahead. Stein's reward was a great Hibs performance in front of a crowd of nearly 50,000 which led to a 1–0 victory through a magnificent headed goal from Neil Martin, who must have been four feet off the ground when he met the ball.

We were also in the Scottish Cup quarter-final and were drawn against Rangers at Easter Road. Rangers were boosted for this match with the return from serious injury of their top player Jim Baxter, but again it was Hibs who came out on top. With the teams locked at 1–1 and two minutes to go, John Fraser overlapped down the right flank of the slope. He fired over a waist-high cross and there, flying horizontally through the air, was the great Willie Hamilton to head-glance home his second and Hibs' winning goal. Hibs had beaten Rangers three times in one season, were in the Scottish Cup semi-final and were well placed to win the league. Easter Road erupted with unconfined joy but that joy was to be much diluted before this Saturday night was out.

In those days, the pubs closed at ten o'clock. You were allowed a few minutes to finish your last drink and then you were turfed out into the street. Our Saturday night custom after a great Hibs victory was to celebrate with a few drinks in the pubs of Leith Walk and then to make our way at closing time up to the top of the Waverley Steps where the early editions of the Sunday papers went on sale from around eleven o'clock. We followed our usual routine that March Saturday evening but our happiness turned to despair when we saw the billboards.

The message on the boards was clear and chilling. It simply read 'STEIN FOR CELTIC'. After only one year at Easter Road, Jock Stein had accepted an offer to return to Parkhead and Hibs Chairman William Harrower was allowing him to go straight away. I have never understood why Harrower did not keep Stein until the end of the season. Perhaps he just felt that it did not make sense to retain Stein when his heart was somewhere else.

Whatever the reason for Stein's early release, his departure knocked the heart out of Hibs' season. We lost to Dunfermline in the Scottish Cup semi-final and our league challenge fell away. We did beat Celtic 4–2 at Parkhead with Neil Martin scoring a hat-trick but even this great result did little to console us. Stein won the Scottish Cup with Celtic and two short years later he was winning the European Cup with them. What he would have achieved if he had stayed with Hibs can only be guessed at. Of one thing I am completely certain though. If Celtic had left their approach for Stein until the end of season 1964–65, Hibs would have won the league, the cup or both that season.

I managed to get some more major consolation at Tynecastle on the last day of the season. Hearts played Kilmarnock and only needed to avoid losing by two clear goals to win the league. Their goal average would have been way beyond Kilmarnock if they hadn't lost 7–1 to Dundee at Tynecastle earlier in the season. Hibs were playing Morton at Cappielow that day. On the way back the bus convenor ordered our coach driver to re-enter the city via Gorgie. As we approached the west of the city, he instructed us to conceal our scarves. Coming through Ardmillan we saw a lot of disgruntled looking Hearts fans coming out of pubs having clearly failed to drown their sorrows.

Alan Middlemist, the convenor, asked the driver to stop the bus. He opened the door and spoke to the Jambos. 'Excuse me,' he said. 'We're tourists. Is there a football team plays around here?' Having received confirmation that there was, he continued, 'Were they playing today?' He was told they had been. With exaggerated innocence, he then asked what the score had been. When the Hearts supporters told us through gritted teeth that their team had lost 7–1 to Dundee, our bus erupted and the previously hidden scarves reappeared to be triumphantly waved as we headed swiftly for the safety of Princes Street.

I am not sure why I went along to Hearts title showdown with Kilmarnock, but I did. I stood in joyful amazement as, against all expectations, the Ayrshire team achieved a 2–0 victory. This victory gave Killie the league title and broke the hearts of the Tynecastle faithful. I perfected the art of silent celebration as I watched grown men cry.

In truth, I felt like crying myself as the great Stein dream had proved to be short-lived. As they had done in the past, and as they would do in the future, Celtic had robbed Hibs of a major asset at a time when we could least afford for this to happen.

6

BOB SHANKLY AND THE NEVER-ENDING SALE

Jock Stein was replaced as Hibs manager by Bob Shankly. Stein apparently had recommended Shankly to the board. He was great friends with Shankly and his more famous brother Bill, the legendary manager of Liverpool. It would be Bill Shankly who told Stein in 1967 after he had won the European Cup: 'John, you're immortal.' Sadly, as tragic events in Cardiff in 1985 were to show, these words were not literally true. However, back in 1965 Stein certainly seemed irreplaceable.

Someone had to succeed him though and Bob Shankly was that man. Shankly was not without pedigree. He had won the league with Dundee and had led the Taysiders in an impressive European Cup campaign. He had agreed to come to Hibs because he was disenchanted with Dundee for continually selling their best players. As we shall see there was to be a certain irony in that situation. Shankly failed to stop the final part of the 1964–65 season turning into a major anticlimax for Hibs. Such was the severity of the blow dealt to the club by Stein's sudden departure, that Hibs supporters were prepared to reserve judgement on his tenure until the following season.

He did not endear himself to his new fans though by one of his early actions. He sold Willie Hamilton to Aston Villa for £25,000. Hamilton must have been a difficult player to control. Football was something he fitted into his social calendar but Stein had proved that with firm handling he could be a match winner without equal. Shankly had clearly decided that Hamilton was more trouble than he was worth. During the close season of 1965, the new manager had taken Hibs on tour to Canada. In one match Hamilton had displayed his footballing prowess by scoring seven goals. He was presented with a handsome and valuable silver salver as man of the match. He proceeded to show his attitude to life by bending the salver in half to fit it into his bag.

One of my friends at that time, Walter Easton or 'Waldo' as he was known, idolised Willie Hamilton. He slept with his picture above his bed and, no mean amateur football himself, he tried to model his own playing style on the great man. On the day the news broke that Hamilton had been transferred, Walter was having a haircut in a barber's shop on Leith Walk. When he heard the news of Willie's transfer on the shop radio, he leapt from the chair, threw some money at the startled barber and headed for the door.

'Where are you going?' the barber asked.

'To get a paper. Hibs have sold Willie Hamilton.'

'But your hair's only half cut,' spluttered the barber.

'Aye and so will I be before the night's out,' replied the bold Waldo.

I wonder if Aston Villa knew what they were getting for their money. They were acquiring a footballing genius who could drift effortlessly past opponents, pick out and execute exquisite passes with nonchalance and score wonderful goals. They were also signing a man for whom training was an inconvenience, only to be tolerated at the manager's insistence and for whom the consumption of alcohol and carousing was as natural as breathing.

Shankly made another sale in his first season, but this time he did so reluctantly. Neil Martin, another much loved player who could be relied on to score goals galore, was sold to Sunderland for a large fee. Despite all this, Hibs were playing well. With the exception of the two players mentioned, Shankly had retained the core of Stein's team. He made more use of Jimmy O'Rourke and Eric Stevenson than Stein had done. These two were excellent players and true Hibees. He also gave promising young players like John Blackley and Peter Marinello the opportunity to become first-team players. Under Shankly, Hibs always looked capable of winning a trophy but I don't think that we fans ever really thought that they would. His team played an exciting brand of attacking football and we were never short of entertainment. However, the team did lack solidity and too often we were beaten by inferior teams who were more physical in their approach.

During the Bob Shankly era, I met the lady who would become my wife and who remains my best friend and fellow Hibbie to this day. We are now approaching forty years of happily married life and, unsurprisingly, we met through the Hibs connection. I travelled on the supporters' bus to Parkhead one grey October day. On the bus that day were a couple of very attractive young ladies making their first trip. When we got to Celtic Park, there was a thick mist. The game was called off and the bus convenor decided that we should spend the afternoon in Glasgow so that our journey wasn't completely wasted.

I got talking to our two new female supporters and by the time I got off the bus back in Edinburgh, I had made a date with one of them. Making that date was probably the best move I ever made in my life. By this time, I had left school and was training to become a teacher. Given our shared love of all things Hibernian, our romance blossomed quickly and we got engaged in October 1967. On the day of our engagement,

Hibs beat Airdrie 4–1 at Easter Road. Our celebration party was the following Saturday and I had a great time having returned from watching Hibs demolish Dundee 4–1 at Dens Park. These high-scoring encounters were typical of Shankly's Hibs. In that same season, Partick Thistle were defeated 7–0 and Hamilton Accies were humiliated 11–1.

Our engagement was not always straightforward. One Wednesday we went up to Pittodrie for a Scottish Cup replay. I was wearing my best suit which was, in fact, my only suit. When we got there, the gates had been locked. Quite a number of supporters' buses arrived at around the same time. The fans were disgruntled to say the least at the prospect of missing a game they had travelled so far to see and began to push against the gate. The gate soon gave way and everyone started racing into the ground. I was knocked over in the rush and ripped the knee out of the trousers of my one and only suit. By the time I picked myself up the gates had been locked again. My ever-loving fiancée and her brother had gone in, leaving me lying in the dirt. I had to spend the game with a lot of other fans outside the ground with a cut knee and torn trousers. To make matters worse, Aberdeen, managed by Eddie Turnbull, won the game 3–0.

By this time Shankly had a settled team. John MacNamee had also moved on. He had been sold to Newcastle and replaced by John Madsen. Big MacNamee had been a huge character in every way. In a League Cup match against Rangers, he had risen to head home the winning goal in the last minute, scattering Rangers defenders including John Greig as he did so. As he had picked himself up to celebrate, he had further nonplussed the Ibrox men by uttering the immortal line, 'That's sunk your submarine then.'

His successor was smaller of stature but no less hard. Madsen had a blond skinhead which gave him a bullet-headed appearance. He looked like a mini version of Manchester United's Nemanja Vidić and played in a similar style. His commitment was total and the fans took to him very quickly. He was now partnered in central defence by the youthful John Blackley, with an exciting young attacking talent in local lad Bobby Duncan at right back and the ever-reliable Joe Davis at left back. Willie Wilson was still first-choice goalkeeper although by this time his weight problems were, if anything, more pronounced than before. Willie was being challenged for his position by a promising goalkeeper called Thomson Allan.

Pat Stanton and Pat Quinn formed a classy midfield partnership with Alan McGraw also doing sterling work in that area when selected. Up front, we had a wealth of talent.

Jim Scott had also been sold to Newcastle. Just as Hibs had replaced Joe Baker with his brother Gerry in the early '60s, now, at the end of the decade, Jim Scott was replaced by his brother Alex. Alex had been a star at Rangers before making a big money move to Everton when Willie Henderson had emerged at Ibrox. He had pace and skill and was a magnificent crosser of the ball from his right-wing beat. On the other flank, Eric Stevenson had now established himself as the regular choice which his talent had long suggested he should be. Eric was full of tricks that he performed at pace. He was able to wrong-foot every full back he came up against and earned Hibs a lot of penalties by being brought down by desperate lunges from the defenders he was facing, as they just could not cope with his balance and elusiveness. He also scored his fair share of goals.

Hibs twin strike force was Peter Cormack and Colin Stein. Cormack had started out under Jock Stein as a right winger but Shankly had converted him into a striker. He was brave, mobile, superb in the air and a highly accomplished finisher.

Stein was an all-action centre forward who had burst onto the scene with a real flourish. He could dribble, head, shoot and score. He never stopped running and foraging and defenders hated to play against him. These two were backed up by Jimmy O'Rourke, still just in his early twenties and developing all the time as a footballer, and Peter Marinello. Jimmy stepped in whenever anyone was injured and did a great job across all the forward positions. Marinello had exciting potential and was being brought along selectively and sensibly by his manager.

A great example of Jimmy O'Rourke's value to Hibs was a derby match at Tynecastle during the Shankly era. Making one of his regular stand-in appearances, Jimmy scored two great goals in the first ten minutes as did Eric Stevenson and, unbelievably, we were 4–0 up by ten past three. Hearts fans coming in late heard the score in disbelief, turned round and went straight back out again. We Hibs fans stayed to celebrate. The team was content to maintain its early lead and there was no further scoring. I have always felt that if Hibs had kept their foot on the pedal that day, a certain 7–0 scoreline at Tynecastle might just have happened a few years earlier than it eventually did.

Bob Shankly had a great record against Hearts. Another notable victory at Tynecastle took place in September 1967. Just prior to this, Willie Hamilton had returned to Edinburgh. Having started his Aston Villa career brilliantly, he had then been injured in a car crash. Villa had decided to release him shortly afterwards. Willie was now a free agent and had headed for Easter Road. One of Hibs' directors at that time, Sir John Bruce, was an eminent surgeon. He apparently told Bob Shankly that Hamilton's health was not good and that it would be too big a risk to sign him. This news hugely disappointed the Hibs support. To make matters worse, Hearts stepped in and signed Willie, although the player himself had made it clear that Easter Road was his preferred destination.

Anyway, Willie was in Hearts' line-up for this early season derby. It is the only time that I have ever seen the Hibs support applaud a Hearts player as he ran onto the pitch. In the event it was Hamilton's old midfield partner Pat Quinn who took the plaudits. Hibs won 4–1 and Pat scored three of them. The fans sang 'Hat-trick for Patrick' and after the game the wee man announced that if he had known scoring a hat-trick against Hearts would make him so popular, he would have done it years ago!

After the game, a few of us went round the back of the stand to congratulate Pat Quinn on his feat. When he emerged he was in the company of a certain W. Hamilton. The Duke was dressed in a Hearts blazer but was singing a duet of a Hibs song in harmony with wee Pat. Willie's second coming at Hearts didn't last long and sadly he slid down the leagues before dying a tragically young death in South Africa at the age of thirty-eight. He was a victim of naturally poor health and a lifestyle completely unsuited to a professional sportsman. He only played for Hibs for two years but in that short time he had made such an impression that, to this day, he is still revered and loved by Hibs supporters of my vintage.

If Hibs fans of today want to appreciate fully just how good Willie Hamilton was, they need look no further than a story which Pat Stanton never tires of telling. When Pat was at Celtic in the late '70s, he was having a dressing-room chat with Roy Aitken and the late Tommy Burns after training. They were discussing who was the best player they had played with, or against. Pat said that he had no doubt at all about his choice. It had to be Willie Hamilton. Displaying the type of tunnel vision which characterises the Old Firm to this day, Aitken and Burns said that they had never heard of Hamilton.

At this point, Jock Stein who had been listening to their conversation came out of the showers. He said, 'Pat is absolutely right. He's not only the best player who Pat Stanton has ever seen, he's also the best player Jock Stein has ever seen.'

Another famous victory over Hearts was at Easter Road in the New Year derby of 1968. Hibs hadn't won a home Ne'er-Day derby for twenty years, but this time they were determined to break that long-standing hoodoo. Just before the end of a closely-fought match, Eric Stevenson burst into the Hearts box at pace and was sent flying by Hearts' George Fleming. Referee Willie Syme (father of David of later infamy) had already turned down two strong penalty claims but this time he pointed to the spot. Up stepped Joe Davis. I was at the game with my fiancée Margaret, her dad and her dad's friend Frankie Dearie. As Davis placed the ball on the spot, Frankie said, 'It's not really important whether he scores or not. It's only a game.' Our left back and captain did his usual reliable job despatching the ball past Jim Cruickshank with aplomb. I looked over to Frankie to see how he was reacting but the man, who didn't really care whether Hibs scored or not, was oblivious to the outcome of Davis' kick. He had had his eyes covered by his hands and his head bowed in prayer as he invoked the beneficence of the Almighty to ensure that elusive New Year derby day victory at Easter Road. His prayers were answered and that night's New Year celebrations were even better than usual.

Shankly's record against Celtic at this time was less impressive. Celtic were the best team in Europe and had outstanding attacking options in every area of the pitch. Other teams defended in depth against them but Shankly attacked them head-on. The outcome was usually a highly entertaining game that Celtic won comfortably. In the autumn of 1966, Hibs and Celtic met at Easter Road. Both teams were unbeaten and both teams went on an all-out attack. Celtic prevailed in a 5–3 classic. In 1967, while the Beatles were singing 'All you need is Love', Hibs and Celtic were operating on the principle that all you need is goals. Again they met at Easter Road as Scotland's two highest scoring teams. A titanic struggle was locked at 1–1 when Hibs were awarded a seventy-second-minute penalty. Joe Davis sent Ronnie Simpson the wrong way from the spot, but all he succeeded in doing was galvanising Celtic. Stein's mighty men stormed down the slope for the remainder of the game, scoring four times and putting a totally deceptive gloss on the final 5–2 scoreline.

Hibs reached the League Cup Final in 1968. The match was held over until early 1969 after a fire in the stand at Hampden. Again Hibs adopted a gung-ho approach and again they paid for it. This time Celtic won 6–2. Indeed they were six goals up at one stage before O'Rourke and Stevenson scored late goals to achieve a modicum of respectability.

Shankly also led Hibs into some classic European matches. In November 1967 we met Napoli in the Fairs Cup. The Italian league leaders won the first leg comfortably 4–1. Everyone assumed that they were safely through to the quarter-finals. Everyone except Bob Shankly. The normally reserved Hibs boss was convinced that his team could still go through and he relayed this message to anybody who was prepared to listen. Napoli trained at Easter Road the night before the game. Their renowned goalkeeper Dino Zoff looked well-nigh unbeatable. Their manager was so confident that he sat in the directors' box sipping a large whisky.

The night of the game was my twentieth birthday and what a present the Hibees gave me. Within minutes of the start of the match Bobby Duncan scored a thirty-yard rocket, which he fired with his left foot high into Zoff's net. Just before half-time, Pat Quinn slipped home a second from close range and the impossible was becoming distinctly possible. Hibs roared down the slope in the second half and amazingly scored three more goals. A towering header by Peter Cormack from an Alex Scott corner was followed by another header from Pat Stanton. A run and shot by Colin Stein finished things off. The crowd staggered out of Easter Road drunk on adrenalin and headed for the local bars to get drunk on something else. I had arranged to meet friends for a birthday celebration at Tiffany's in Stockbridge, which was the fashionable nightspot in Edinburgh in those days. I went because I had to but in all honesty I would rather have joined the celebrations in the Hibs Supporters Club.

Dino Zoff looked shell-shocked at the end of the game. I don't know if his manager had a whisky that night but he would certainly have needed one. The headline above the *Daily Record* match report screamed, 'THIS WAS HIBS NIGHT OF MIRACLES'. Bob Shankly, in rather more subdued fashion, permitted himself the satisfaction of stating, 'I knew from what I saw over there that we could beat them but I didn't expect a victory as complete as this.' Hibs being Hibs followed that magnificent performance and historic result by losing 1–0 at home to Morton three days later.

Next in line in the Fairs Cup was mighty Leeds United. Don Revie's combination of class and callousness was the best team in England at that point, as well as one of the best teams in Europe. The first leg was played at Elland Road just before Christmas. Hibs played magnificently and un-deservedly lost 1–0. The return leg, in January 1968, was played on the night after one of the worst storms in Edinburgh's history. Severe gale-force winds had ripped into the city's buildings causing major damage. Hibs started this match at hurricane force pace and scored an early goal from Colin Stein. Hibs retained the upper hand throughout the match and with only a few minutes remaining, extra time appeared imminent.

Then fate, in the form of referee Clive Thomas, took a hand. FIFA had just introduced the four-step rule for goal-keepers. The rule, which was designed to prevent timewasting, decreed that if a goalkeeper took more than four steps before clearing the ball, he should be penalised by an indirect free kick. All through the game, Leeds goalkeeper Gary Sprake had been allowed to take as many steps as he liked. Television evidence after the game showed that he had actually taken nine steps before clearing on one occasion. Mr Thomas liked nothing better than being at the centre of controversy (he had once disallowed what would have been a winning Brazilian goal in a World Cup match by blowing for full time as the ball passed through the air into the net) and he excelled himself on this occasion.

As Willie Wilson tried to clear the ball, he was jostled into an extra step by a Leeds forward. The whistle sounded and everyone expected a free kick to be awarded to Hibs. Incredibly the Welsh referee penalised Wilson for over-carrying and gave Leeds an indirect free kick inside Hibs penalty area. What happened next was inevitable. Johnny Giles floated over the free kick and Jackie Charlton headed it in to give Leeds a thoroughly unmerited victory. The controversy-loving Mr Thomas no doubt went home happy. We Hibs fans departed experiencing a very different set of emotions indeed.

Bob Shankly hated to sell his best players. A case in point was Colin Stein. Stein was the original action man of a centre forward. The Hibs fans loved him until one day out of the blue he asked for a transfer and announced that he had always wanted to play for Rangers. Obviously Rangers had always wanted Stein to play for them too, because in no time at all they had offered £100,000 for him. Even though this was a huge amount of money in those days, there was embarrassing haste about the alacrity with which our board accepted this bid. The Hibs fans never forgave Stein for deserting them as he did. For a few years after his departure, every stray dog which ran on the pitch during a game at Easter Road was met with a chant of 'Colin, Colin, Colin Stein!'

As luck would have it, Hibs met Rangers and Stein at Ibrox not long after the striker's move had taken place. Predictably Rangers won 6–1 and Stein scored a hat-trick. The Hibs scorer in that match was Joe McBride. Shankly had signed McBride for £20,000 to replace Stein. He followed his goal in that debut match with two in mid-week against Hamburg in the UEFA Cup, and four against Morton in the league on the Saturday. He went on to be Hibs top scorer for two consecutive seasons. He also repaid his old club Celtic for deeming him surplus to requirements by scoring two goals against them at Easter Road to give Shankly one of his few triumphs over Stein. McBride's first goal in that match was an exceptional overhead kick – one of the best Hibs goals I have ever seen. His son Joe Junior also played for Hibs in the 1980s and was a highly skilled left winger who graced his father's illustrious footsteps.

Shankly had an eye for a player as his bargain basement signing of Joe McBride proved. He liked to buy, but he was totally opposed to selling players he wanted to keep. He had encountered this problem at Dundee and was now experiencing similar difficulties with Hibs. More and more, the board forced him to sell his good players. This was a shame as he had built an excellent team. It was always exciting to watch Hibs under his astute management. He may not have been as flamboyant a character as his more famous brother but he knew the game inside out and, in his own quiet way, was capable of producing a Hibs team which could match the best.

In particular, I remember one game at East End Park in the late '60s. Dunfermline were a side to reckon with at that time and very few sides got the better of them on their home patch. Hibs played sublime football that day and early in the second half were 5–2 ahead. Unfortunately, we took our foot off the gas and Dunfermline fought back to level the match at 5–5. However, there was to be a happy ending. In the very last minute Jim Scott, a centre forward who possessed exquisite skill but who was not always a certain finisher, broke through and converted a difficult one-on-one opportunity to seal a famous win. We fans on the old East End Park terracing, who had gone from the heights of happiness to the depths of despair all in the one afternoon, danced with delight as our Hibee heroes treated us to another roller coaster ride which, thankfully, this time had ended in success.

Since arriving at Hibs, Bob Shankly had been forced to sell John MacNamee, Neil Martin, Jim Scott and Colin Stein and had chosen to transfer Willie Hamilton. All of these were players of the highest class. Peter Cormack had been eying a move for some time but Shankly had resisted all his overtures. However, speculation mounted that Arsenal were poised to move for Cormack. I am sure that Shankly thought that it was inevitable that when an offer came in, the board which always said 'yes' would answer in the affirmative once more. Cormack would have been a huge loss and the prospect of that loss was just too much for Bob Shankly. The man who loathed having to sell his best players had had enough. He tendered his resignation and Hibs were once again looking for a new manager.

7

MCFARLANE, MARINELLO AND THE BAKER BOY RETURNS

When Bob Shankly left Hibs in 1969, he had had enough of leading a selling club. However he signed off in style. His second-last game in charge was against Celtic at Parkhead. This was the Celtic team that had won the European Cup two years earlier and was to reach the final of the premier European competition again that very season. It was almost unheard of for them to lose at Parkhead at that time. Come to think of it, they don't lose too many home matches these days either. Anyway, on 13 September 1969 Hibs went to Glasgow and beat Celtic 2–1 with goals from Johnny Hamilton and Pat Stanton to make it a special day. It was even more special for me because it was my wedding day. Margaret and I were uttering our marriage vows as Hibs achieved their famous victory and that outstanding result helped the wedding speeches to go with a swing.

The priest who married us was called Father Stephen McGrath. He was a Mancunian and a football man. Indeed, he claimed to have played in goal for England Schoolboys before he went off to the seminary to train for his religious life. His teams were England and Manchester United but he didn't take much of an interest in Scottish football. He had already performed the marriage ceremonies for Margaret's two older sisters. Tricia's wedding took place on the day of the 1966 Word Cup Final so, of course, Father Stephen used his speech at the reception to praise Bobby Moore and company to the heights. When Frances was married in 1968, her wedding came three days after Manchester United's European Cup Final win over Benfica. This time Father Stephen's speech lauded the achievement of his beloved Reds. When he rose to speak at our wedding reception, he began by saying that he was sorry that he wouldn't be able to continue his tradition of starting his speech with news of a footballing triumph. I immediately rose to correct him and pointed out that Hibs had just beaten Celtic at Parkhead and although, as an Englishman, he might not realise it, this was far more important than England winning the World Cup or Manchester United capturing the European Cup. He took my remarks in good part although I'm not sure that he agreed with them. The rest of the guests did though because, when I made my announcement of the score from Celtic Park, a huge roar went round the room from the predominately Hibernian company. Later that night, the music and dancing stopped for half an hour as most of the guests filled the television lounge in the hotel to watch the *Sportscene* highlights of Hibs' success earlier in the day.

We went off on honeymoon to the less than exotic location of Aberdeen but returned a day early so that we could attend Hibs match with Raith Rovers. We were rewarded by a sound 3–1 win, which included a rare goal from Chris Shevlane in what turned out to be Bob Shankly's last match in charge of Hibs.

Shankly's successor was Willie McFarlane, who up to that point had been the manager of Stirling Albion. McFarlane had played for Hibs in the 1950s, owned a local betting shop and was a colourful character. He had been a rugged full back with a reputation as a penalty expert who had never quite held down a regular first-team place. He had two nicknames. His fellow players called him 'Packy' but I'm not sure where that came from. There was a character in the 1950s John Wayne film *The Quiet Man* called Packy McFarlane so it may have come from that. To the fans he was known as 'Killer' because his tackling style put his opponents in serious physical danger.

I discovered McFarlane's love of horse racing when I attended a reserve match at Easter Road towards the end of his career. As the players came off at the end of the first half, I was positioned above the tunnel, in what used to be the standing enclosure, to clap them in. As they headed for the dressing rooms, the players were asking the fans if we had heard how the first team were getting on. The bold Packy, however, was in search of rather different information. He was only interested in the name of the horse that had won the 3.30p.m. race at Kempton Park. At that time my mother worked in a café in Leith. Willie McFarlane was a regular customer there and according to my mum, he was 'an awfy man!'

Our new manager might have got his nickname from *The Quiet Man* but he was most certainly not a quiet man himself. Nor was he a modest man. No sooner had he arrived at Easter Road than he was telling the world how good Hibs were and making it clear that under him Hibs would fear no one. His first match in charge was against Hearts at Tynecastle. A victory for Hibs would put us top of the league. Willie McFarlane promised the Hibs fans that a victory was exactly what they would get. He was proved right. Hibs won 2–0 with goals from Peter Cormack who, for the time being at least, was still in Hibs ranks and Joe McBride who continued to bang in the goals. This win put Hibs top of the league and McFarlane announced after the game, 'We're top of the league and that is exactly where I expect us to stay.' I was a newly and happily married man, I had just bought the Beatles' new album *Abbey Road*, Hibs had just beaten Hearts and were on top of the league. That day I felt on top of world.

Hibs next major challenge was a match against Rangers at Ibrox. Our manager once again did not lack confidence. He declared that Hibs would win and win well. Once more he backed his words up with actions. Hibs went to Ibrox, played brilliantly and won 3–1. The prolific McBride was again on target but the star of the show was young Peter Marinello. With his long black hair and intricate dribbling, Marinello looked like George Best. Sometimes he played like him too. He scored two great goals at Ibrox and his performance drew comparisons with another soccer great. Alex 'Candid' Cameron wrote in the *Daily Record*, 'Marinello has a balanced grace when he runs. He is reminiscent of Gordon Smith.' Praise indeed, but on this occasion well deserved. Marinello looked an outstanding prospect.

McFarlane next declared that he intended to keep Peter Cormack at Easter Road. He did, but not for very long, so this was one boast which he failed to deliver on. However, to begin with, the momentum was well and truly with Willie Mac. He signed Erich Schaedler from Stirling Albion. Schaedler was not the finished article at this point but his promise was there for all to see. The next new arrival was Johnny Graham who came from Ayr United. Graham was a very good player. He made a tremendous start to his Hibs career, which sadly he didn't manage to sustain. Results continued to be good and Hibs fans were more than happy with the new man in charge. By this time, McFarlane's popularity was such that he had his own column in the *Pink News*.

Just when it seemed that everything was going perfectly,

Arsenal made a bid of £100,000 for Marinello. Hibs, of course, accepted the offer. Marinello didn't want to go but Hibs made it clear that they wanted the money more than they wanted him. Marinello had been oblivious to Arsenal's interest until one day when he was waiting at a bus stop to go to training at Easter Road, a car stopped and Arthur Duncan, who was then making his name as a flying winger with Partick Thistle, wound down the window and offered him a lift. When Peter asked Duncan why he was heading for Easter Road, he received the reply, 'I'm going for signing talks. I think that they're going to buy me to replace you.'

Marinello reluctantly signed for Arsenal but, sadly, it wasn't too long until his career, which had started so meteorically, went on a downward spiral. At this point, Hibs fans were unaware of the impending acquisition of Arthur Duncan, and McFarlane put his first foot wrong. In his *Evening News* column, he asked fans, 'Who would you rather have – Peter Marinello or Johnny Graham?' The fans response of course was, 'We would rather have both!' But the Hibs support stuck with McFarlane. They liked his brash style and they liked the way his team played. When Duncan arrived and showed how good he was, people began to realise that the sale of Marinello had probably been a shrewd bit of business. When Peter Cormack was sold to Nottingham Forest for £125,000 though, the fans were less convinced. Season 1969–70, which had begun so excitingly and entertainingly, eventually fizzled out in anti-climax as the team ran out of steam.

The new season got off to a mixed start. League form was patchy but Hibs made an outstanding start to their Fairs Cup campaign. Swedish team Malmo were demolished 6–0 at Easter Road and Joe McBride contributed an explosive hat-trick. The *Daily Record* said, 'Willie McFarlane's men were magnificent in a second half goal blitz.' However, Willie's days as Hibs manager were numbered. He resigned after what was rumoured to be a fallout with the club's new owner Tom Hart. He had only been in charge for a little over a year and was replaced by Dave Ewing, who wasn't well known in Scotland. A Scot himself, he had been a no-nonsense centre half for Manchester City and came to Hibs from a post on their coaching staff.

Ewing's stay at Easter Road was short-lived but marked by two notable events. In January 1971, he brought Joe Baker back to Hibs and it goes without saying that this move was warmly welcomed by all the Hibs faithful. It was almost ten years since Joe had left for Torino and his career had been nothing less than eventful in those years. In his one season at Torino he had experienced a real roller coaster ride. He had become the fans' hero through scoring the winning goal in their derby against Juventus. Beating their great and much wealthier rivals was a significant event for the Torino supporters and after the match, hundreds of them headed for the apartment where Joe was staying with his team mate Denis Law. They stood outside chanting Joe's name until the early hours of the following morning. Joe's joy was short-lived. He had treated himself to a new car, an Alfa Romeo Giullietta Sprint. Driving the car on unfamiliar Italian roads, Joe had crashed and been seriously injured. He told me later that he had 'cheated death.' It was only after five operations and suffering 'pain of indescribable intensity' that Joe pulled through. Incredibly he was playing and scoring again before the end of the season.

Joe moved from Torino to Arsenal where he became a huge favourite with their fans. He scored ninety-four goals in 114 league matches and over 100 goals in all competitions. His next port of call was Nottingham Forest where he notched up forty-nine goals in two years. Joe had come back to Easter

Road for a friendly match during his time with Forest. The match had finished 2–2 with the Baker Boy getting both goals. For one of them, a trademark power header, he comprehensively outjumped big John MacNamee who was six inches taller than Joe and no slouch in the air. Joe had next been signed by Sunderland where things hadn't worked out for him. Amid great euphoria among the Easter Road support, Dave Ewing then brought this all-time great Hibernian back to his true home.

Joe's homecoming was in a league match against Aberdeen at Easter Road. Hibs had been struggling. Indeed they hadn't won in ten games. Aberdeen, on the other hand, under the stewardship of Eddie Turnbull, were the reigning Scottish Cup holders, were unbeaten in fifteen matches and had just set a new record in Scottish league football for the length of time they had gone without conceding a goal. Their goal-keeper Bobby Clark had been in such unbeatable form that he had been quoted as saying that he had forgotten what it was like to pick the ball out of the net. Hibs and Joe Baker were about to remind him.

Easter Road was packed for the match and there was an amazing atmosphere. Those of us who remembered Joe from his first spell were like children again at the prospect of his return. The young fans, who were there to see him for the first time, wanted to see if all the stories they had heard about this player were really true. When Hibs took the field there was an incredible roar and I don't mind admitting that I had tears in my eyes. There, back where he belonged and back in the emerald green of Hibs, was a slightly older Baker Boy. Resplendent in white boots and sporting a splendid pair of seventies-style sideburns, Joe Baker made a sensational return.

At first Aberdeen maintained their previous defensive excellence. They extended their newly-achieved record by reaching half-time with their goal still intact. However, down the slope in the second half, Hibs were irresistible. Roared on by a passionate crowd, we scored not once but twice. Pat Stanton gave Hibs the lead then the ground erupted when a diving header from the returning hero made it two. Joe scored again shortly afterwards but the referee wrongly ruled the goal out for offside. Nothing could spoil Hibs' day though. Aberdeen's defence was breached for the first time in many weeks, Hibs had won at last and the Baker Boy had returned in triumph.

Joe recalled that day fondly: 'It was an incredibly emotional reunion. The reception I got when I ran onto the pitch made me realise just what I had been missing all these years.' Baker had arrived with only a third of season 1970–71 left, but he still managed to finish the season as Hibs' top scorer with eight goals. I discussed that great occasion recently with one of the lads with whom I play five-a-side football on a Thursday night. He is a bit younger than me and had only heard about Joe Baker's exploits during his first spell with Hibs from his father. He had gone along in January 1971 to see for himself how closely the reality resembled the legend. He wasn't disappointed. 'I was transfixed. There was non-stop noise and Baker was unbelievable. I just remember thinking that if he was that fast and that good at thirty-one, he must have been some player ten years earlier.' He was.

Hibs reached the Scottish Cup semi-final that season and that was when Dave Ewing made his second lasting contribution to Hibernian folklore. Hibs were drawn against Rangers and when asked at a press conference if he was concerned at facing the mighty men from Ibrox at Hampden, Ewing retorted that he wasn't because in his opinion Rangers 'were rubbish.' This remark was nearly as well received by Hibs fans as the return of the Baker Boy. Needless to say the press had a field day.

Typical of their coverage was a cartoon which showed a dustbin lorry pulling up outside Ibrox with the driver leaning out the window saying, 'We've come to collect the rubbish.'

If Ewing expected his remark to upset Rangers, he miscalculated. Rangers beat us in the semi-final. By this time I had become a teacher and went to the match with my Head Teacher who was a wonderful Irish character called Carl Carney. Carl had gone through a back operation not too long before the semi-final and was still in pain. We had to park miles from Hampden and walk up to the ground and every step must have been agony for him. The journey back after defeat must have been even more painful but he refused to let his spirits droop. Every time he felt a bit down, he would recall Dave Ewing's description of Rangers and collapse into helpless laughter.

Hibs at that time did not fit Ewing's rubbish category either. We weren't bad but we weren't great. The fans didn't really warm to Ewing and after a few short months he was gone. Eddie Turnbull left Aberdeen to return to Hibs in the summer of 1971 with great joy amongst Hibs fans. Eddie, of course, had been a member of the Famous Five and a great player. He was also a great character, renowned for his plain speaking and salty language.

Eddie Turnbull's spell as manager at Pittodrie had been marked by success. He had beaten Celtic in the Scottish Cup Final in 1970 and had built a top team. I mentioned earlier that I had spent my honeymoon in Aberdeen. When we were there, we had spotted Turnbull in the lounge of our hotel one afternoon. He had been there to sign a Highland League player called Derek McKay. Less than a year later, the same McKay was to score two goals in Aberdeen's 3–1 Scottish Cup win over Celtic. Little did we think, as we looked over at the great man that day, that less than two years later he would be back at Easter Road as manager.

8

TURNBULL'S TORNADOES

When Eddie Turnbull returned to Hibs as manager, we supporters were delighted to have him back. He had been a legendary player for our club, had established a high reputation for his coaching when he was Hibs 'trainer' and had proved himself to be a top class manager at Aberdeen. As fans, we took it for granted that Turnbull had jumped at the chance to return to Easter Road. Apparently not. Years later, after he had left Hibs, Turnbull revealed that he had come very close to rejecting Tom Hart's approach. Claiming that he was considered 'a God' in Aberdeen, he admitted that he only came back to Hibs because his wife was homesick up North and he and Tom Hart were great friends. I consider this a very strange statement for a man whose adult life has been inextricably linked to Hibs. As you will see over the next couple of chapters, Eddie Turnbull is a very complex man to whom paradox and contradiction are no strangers. However, as the new season dawned in August 1971, all we knew was that Eddie was in charge and the future was exciting. Even the most ardent Hibees among us failed to appreciate at this stage just how exciting the next few years were going to be.

In those days, the League Cup started the season off. Each team played six sectional matches and the sectional winners qualified for the quarter-finals. Hibs won their section in style.

They won their first game away to Motherwell and Turnbull wrote his first set of competitive match programme notes before the following game against Dundee United. He praised the team for their opening day victory but sounded a cautionary note by declaring, 'It will take a fair bit of time for the players to think and act the same way as I do.' Events were to prove that this prediction was on the pessimistic side. He also paid tribute to the fans for turning out at Motherwell in large numbers but ticked them off for invading the pitch when Hibs scored. Eddie the autocrat was already making his mark.

At this point, Turnbull had already made one signing. He had signed Jim Herriot to play in goal instead of the goal-keeper he had inherited – the talented but inconsistent Roy Baines. Herriot had been an excellent servant to Dunfermline and Birmingham City, had been capped by Scotland and, at the age of thirty-one, was at the ideal stage of his career for any club that needed an experienced last line of defence. Aside from his goalkeeping prowess, Herriot had another claim to fame. When the author of the famous series of James Herriot veterinary tales was looking for a pen name to append to his books, he had attended a Birmingham City match. On reading the programme, he had come across the name Jim Herriot in the home team's line-up. He liked the name and decided to adopt it as his nom de plume. The rest, as they say, is history.

At this early stage of the campaign, Joe Baker was flying and seemed set for a great season. He was being ably assisted by young Alex Cropley. Willie McFarlane had blooded Cropley after Peter Cormack had moved to Nottingham Forest and now, under Turnbull, he was beginning to flourish. Unfortunately, Baker sustained what turned out to be a long-term injury and, in his absence, Hibs went out of the League

Cup over two legs to Falkirk. The club's league form was good though and, in November, they lay third in the table behind Celtic and Aberdeen. At this point, Turnbull made a superb signing. He bought Alex Edwards from Dunfermline for a mere £15,000. Edwards was a magnificent player and had only been sold by Dunfermline because they needed the money and he had a suspect temperament. It was amazing that neither Old Firm club nor a top English team had moved to sign Edwards. He was certainly good enough to grace any footballing stage. We Hibs fans weren't complaining that this little genius had slipped through the net of the bigger clubs. This was especially the case after Edwards had made an outstanding debut in a 3–2 home win over Kilmarnock. He completely controlled the game and topped off his performance with a rocket shot from twenty-five yards to secure the points.

As 1971 gave way to 1972, Turnbull moved into the market again. He signed Alan Gordon from Dundee United for £13,000. Gordon was a tall, elegant striker who had started his career at Hearts. Again he was an excellent acquisition and the new manager's team was starting to come together nicely in time for the Scottish Cup.

Hibs got a difficult draw. That season Partick Thistle had shocked the football world by beating Celtic 4–1 in the League Cup Final. They had an excellent team and we had to travel to Firhill to meet them. By this time, my wife Margaret was pregnant and not able to travel to away games any more, although she was still a regular at home matches. I had started to travel to away games with one of my teaching colleagues, Ian Mooney, who was as big a Hibee as me. Ian and I travelled to Firhill that day in some trepidation. We needn't have worried. Alan Gordon gave Hibs an early lead and Erich Schaedler added a tremendous second to secure the game.

Schaedler had many qualities, one of which was the ability to take seriously long throws. This day he hurled one of his specials into the Partick six-yard box. One of the defenders headed the ball back towards Schaedler on the left touchline. He met the ball on the volley and sent a thunderbolt into the roof of the Partick net.

So the first hurdle had been successfully overcome. As we left the ground, Ian and I wondered if this could at last be the year when Hibs Scottish Cup hoodoo – which now stretched to seventy years – could be laid to rest. Next up was Airdrie at home. Joe Baker was fit enough to play in this game and he and Gordon scored to give Hibs a comfortable 2–0 victory. This was Gordon's first goal for Hibs and things were looking up for him after his debut which had resulted in a 2–1 defeat to Motherwell. In that game, Pat Stanton missed a penalty. As he trotted back to the centre spot after his miss, Pat had said to Gordon, 'I am not to be trusted with penalties.' The accuracy of this remark was to be borne out in a classic European match with Leeds United in a couple of years time, but for now everyone's thoughts were on the 1971–72 Scottish Cup and Hibs' quest to win it.

The quarter-final draw presented Hibs with a home tie against Turnbull's old team Aberdeen. Jimmy O'Rourke scored within ten seconds of the start, Joe Baker added another after half-time and Hibs went through with ease. Again we asked ourselves: 'Could this be the year?' Our semi-final opponents were Rangers. Before the semi-final came round, I had a major personal milestone. Margaret gave birth to our first child. Margaret had gone into hospital early because the doctors were concerned that the birth might not be straightforward. On the Saturday, Hibs played St Johnstone at Easter Road and won 7–1. I was there, of course, and our forwards were irresistible and superbly led by Joe Baker. After the match I met one of my old school friends and he invited me to join him for a post-match refreshment in the Hibs Supporters Club. This invitation proved equally irresistible as did the pints of Guinness which they were serving in the club.

At seven o'clock, I realised that I should have been at Elsie Inglis for the evening visiting. I raced up the road and reached the maternity hospital breathless and desperate to find a toilet. My expectant wife looked beautiful and serene but her mood soon changed when she smelled my breath. It took a further turn for the worse when I informed her how desperate I was to relieve myself. 'You can't go in here,' she whispered with intent. 'It's a women's ward. There are no male toilets.'

I pointed out that if I didn't go in the next couple of minutes, what was left of my self-control might desert me. To Margaret's great embarrassment, she had to call the nursing sister over and ask her if I could use the ward toilet. The sister was very much of the old school and to my even greater embarrassment, she insisted on escorting me to the toilet, checking it was empty before granting me entry then standing guard outside until I had finished. She completed her performance, to the amusement of everyone else in the ward, by asking me in a loud voice as I made my exit if I had remembered to wash my hands.

By the end of the visiting hour I was forgiven and by the end of the following Monday I was euphoric. Our son was born handsome and healthy. We decided to call him Patrick Joseph. St Patrick and St Joseph were Margaret's two favourite saints and Patrick Stanton and Joseph Baker were two of my all time favourite Hibs players so we had no trouble agreeing on a name.

Shortly after our happy event, it was semi-final time. Could this be another happy event? The first match at Hampden ended 1–1 with Jimmy O'Rourke scoring for Hibs. This match was to prove to be Joe Baker's last game for Hibs. The replay was scheduled for a Monday night. Before the game, the Hibs players were resting in their hotel rooms. Joe told me that he was keyed up for the game and couldn't settle. He ordered a pot of tea and a sandwich. Later as the players prepared to leave for Hampden, Eddie Turnbull presented Joe with the bill for what he had had. When Joe said that he would expect the club to pay for it, Turnbull told him that if he didn't pay the bill, he wouldn't play that night. Joe again refused to pay. Turnbull did not select him for the semi-final replay and, indeed, did not select him again. He was freed at the end of the season and moved to Raith Rovers. He did well enough there to score six goals in one game and to score two goals against Hibs in a League Cup tie at Easter Road. Injuries were a problem for Joe by this stage of his career but he still had something to offer Hibs. However, he and Eddie Turnbull had never had an easy relationship and at this point in Hibs' history, Turnbull deemed Baker surplus to requirements. When Joe told me this story he was deeply disappointed that he hadn't been able to contribute to the great matches that were to follow under Turnbull's stewardship.

However, the team was on a high and Baker's departure was met with equanimity due to the continuing excellence of the team that Turnbull was starting to build. Rangers were played off the park in the semi-final replay. To that point, I had never seen Hibs outplay the Ibrox team quite so comprehensively. Pat Stanton and Alex Edwards supplied the goals in a 2–0 victory and, in all honesty, the margin of victory could, and should, have been much wider.

We were in the final for the first time since 1958 and inevitably we were up against the might of Jock Stein's Celtic. Stein's team at that time was well-nigh unbeatable in a domestic context. They were also highly successful in Europe.

Hibs were playing so well, however, that most Hibs fans genuinely believed that we could match the Parkhead men in the final. So hopeful of victory were Margaret and I that we had arranged Patrick's baptism for the day after the final. As most of our friends and family were staunch Hibees we planned for the day to be one big celebration party.

How wrong we were! In front of a crowd of 106,000, Hibs froze and Celtic played magnificently. They were used to big occasions and used to winning on big occasions. Billy McNeill scored an early goal, Dixie Deans had the game of his life and scored a hat-trick and quite a few of Hibs best players came nowhere near their normal form. We were comprehensively beaten 6–1. Our defensive play was naive and Celtic took full advantage. Going forward, we created many chances but, with the exception of an early goal from Alan Gordon, failed to take them. Jimmy O'Rourke said afterwards that the game could have finished 8–4. He was right but it didn't alter the fact that Hibs had been humiliated and a great season had ended in a depressing anticlimax.

Our baptism next day was initially a very subdued affair. We were proud of our new baby and happy to celebrate his big day but the events of the previous afternoon at Hampden hung over the occasion like a spectre at the feast. However, as the day progressed and the healing powers of the refreshments began to take effect, we consoled each other that it had been a great season and that even better days lay ahead. We also agreed that our team could only learn from the traumatic experience of the day before and would come back from it with renewed strength. The evening ended with the singing of Hibs songs.

When season 1972–73 dawned, it was clear from the outset that the disappointment of the Scottish Cup Final capitulation to Celtic had only served to make Eddie Turnbull and his players even more determined to show their true worth in the months ahead. There could be no doubting the quality of the team which Turnbull had assembled.

Jim Herriot was proving to be an excellent goalkeeper. He was safe and unflappable but had one eccentricity. In night matches he rubbed soot under his eyes because he claimed that it took away the glare from the floodlights. John Brownlie at right back was simply the best right back ever to wear a Hibs jersey. He was a sound defender but his talents lay in attack. Time and again he would surge forward at pace to score brilliant goals or create chances for his colleagues. Erich Schaedler at left back approached the game differently. He made sledgehammer tackles and ran like an Olympic sprinter. He too could go forward with intent.

In central defence, Jim Black was a football playing centre half. He read the game well and always tried to use the ball intelligently when he was in possession. He was good but he would have been even better if he had been more physically imposing. Partnering Black was John Blackley. 'Sloop' (John B), as he was known, had it all. He was good in the air, brilliant defensively and a highly-skilled footballer who turned defence into attack with regularity and ease.

The midfield trio was immense. Alex Edwards displayed tremendous vision and was able to dispatch sixty-yard defence splitting passes with unerring accuracy. He had formed a tremendous partnership with the marauding Brownlie on his right and both these players also linked smoothly with Pat Stanton in the centre. Pat captained the team by example. He was naturally undemonstrative but he was also naturally gifted. For the sake of the team, he had stepped forward from his original role as sweeper to allow John Blackley to play in defence. He had become the complete midfield player. Composed on the ball, expert at retaining possession and able to score goals with head or foot, Pat was the fulcrum of the team. To his left was Alex Cropley. Known as 'Sodjer' because he had lived in Aldershot when he was young, Alex had gone to school at Norton Park in the shadow of the old North Stand at Easter Road, and was the perfect complement to his midfield partners. Although small and slim, Alex's slightness was deceptive. He could tackle with ferocity and used the ball brilliantly with his educated left foot. He could also strike the ball cleanly and was always liable to come up with a goal when it was needed.

Turnbull's team also had quality in abundance in attack. Alan Gordon at centre forward was an exceptional player. He was absolutely outstanding aerially. Like all great headers of the ball, he seemed to be able to hang in the air. He could also leap prodigiously and was able to direct the ball with his head to on-coming midfield players or his strike partner Jimmy O'Rourke with the utmost facility. He was also skilful on the ground. His finishes were deadly and he held the ball up superbly. Jimmy O'Rourke was the perfect foil for the tall Gordon. Small and nippy and with a born poacher's eye for goal, Jimmy was playing the best football of his career in the early part of Eddie Turnbull's reign. The experience of playing in all forward positions and also in midfield in his formative footballing years had made Jimmy the complete attacker. Although it was ten years since his first team debut, he was still just twenty-six and possessed what Tommy Docherty called 'that terrible disease – he just couldn't stop scoring goals.'

Arthur Duncan completed the team. Arthur could run like a pedigree racehorse and was an underrated finisher. He always weighed in with his fair share of goals and when Turnbull played him at centre forward in one game, he scored four times to confirm his capabilities in the goal scoring department. His pace was his main asset and when he hit the dead-ball line, he was capable of delivering a telling cross. He was also capable of blasting the ball behind the goals but this unpredictability was part of Arthur's charm and it probably made him more difficult to read if you were playing against him.

These were the eleven men, who in the opinion of most Hibs supporters, constituted our strongest team. Occasionally, Turnbull would change his selection and when he did this the players who usually missed out were Alex Edwards and Jimmy O'Rourke, but for the most part he fielded his top team. This team was such a powerful and unstoppable force that it earned the name of 'Turnbull's Tornadoes.' The last few months of 1972 were to see these players play the best football by any Hibs team since the peak of the Famous Five. The team also lifted two trophies in this short time. As for us fans, we were on cloud nine. We couldn't believe how much progress in his team-building Eddie Turnbull had made in such a short time and we were privileged to watch football from heaven.

The season started with the introduction of a new competition sponsored by a well-known Scottish brewery called the Drybrough Cup. The four highest scoring teams in the two top leagues qualified and Hibs of course were there. We eased into the semi-finals with a routine 4–0 demolition of Montrose. Our opponents were Rangers at Easter Road on the first Wednesday in August. Rangers had just won the European Cup Winners Cup by beating Moscow Dynamo in Barcelona so they must have travelled east in a confident frame of mind. It was a warm night and Hibs absolutely roasted Rangers. If our win in the Scottish Cup semi-final replay at the end of the previous season had been comprehensive, this demolition was decisive, destructive and delightful for all Hibs fans to watch. A measure of how seriously supporters were taking this tournament can be seen from the attendance, which was more than 27,000. The fluidity of Turnbull's team over-whelmed Rangers. We came forward in waves with each player showing skill, inventiveness and the ability to interchange and improvise to devastating effect. Stanton and Gordon who had both scored in the previous round were on target again and such was the extent of Rangers discomfort that they had to resort to rough-house tactics. It did them little good, however, and Hibs swept into the final by a margin of victory that, although conclusive, actually flattered Rangers.

So only three short months after being embarrassed 6–1 in the Scottish Cup Final by Celtic, Hibs returned to Hampden. Once again Jock Stein's great team lay in wait for us. What we did not know was what fate had in store for us. Would our pride be restored or were we in for further humiliation? I have to be honest here and admit that I was not among the 50,000 who attended the final. I just could not have taken the tension after the trauma I had suffered back in May. That afternoon, Margaret and I took our baby son to see his grand-parents. My dad had a massive old radio which he kept on a shelf in the kitchen. I have no idea how old it was but it was the size that televisions used to be before flat-screen technology was introduced, and it had a wide range of knobs and dials. It seemed to be able to pick up almost any station but this day the only channel we were interested in was Radio Scotland. We asked my dad to put the Drybrough Cup Final on and promised that if Celtic were hammering Hibs again, we would turn the wireless off.

Well that trusty old wireless set was to crackle and squeak and capture our attention for the next two hours and more. Eddie Turnbull had included Johnny Hamilton and John Hazel and, inexplicably, left out Alex Edwards and Jimmy O'Rourke.

However, these unenforced team changes did not deter Hibs. Brownlie and Schaedler marauded with purpose, Stanton and Cropley dominated midfield and Alan Gordon was in prime form. By half-time, Hibs were 2–0 up courtesy of a Gordon double and in the sixty-second minute Billy McNeill diverted a Duncan cross, which was heading for our brilliant centre forward, into his own net to give us a three-goal advantage. Back in the kitchen in Leith, there was an air of celebration. Surely not even Hibs could throw it away now? Margaret and I kept saying, 'Why didn't we go?'

Then things began to change. There was a disturbance in the crowd at the Celtic end of the ground and play was stopped. When the match restarted, Hibs seemed to have lost both their momentum and their concentration. First Paul Wilson and then Jimmy Johnstone pulled goals back for Celtic. The air of relative relaxation, which had prevailed around my mum and dad's kitchen table, had now given way to outright tension.

Celtic were now displaying their greatness by launching wave after wave of attacks on the Hibs goal. Our mouths were dry and the palms of our hands were soaked in perspiration. The commentator was David Francey, who was then the doyen of Scottish radio commentators. He had a style all of his own and a very distinctive voice. All his voice seemed to be saying now was, 'Here come Celtic again.' The time seemed to stand still but Hibs to their credit managed to hold out until with just two minutes left, Francey's voice reached a crescendo as he announced that Johnstone had saved the game for Celtic. We stared at each other in depressed disbelief. All we could say was, 'Thank goodness, we didn't go. This would have been just too much to take.'

When Germany equalised in the last minute of normal time against England in the 1966 World Cup Final, Alf Ramsey told his team before the extra time, 'You've beaten them once, now go out and beat them again.' Wise words and they did the trick. Now Eddie Turnbull faced a similar challenge as he gathered his Tornadoes around him at Hampden. The stakes could not have been higher. The force was now with Celtic and if Stein's team were to win again, they would have established an unassailable psychological advantage over the team which Turnbull was in the process of building. Whatever our manager said that day must have been rhetoric of Churchillian quality because when extra time began, Hibs were right back in their stride.

Jimmy O'Rourke came on for Johnny Hamilton and almost immediately proved why he should have played from the start. He picked the ball up thirty yards from the Celtic goal. As the defenders around him backed off, Jimmy weighed up his options and decided to go for broke. He let fly with a rocket shot and from the moment the ball left his boot it was only going to end up in one place and that was the roof of the Celtic net. Jimmy O'Rourke had scored some great goals for Hibs and had struck some ferocious shots but none of his previous efforts matched this collector's piece of a cannon-ball which restored Hibs' lead. In the grandparental kitchen, we jumped for joy and hugged each other in relief. Little Patrick, all of four months old, looked at us as if to say 'What is all this?' I looked back at him thinking, 'It's called supporting Hibs, son. It can be great but it's never easy!'

As extra time roared on, with both teams committed to all-out attack and play raging from one end of the pitch to the other, we sat in nerve-ridden silence wondering if this time Hibs could hold out or if Celtic would break our hearts again. We needn't have worried. In the final minute of the match, Arthur Duncan, showing incredible reserves of stamina and displaying all his legendary pace, outran the Celtic defence. He reached the byline leaving Danny McGrain in his wake as he did so and smashed a tremendous shot into the Celtic net from the most acute of angles.

Hibs had won the Drybrough Cup and in doing so had displayed a combination of class and courage. Around the radio in Leith, we were suffering from nervous exhaustion and delirious happiness in equal measure. Margaret and I looked at each other and mouthed, 'If only we had gone.' Our baby son gurgled contentedly, totally unaware that in his first four months of life he had managed what it had taken his mother and father the best part of twenty-five years to achieve. None of us were worrying about the disparity in timescale though. Hibs, at last, had won a cup at Hampden and that was all that mattered.

Watching the highlights on *Sportscene* that night was wonderful. There were no video recorders or DVDs then of course so we had to watch it and remember it. That was not a problem though. As I lay in my bed that night, a cup winning supporter at last, I played the days events over and over in my head. The images I had just watched on our black and white television set filled me with joy and were etched in my mind forever.

As the season proper got underway, Hibs continued their exciting form. They were faring well in the league and making great progress in another two cup competitions.

Hibs were competing in the European Cup Winners Cup as Celtic were both league champions and Scottish Cup winners and naturally had chosen to compete in the premier tournament, which was the European Cup. In the first round, we drew Sporting Lisbon who had a very strong team at that time. The first leg in Lisbon was watched by 100,000 fans and Hibs played in a purple strip. Although Sporting won 2–1, Hibs played brilliantly. Many of the players of that time consider that match to have been Turnbull's Tornadoes best-ever performance, which is really saying something. On the plane back to Edinburgh after the match, Alan Gordon sat next to Gordon Smith, who had gone out to Portugal to support the team. Smith paid Turnbull's men the ultimate compliment when he told his fellow passenger that the team he had just seen playing would have been too good for the Hibs team of the Famous Five era.

In the return leg at Easter Road, Hibs changed their strips again and wore all-green tops. They may not have played in purple this time but they certainly struck a purple patch. Sporting were demolished 6–1. Jimmy O'Rourke scored a hat-trick and Alan Gordon contributed two more. Like the rest of the 26,000 crowd, I was spellbound as Hibs roared down the slope in the second half to give a captivating display. Brownlie and Schaedler rampaged forward, Edwards, Stanton and Cropley dribbled past players and provided a non-stop supply of inviting passes and Gordon and O'Rourke were just too hot for the Portuguese defence to handle. It was a privilege to watch football of this quality and the *Daily Record* got it exactly right when it declared 'Hibs join the European greats' and added 'All Scotland must salute super Hibs.'

Next in line was the Albanian club FC Besa. This time the first leg was at Easter Road and Hibs went one better than they had done against Sporting by scoring seven goals. Again O'Rourke notched a hat-trick and Cropley, Duncan and Brownlie shared the other four goals to keep him company. The atmosphere was amazing and Hibs could have scored even more. They led 7–0 after sixty-five minutes but took their foot of the pedal to allow Besa a late consolation goal. This time, the press described Hibs performance as 'a green and white blitzkreig.'

Almost 23,000 packed the stands and stood on the old

terracing for this game and we Hibees all watched proceedings with a mixture of pride and disbelief. 'Could this team of all talents really be our Hibs?' was the question we asked ourselves. The answer was a resounding 'yes,' and those of us who remembered the bad old days under Walter Galbraith were beginning to realise that we were now in the midst of something special and that we should cherish it.

A 1–1 draw in Albania completed the formality of qualification for the quarter-final and Hibs were paired with Hajduk Split from what was then Yugoslavia. However, the Cup Winners Cup now went into cold storage until the following March and that left the team and the fans to concentrate on another cup competition in which Hibs were also doing rather well. Hibs were steamrollering their way through the League Cup. This competition had been revamped and teams, which had qualified from the initial section, had to play two further two-legged rounds before they reached the semi-final.

In the first post-sectional round, Hibs took on Dundee United with the first match away. Tannadice was an intimidating place for visiting teams in those days but it didn't present any problem for this unstoppable Hibs team. The Tornadoes blew United away 5–2. The amazing Mr O'Rourke scored yet another hat-trick and Alex Cropley weighed in with two beauties of his own. Once again though the whole team performed impressively and completely outplayed a very good United side.

I was still going to matches with my friend Ian Mooney. We were teaching together in Bonnyrigg and our Head Teacher Carl Carney was also a real Hibs man. Sometimes Carl joined us on our jaunts to away matches. Ian and I had travelled through to the League Cup match at Tannadice with Ian's dad Jackie. Jackie was a man of quick wit and lively opinion. In the pub before the match, he told us that he had heard a lot

about this team that Eddie Turnbull was building. He added
that he would take a lot of convincing that Turnbull's team
would ever come close to matching the exploits of the Famous
Five side, which he had watched when he was younger.
Reflecting after the match on the virtuoso performance that
he had witnessed, he informed us that he had reconsidered
and was now well and truly convinced! Turnbull's Tornadoes
had another convert.

The second leg with Dundee United was a quiet goalless
draw but we were now in the quarter-finals where we would
meet Airdrie. Airdrie had a strong side at that time with top
players such as Drew Busby, Drew Jarvie and Derek Whiteford.
On their own tight Broomfield pitch they were a match for
anyone, especially in a floodlit match when their raucous crowd
seemed to raise their noise levels by an extra few decibels. This
was the kind of match in which previous Hibs teams would
have struggled. This team was different though. On this cold,
windy Wednesday night in October, they provided a footballing
masterclass. Twice Airdrie led, the referee did Hibs no favours
and the Lanarkshire crowd was even more vociferous than usual.
None of this deflected Hibs from the task in hand. We just kept
playing our cultured football and gradually the goals came and
class told. Hibs won 6–2. It was Arthur Duncan's turn to score
a hat-trick this time, O'Rourke weighed in as usual and the
brilliant Brownlie served up two sensational goals. This was a
man playing right back who did more attacking than most other
teams' centre forwards. The second leg was comfortably won
4–1 and Hibs were now in the semi-finals. Yet again we would
face Rangers. The Ibrox team must have been sick of the sight
of us and they had good reason to be. Hibs beat them again,
1–0 this time, and Brownlie was on target once more. He drove
at the Rangers defence, played a one-two, collected the return
pass and smashed it past Peter McCloy.

We were now in the League Cup Final. Inevitably we would face Celtic, who no doubt would be intent on revenge after the Drybrough Cup Final. Margaret and I had now recovered our courage. Slightly embarrassed that we had 'bottled out' of the Drybrough Cup Final due to our post 6–1 Scottish Cup Final thrashing trauma, we were determined that this time we would be there. We arranged for Margaret's mum to look after Patrick and we booked ourselves onto the Eastern Branch supporters' bus. This was the bus we had originally met on so in some ways we were taking a sentimental journey. The big question was – would it be a happy one? It was good to see old friends again and there were new faces on the bus too. Everyone, though, was in the same frame of mind. We were hopeful but apprehensive. We knew our team was good enough to win but we also knew that the Stein Machine could overrun any team. We arrived early in Glasgow and had a few drinks in a pub near Hampden. The drink emboldened all of us and we sang Hibs songs all the way up to the ground.

The first half was a cat and mouse affair but it was significant that Stein had moved Jimmy Johnstone to the left wing to counteract the attacking threat posed by John Brownlie. By half-time, Hibs were feeling their way into the match and were more than holding their own. As the teams left the field for the break, the huge Hibs support cheered their team to the echo. Jimmy O'Rourke said afterwards that he had known at half-time that Hibs would win after the fans cheered them off the park. He declared that the players felt ten feet tall. Jimmy was certain that it was easily the best support that Hibs have ever had outside Edinburgh.

Hibs took command of the second half and Pat Stanton played the best forty-five minutes of his life. First, Alex Edwards found Pat in space in the Celtic box with a neat free kick. Pat stayed composed and placed the ball high in the

Celtic net. Next, Edwards split the Celtic defence with a dream pass and Stanton raced on to it. When he reached the byline, he crossed the ball to the near post. Jimmy O'Rourke came racing in at full pelt to bullet a tremendous diving header past Evan Williams. Pat and Jimmy had played together since their schooldays at Holy Cross and were true Hibs men. Their combination for this goal was as fitting as it was brilliant but our super skipper wasn't finished yet. He hit the post with a twenty-yard drive. Then Alan Gordon had a shot cleared off the line. Hibs should have been out of sight. The Hibs support chanted 'Hibees, Hibees' over and over again. The noise and atmosphere were unforgettable. Surely triumph lay in wait. Then with eight minutes to go Celtic scored. Erich Schaedler missed a through ball and Kenny Dalglish supplied a measured finish. Was our dream about to be snatched away? Happily no. When the final whistle sounded, our victorious heroes ran down to the end of the ground where all we Hibs fans were stationed. They applauded us and we acclaimed them. This was what I had longed for for all of my fifteen years supporting Hibs. Yes we had won the Summer Cup and the Drybrough Cup but this was the real thing – one of Scotland's major trophies at last. Indeed it was the club's first major trophy since the Famous Five team had won the league in season 1951–52. I was proud and happy and on a bigger high than the Man in the Moon.

We cheered the presentation and as Pat Stanton held the cup aloft, he must have reflected on his own performance that day, which had been truly monumental. Back in Edinburgh, many, many thousands lined the streets as the open-top bus made its way to the Balmoral Hotel where the team was to have its celebratory meal. The players took it in turn to come to the open windows of the hotel and display the cup to the fans. We took it in turn to chant their names.

Eventually the team made their way to their meal and we fans headed for home. In 1958, I had been part of a crestfallen crocodile of Hibs supporters which had made its weary way along Princes Street after the Cup Final defeat to Clyde. Fourteen years on, things were very different. We had a spring in our steps and a song in our hearts. Margaret and I headed back to her mum's house. There we were reunited with our baby boy. I hugged him and told him that in the eight months in which he had been alive, Hibs had won two trophies. I assured him that he was 'some boy.' Next to arrive was Margaret's dad Arthur. He had done a bit of lubricated celebrating before heading for home and as he came up the entry stair, he was lugging a weighty carry-out of the liquid variety. His carrier bag was too weighty as it turned out because as he approached the top of the stairs, the bag burst and the bottles it had been holding fell into the stairwell before smashing to pieces as they landed on the ground floor of the entry.

Arthur was not downhearted. He was too elated for that. His emotions were running so high that he even conceded that Alex Edwards was 'the best Hibs number seven since Gordon Smith.' We settled to watch the BBC highlights and only then, when we were able to watch the match without tension, did we realise how good our team had been on that historic day. Margaret and I then caught the last bus back to Bonnyrigg. The next day was the original 'Super Sunday.' We enjoyed a massive breakfast while talking about nothing but the match. I then went and bought every Sunday paper, and when I say *every* I mean *every*. The headlines made wonderful reading – 'HAIL HIBS', 'PAT THE KING', 'ENTER EDDIE EXIT HIBS CUP HOODOO' and 'HIBS CUP TRIUMPH' were only a few examples. Hibs Chairman Tom Hart proclaimed, 'We will go on to even greater things. I am convinced of that. Eddie

Turnbull has built a great team and all of our players will be staying at Easter Road.'

The chairman's words were exactly what we wanted to hear although time was to prove them less than prophetic. We ended the day by watching the *Scotsport* highlights of the previous day's glorious events. Arthur Montford, in commentary, was lavish in his praise of Hibs. Archie MacPherson had been exactly the same the night before when commentating for the BBC. It was unheard of for these two institutions of Scotland's commentary boxes to be quite so effusive about any team outside the Old Firm. However, Turnbull's Tornadoes were now so good that they could not be denied the level of praise which they so richly deserved.

The Saturday after the League Cup Final, Hibs entertained Ayr United at Easter Road. They also entertained their fans by slamming Ally McLeod's team 8–1. McLeod was at that point a promising manager and his 1978 Scotland World Cup adventure was something for the future. When he came to Easter Road in December 1972, he was simply a man with a growing managerial reputation. By the time he left, that reputation had been somewhat diminished.

Eddie Turnbull set the tone by declaring in the match programme, 'Only two competitions have been concluded in Scotland this season and Hibs have won them both.' You can imagine the Hibs supporters' pride as we carried out our pre-match reading. Before the game kicked off, the Hibs youth team ran round the pitch carrying the League Cup and the Drybrough Cup. By the time the teams appeared, the crowd was in a ferment, which is sometimes the cue for anticlimax to follow. Not this day though. Hibs followed the script perfectly and annihilated Ayr. It wasn't just the score that impressed, it was the quality of the team's play. Pace, skill and virtuosity all combined to sweep Ayr away. There were hat-tricks for Alan Gordon and almost inevitably Jimmy O'Rourke. After the match, a gracious Ally McLeod declared, 'Playing the way they did today, Hibs would have been too good for Real Madrid.' Pat Stanton responded by saying, 'He didn't need to tell us that. We knew it already because we beat them just a few years ago.'

If Hibs needed something to keep their feet on the ground and concentrate their increasingly confident minds, it came in the shape of a game against Celtic at Parkhead two days before Christmas. Margaret and I had invited our parents for Christmas dinner and we were planning to celebrate a great year for Hibs and for ourselves in some style. We didn't want Celtic to put a dampener on those celebrations by handing Hibs a pre-Christmas caning. We needn't have worried. Once again Turnbull's Tornadoes rose to the occasion. In front of a massive home crowd, Celtic were desperate for revenge and could not have been any more motivated than they were. They threw everything at Hibs but we took all they could offer and came back in style. A great game finished 1–1 with Alan Gordon scoring a fine header and most critics agreeing that, despite the level of Celtic's performance and commitment, Hibs could have, and probably should have, won the match.

Our baby son Patrick was now eight months old and among his collection of Christmas presents was his very first Hibs strip, bought for him by his proud Grandad Arthur. Patrick wore his strip throughout Christmas Day and we still have a great photograph of him posing proudly in his new garb after we had finished opening his presents with him. We had a marvellous family day and many toasts were proposed. The recurring theme of those toasts was 'To Eddie Turnbull, his Tornadoes and continued success.'

The last home match of 1972 was against Aberdeen and

Hibs won a game of top quality football 3–2. The highlight of the game was a classic goal scored by Alan Gordon. Alex Cropley picked up the ball at the halfway line just in front of the players' tunnel. He signalled to Arthur Duncan to start running. As Arthur did so, Cropley placed a perfect pass inside the Aberdeen full back. Alan Gordon matched Duncan's run down the wing by sprinting through the centre. Duncan caught the ball just before the goal line and whipped over a fast, first-time cross. Gordon launched himself horizontally and met the ball flush on his forehead to send it rocketing into the Aberdeen net. So perfect was the conception and execution of this goal that Gordon recalled after he retired that for the only time in his career, the crowd applauded him all the way back to halfway after he had scored a goal.

The scene was now set for the New Year's Day derby match against Hearts at Tynecastle. Hearts were third in the league and hopeful. Hibs were second in the league and confident. We also knew that a convincing derby victory would send us to the top of the table. I am always apprehensive when Hibs play Hearts, irrespective of the strengths of the respective teams at any given time. On this occasion however, I was more confident than usual.

At this time, I was living in Bonnyrigg as I taught in the local school there. Not being in a position to own a car, I set out for Edinburgh on what, in those days, used to be called the SMT bus. When I arrived at St Andrew Square bus station, I met a parent from the school with her two sons. The boys, Bernard and Michael Kelly, attended my school and had tragically lost their father in a car accident just a short time before. They were going with their mum to visit a relative in hospital and didn't look too pleased at the prospect. They were enthusiastic football fans although their team was Celtic rather than Hibs. Nevertheless, I asked them how they fancied going to see the Edinburgh derby (matches were rarely all ticket affairs in those days). They were very keen to go to the match and their mum was happy to let them go. This chance encounter was to enable two young Celtic fans to be present at one of the greatest days in Hibs history.

While I was travelling through, Hibs were training at Easter Road. Eddie Turnbull had called his team in on the morning of the match and he told them that they should be proud to be the only team in Britain which was training on New Year's morning. Jimmy O'Rourke meanwhile was telling all his team mates that he could feel in his bones that this was going to be a special day. He had been watching *Zorro* on television and he couldn't stop focusing on the letter Z which kept flashing up on the screen. He knew it was significant but couldn't work out why. After the game, of course, Jimmy realised that it wasn't Z he was seeing but 7.

Hearts started the game well and missed two early chances. After that, they didn't get a look in. With Black and Blackley rock solid in central defence, Edwards, Stanton and Cropley dominating the midfield in imperious fashion and Duncan, O'Rourke and Gordon proving absolutely unstoppable in attack, Hibs recorded a famous and unforgettable victory. At half-time it was 5–0 and many Hearts fans had already gone home. Being a natural pessimist, I was hoping that Hearts wouldn't mount a second-half comeback. Most of my fellow Hibs fans were in rather more positive vein and were discussing the possibility of Hibs scoring double figures. At half-time, I met Alan, the brother of my friend Ian Mooney. Alan was in a state of euphoria, induced by a combination of the score line and the drinks he had consumed in celebrating the goals. He wrapped me in a bear hug and informed me that I was 'the greatest man since Winston Churchill.' At that moment, I would have preferred a comparison with Pat

Stanton. Pat it was who made a fifty-yard run through the Hearts defence to create goal number six for Jimmy O'Rourke. Pat claims that his effort was going in anyway. Jimmy insists that he had to make sure that the ball crossed the line. This run summed up Pat Stanton's elegance as a player. He hardly seemed to exert himself at all yet he effortlessly left several Hearts players in his wake. Pat was a class act indeed.

Alan Gordon completed the scoring with a trademark header from an Arthur Duncan cross. Arthur had been set up by Erich Schaedler who had won the ball from Hearts' Dave Clunie with a bone-shuddering tackle, which left the Hearts man in a crumpled heap on the grass. When Gordon scored, there was plenty time left for Hibs to add more goals. They did not do so although they did create and miss several additional opportunities. However, almost forty years later, Hibs fans still talk and sing about the magical 'seven' and, on reflection, the scoreline we achieved on that historic occasion had the perfect resonance. I don't know why but 7–0 just sounds better than 8–0 or 9–0.

Hugh Taylor summed up Hibs' performance next day when he wrote in the *Daily Record*, 'Enchanting play by Alex Edwards and Alex Cropley carved fantastic gaps in the Hearts defence. Hibs are now playing with all the flair, polish and venom of a top team and when I say top team, I mean one of the top teams in the world.' I travelled home to Bonnyrigg as the happiest man in the world. I knew that I had witnessed something unique and I felt privileged to have been present. I was on a rickety old SMT bus but I felt like I was flying on a magic carpet.

Clearly the first day of 1973 was a very special day indeed for all Hibs fans. You would have thought that I would have gone home that night and thrown the party to end all parties. I didn't. We had a quiet family night and a few drinks, but nothing excessive. In those days, there were no video recorders so if you didn't watch the television highlights live, you didn't see the television coverage of the match. We all wanted to be able to watch *Sportscene* that night and take in every aspect of the momentous match that had taken place earlier that day. Alistair Alexander was the commentator and he didn't disappoint as time and again, he heaped praise on Hibs' flowing football. Just before we settled down to watch the football, there was a knock at the door. Our New Year visitor turned out to be a Hearts-supporting friend of mine. He had been so certain that Hearts would win the derby match that he had bet me £5 and even given me the benefit of a draw. Now, like the true sportsman he was, he had come to pay his debts. We invited him in to have a drink and watch the match on television with us. Not surprisingly, he declined our invitation, handed over his fiver, wished us Happy New Year and left. His parting shot was to tell us that Hibs had been lucky. He was totally wrong there. Hibs' most famous derby victory owed nothing to luck and everything to ability.

Looking back now it is interesting to reflect that two men who were in the Hearts ranks that day are very much involved in the cut and thrust of today's SPL. Jim Jefferies was the Hearts captain that day and Hibs have made him suffer again since. Jefferies was in charge of Hearts when Hibs hammered them 6–2 in October 2000. He was also, of course, the manager of Kilmarnock when Hibs thrashed them 5–1 in the 2007 CIS Insurance Cup Final. The other Hearts player who played in the 7–0 game, and survived to tell the tale, is Donald Park. Donald, of course, has seen sense in recent years and moved to the east of the city where, in a number of spells at the club, he has provided Hibs with exemplary service as a coach.

Turnbull's Tornadoes were riding high. They had two cups in the trophy cabinet, looked a good bet for the league and the Scottish Cup and had even released a record. The team had recorded a double A-side featuring 'Hibernian, Give us a Goal', which had been written by chairman Tom Hart's wife Sheila. The other song on the disc was called, not surprisingly, 'Turnbull's Tornadoes.' The composer this time was the famous music arranger Johnny Keating. Johnny was probably best known at that time for his arrangement of the *Z Cars* theme which accompanied the popular BBC police drama series. As a lifelong Hibee, he was only too happy to write a song about his favourite team. The tune was the same as that used by John Lennon for his classic 'Happy Christmas (War is over)' and the lyrics fitted the bill perfectly. The words of the chorus described Hibs play as 'The best brand of football the world's ever seen.' At that particular time, that grandiose claim was not far from the truth. Not only did we not have video players at that time but CD players hadn't been invented either. Hibs record came out in the old vinyl format and sold well to fans, who were on the ultimate of highs.

Sadly, we were just about to be brought back down to earth. On Saturday, 6 January 1973, Hibs entertained East Fife. A larger-than-usual crowd rolled up to Easter Road and, if I am being honest, we were all expecting an avalanche of goals. We weren't expecting the goals to come from East Fife either. We were confident that our high-powered Hibees would completely steamroller the men from Methil. As the match began, there was a carnival atmosphere in the ground but that was to change in the most dramatic fashion over the following ninety minutes. East Fife were managed by a former Hibs favourite, Pat Quinn. Pat had been a footballer of the purest quality and had earned himself the affection of the Hibs support. This day, he went a long way towards diluting his popularity by setting his team up to defend in depth and play with complete cynicism.

East Fife defended, fouled and wasted time throughout the first half. They had given their midfield player, Johnny Love, the task of man-marking Alex Edwards. Love was a local boy and a Hibs supporter but he didn't let this get in the way of his mission to wind up Hibs' little midfield maestro. Edwards was fouled consistently and his other team mates fared little better. The referee was David Syme and he displayed remarkable leniency as he turned a Nelsonian eye to the worst of Quinn's team's excesses and seemed to make little effort to exert proper control or take appropriately firm action. What was turning into a frustrating day took a turn for the worse just before half-time. John Brownlie was driving forward up the right wing when he was tackled by Ian Printy. Brownlie went down in a crumpled heap and silence descended on Easter Road. It looked bad and it was. Our wonderful right back had broken his leg in two places and wouldn't play first team football again for eleven months.

As the game wore on, Hibs could find no way through the iron curtain that East Fife had erected in front of their goal. Then, with minutes remaining, a bad day became significantly worse. Alex Edwards, after being fouled yet again by Johnny Love, picked up the ball and looked at the referee to see what he planned to do. Syme did not plan to do anything and told Edwards to get on with taking the free kick. Edwards, at the end of his tether, threw the ball angrily in the direction of Love. At this point, the referee did take action. He produced his book and cautioned Edwards. This meant that Edwards had reached the disciplinary points' threshold and was due for a suspension.

When Edwards subsequently appeared before the SFA, no Hibs fan was surprised when the denizens of Park Gardens handed out a swingeing eight-week ban. It was as unfair as it was extreme. Edwards was a fiery little character who was prone to retaliation but time and again those who cynically provoked him escaped suspension. That was exactly what happened in the case of Johnny Love in this particular league match, which had now turned into a full-scale disaster. Ironically, Alan Gordon headed home a last-minute winning goal for Hibs. Celebrations though were less than muted – they were non-existent.

That night Margaret and I had been invited to a post New Year party. We had arranged baby sitters and as new parents, we had looked forward to a rare night out. By the time I got home, I had decided that I wasn't going. I was in no mood for partying. Margaret insisted that we go. She convinced me that were was nothing to be gained by brooding on Hibs' misfortunes and that we should go out and take our minds off that day's events at Easter Road. Well we did go but, I for one, was no company for anyone. I was sunk in deep despair and no one's attempts to shake me out of it came close to success. I was not a big drinker in those days (and even less so now) but I was determined to drown out my sorrows and sought oblivion through a glass. Such was the depth of my gloom, however, that no amount of drinks – and I swallowed more than my fair share of whiskies – had the slightest effect on me. At the end of the evening I was as stone-cold sober and as hugely depressed as I had been at the start of it.

In all honesty, Turnbull's Tornadoes were never the same force again and it has to be said that the manager contributed to this state of affairs. Hibs next game was away to Dundee United. Turnbull left out Jimmy O'Rourke and Hibs lost 1–0. This was an inexplicable selection decision. In the first half of the season, O'Rourke had scored thirty-two goals. Prior to the East Fife game, he had scored seven goals in five games. He had spent most of the East Fife match at right back after Brownlie's injury so why was he dropped? Only Turnbull could answer that question. Sadly Jimmy O'Rourke was never again a fully-fledged first team regular. At a time when we had lost an international class right back and an outstanding playmaker, our manager chose to deprive the team of its main goalscorer.

The outcome of all of this was depressingly predictable. Hibs league challenge evaporated and we were knocked out of the Scottish Cup by Rangers. After an excellent 1–1 draw at Ibrox where Alan Gordon scored a fine goal, we dominated the replay but were able to take only one of the many chances we created. Rangers made two opportunities, took them both and won 2–1.

This left us with only one further chance of glory in a season which had started so well but which was now in serious danger of finishing in dispiriting anticlimax. We were still in the quarter-final of the European Cup Winner's Cup and when that tie came round in March everyone felt that we had a really good chance of not just winning our way through to the semi-finals but of winning the competition itself. Our opponents were the Yugoslavian team Hajduk Split and the first leg was at Easter Road. Des Bremner, a young player from Deveronvale in the Highland League had come in to replace Brownlie. Des was to go on to become an excellent midfield anchorman. Indeed his prowess in this role was such that he went on to win a European Cup Winners medal with Aston Villa and gain international caps for Scotland. At this stage of his career, he was a steady replacement for our injured and greatly-missed right back, but he came nowhere near Brownlie in terms of the attacking options which he offered the side. Jimmy O'Rourke was still out of favour although no one could work out why and Alan Gordon was being partnered up front by Tony Higgins. These days Higgins is better known for his work with the players' union and his television punditry.

In 1973, he was a promising young forward who was blessed with great ball control for a big man. He could also score excellent goals although he did not score as often as he should have. On the down side, he tended towards being overweight, was poor in the air especially given his height and was completely lacking in pace. He was Eddie Turnbull's flavour of the month but he was no Jimmy O'Rourke. The good news was that Alex Edwards was available again after his suspension and his return would strengthen Hibs immeasurably.

More than 28,000 crowded into Easter Road for the Hajduk match. There was a great atmosphere and Hibs played magnificently. Edwards gave a towering performance in midfield. The *Daily Record* headline next day proclaimed, 'Edwards puts the sparkle back into Hibs.' They were absolutely correct. The little playmaker's return galvanised his team mates and Hajduk were overrun. Alan Gordon scored a superb hat-trick and Arthur Duncan added a fourth goal. Hajduk had scored a late first half goal in a rare breakaway but with just fourteen minutes left, Hibs were three goals ahead and a place in the semi-finals seemed assured. Our lead could, and should, have been larger. We had missed a host of chances and the Spanish referee had turned down three strong penalty claims. Our peace of mind was slightly disturbed by a late second goal for Hajduk but most of us left the ground thinking that Hibs had done enough and would be capable of safely negotiating the return leg. How wrong we were proved to be.

Hajduk had shown themselves to be a fiery team at Easter Road. In the return match, we discovered that their fans were fierier still. The Hajduk stadium was compact and overflowing. The supporters were close to the play and in a permanent state of frenzy. This made for a testing tie but it was a situation that Hibs should have been able to deal with. Sadly they failed to do so. Jim Herriot, usually so reliable, had a poor match and the rest of the team also allowed themselves to be intimidated by the atmosphere and greatly underperformed. We lost 3–0 and a great opportunity to win a European trophy was squandered.

Eddie Turnbull was incandescent. He revealed later just how disappointed he had been that night when he described it as disastrous and admitted that he had lost faith in his team and was never to regain it. That was a remarkable position for our manager to assume. He had been in charge of Hibs for less than two years, had built an exciting team of all the talents and had won two trophies. Instead of accepting the result in Split for the temporary setback it was, he began the process of dismantling a team in its prime.

Turnbull should have been able to reflect that the disappointing end to the 1972–73 season had owed much to the enforced absences of Brownlie and Edwards and his illogical and totally wrong decision to axe Jimmy O'Rourke. He failed to see this and was so intent on concentrating on his team's late season shortcomings that he forgot all about their early and mid-season brilliance.

Jim Herriot was made to pay for his errors in Yugoslavia and Jim McArthur started the new season as first choice goalkeeper. Jim had been signed a few months earlier from Cowdenbeath and was to prove a good servant to Hibs, although he never quite reached the top level of the goalkeeping spectrum. Jim, of course, is well known these days as a football agent. He was always a man with entrepreneurial flair. In the '70s and '80s, he worked part time as a physical education teacher in primary schools. At that time there was a football league for teaching-staff teams. Most of the sides in the league were secondary-school staffs or further-education-college combinations. I had, however, organised a team of primary teachers. We had a good group of players and we proved ourselves consistently to be one of the best teams in the league.

Our centre forward was none other than Jim McArthur and a very good striker he was too. One night after a match we all went to a nearby pub for a drink. As the evening wore on, a man came into the pub selling fresh fish. He was carrying a box of ice which was full of very appetising looking pieces of haddock. He claimed that the fish had been landed that very day and was offering them for sale at a very reasonable price. We all bought some but no one bought more than Jim who purchased four large fillets. When we met up for the following week's match, everyone was saying how much they had enjoyed their fish. Jim McArthur was uncharacteristically quiet. We asked him if he had enjoyed his fish. He informed us that he had thrown it into the bin. When we asked why, he told us that he hated fish. We then asked him why he had bought it in the first place if that was the case. Jim's reply demonstrated the business instincts which would stand him in good stead in later life. He had bought the fish he said because 'It was too good a bargain to miss!'

Anyway, Hibs began their defence of the Drybrough Cup with McArthur between the posts. Turnbull had also signed Iain Munro from St Mirren. Munro, at that point in his career, was an accomplished and highly promising left-sided midfield player. He was not, however, in the same class as Alex Cropley, the regular occupant of that position in the team, so none of us was really sure why he had been signed. Hibs' first Drybrough Cup match contained a couple of the twists of fate that football so frequently throws up. We met St Mirren, which meant that Iain Munro was making his Hibs debut against the team which he had just left. In goal for the Saints was none other than Jim Herriot who had been given a free transfer by Eddie Turnbull after his rare lapses in Split. Munro played in this match but not at the expense of Cropley who was moved to the left wing. To accommodate this move, Arthur Dunan switched to the right wing. It seemed that our manager would go to any length to keep Jimmy O'Rourke out of the team.

Hibs made heavy weather of a 2–1 win with Duncan and Munro both scoring fine goals. The star of the show, however, was Alex Edwards who was at his majestic best. Even Turnbull was moved to declare that Edwards had showed what tremendous talent he had by spraying a succession of great passes. This tremendous talent did not always prove sufficient to retain a place in the team for Edwards in the months to come.

Rangers came to Easter Road for the semi-final and in front of an excellent 28,000 crowd, Hibs again proved too good for them at the penultimate stage of a competition. We beat them 2–1 with the winning goal coming from Tony Higgins who had come on as a substitute for Alan Gordon. One of the reports of the match described Higgins as 'A teenage titan.' His goal took Hibs back to Hampden and gave them their fourth semi-final victory over Rangers in a period of fifteen months.

So we all trooped back to Hampden for another final. There waiting for us, as usual, was Jock Stein's Celtic. Turnbull left out Cropley and brought in Higgins. At half-time, he took off Edwards whom he had praised so lavishly only a week earlier and replaced him with another promising youngster, Bobby Smith. It was a tightly-contested match in front of just under 50,000 supporters. Alex Cropley came on for Munro on the hour mark (most of us had wondered why he wasn't playing from the start) and made a telling impact. The game went to extra time and with only a minute of this period remaining and penalties looking more of a certainty than a possibility,

Cropley took a hand. He played Alan Gordon in with an astute through pass. Our ultra-cool striker allowed the ball to run past him then expertly placed it beyond Ally Hunter in the Celtic goal. Hibs had won their third trophy in a year. We fans were absolutely elated but it is fair to say that there was a slight tinge of the blasé creeping into our psyche. We were starting to get used to success and were fully expecting it to continue. What we didn't realise on that happy day at Hampden was that it would be eighteen long years before our team lifted another major trophy.

After the Drybrough Cup Final, John Rafferty of *The Scotsman* forecast that 'Hibs are now equipped to take the league title.' Eddie Turnbull was more cautious, preferring to concentrate on the team's forthcoming defence of the League Cup. Rafferty was right because with fine-tuning Turnbull's Tornadoes could have won the league. Rather than taking such a measured approach, the man in charge of our team opted for major surgery instead.

However, it was an excellent start to the season and there was more happiness in store for Margaret and me. On Saturday, 15 September 1973, two days after our fourth wedding anniversary, our daughter Lisa came into the world. When our older son Patrick had been born, Margaret had had to undergo a twenty-seven-hour labour. Being a bit naive about these things, we thought that this was the norm. When Margaret went into labour on that September Saturday morning, she said, 'It'll probably be the same as the last time and take absolutely ages so I think that you should go to the match.' I, of course, should have politely declined and stayed by the side of my imminent wife. However, with what on mature reflection appears like no little selfishness, I set off for Easter Road. We beat East Fife 2–1 with goals from Pat Stanton and Johnny Hamilton and my friends all made jokes about

Margaret's condition back home. Like me, none of them seemed to think that I had done anything untoward in going to the game. Ah well, I suppose we were living in different days.

I returned to be met by a wife who was now in increasingly heavy labour. In no time at all we were in an ambulance en route for the Elsie Inglis maternity hospital. These days it is exceptional for men not to attend the birth of their child. In those days, it was much less common for that to happen and Margaret did not want me around to cramp her style when she delivered. I was keen to be there but was outwitted by my wife and the gynaecologist who hatched a plot to get me out of the way. The doctor told me that nothing would happen before midnight and instructed me to find a pub, have a pie and a pint and read the *Pink News*. 'By the time you come back,' he said, 'things might be starting to happen.'

It was all a dastardly plot and when I strolled casually back into the labour suite a couple of hours later, things, instead of being about to happen, had well and truly taken place. The cries of a newborn baby could be clearly heard. When I asked if I could go in, the midwife answered, 'Not yet but you can look in through the glass.' This I did and saw Margaret fondly holding a beautiful new child. The child seemed to have a rather large appendage and I exclaimed 'it's another boy!'

The midwife shot me a withering look and said, 'No. It's a little girl and what you are looking at is not what you think it is. It's the umbilical cord!' It was indeed and I was now the proud father of a wonderful daughter and another little Hibee had come into the world.

The early weeks of the new season saw Hibs win most of their matches but suffer two significant losses. We went to Tynecastle to play Hearts for the first time since the 7–0 match and lost 4–1. We were also heavily defeated at Ibrox where we went down 4–0. A team as good as Hibs should not have been suffering such defeats so there was cause for concern.

However, the month of November also provided reason for optimism. When Hibs took on Dundee at Easter Road, there were two familiar faces back in the side. After an eleven-month absence John Brownlie returned at right back. He played well but did not fully look the player he had been. Sadly, although he was to continue to play regularly for several more seasons after this comeback and was able to perform at a high standard, he never again scaled the heights which he had reached prior to his leg break.

The other returning hero was Jimmy O'Rourke. Shamefully and ridiculously, Jimmy had been shunned by Eddie Turnbull for months. On this day he scored his first goals of the season to help Hibs to a 2–1 victory. He also had a goal disallowed and, unusually for him, missed a penalty. So Jimmy had returned with a double which could have easily been a quadruple. To put Turnbull's ill-founded obstinacy in the case of selecting O'Rourke into perspective, Jimmy had scored twenty-five goals in season 1972–73 by the time he opened his account for 1973–74. Of course, you cannot score goals if you are not selected to play and O'Rourke's successful come-back completely demonstrated Turnbull's folly in omitting the team's best goalscorer.

The final months of 1973 were times of political turbulence for Britain. The coal miners had decided to take on the Conservative Prime Minister Ted Heath and his government. The miners' strike led to existing fuel stocks being conserved, which in turn resulted in people working in the industrial sector being placed on a three-day working week. There were domestic implications too. Power cuts took place on a daily basis and we all had to resort to using candles to light our homes. We also had to accept that it would not be possible to cook or heat our houses at certain times of the day. All of this had an effect on sport too as floodlit football matches couldn't be played.

Hibs had progressed to the League Cup quarter-finals as they defended the trophy which they had won in such style a year earlier. We were paired yet again with Rangers, this time over two legs. The first leg at Ibrox was lost 2–0 but we all hoped that we could overturn this deficit at Easter Road. The return leg was played on Wednesday, 21 November with a 1.30p.m. kick-off. It was amazing how many people managed to get the afternoon off work to lend their support to Hibs' quest to claw back Rangers lead. There again, maybe they were all on a three-day week! Despite the size of the crowd, though, there was an air of unreality about the proceedings, which took away from the intensity of the atmosphere. This did not help Hibs' cause and Rangers held on reasonably comfortably to secure a goalless draw and, in the process, force Hibs to relinquish their hold on the League Cup.

Hibs were also out of Europe by this stage too. We had again competed against Don Revie's mighty Leeds United side and again we had lost in the unluckiest fashion. Leeds at that time were the equivalent of Arsenal or Manchester United now so victory over them would have been a massive achievement. It was a victory which Hibs richly deserved but failed to deliver. An excellent performance at Elland Road gained a 0–0 draw. At Easter Road Hibs completely dominated the match. Five times Leeds cleared off the goal line. We also hit the post and had a goal disallowed. Again Eddie Turnbull preferred Tony Higgins to Jimmy O'Rourke and again this had a detrimental effect on Hibs' firepower. The outstanding player on the field was Leeds captain Billy Bremner. Bremner played at sweeper and gave a display of breathtaking brilliance. At one point, he stopped a header on the line, insolently performed a keepie-uppie routine then cleared the ball to safety. Standing on the highest part of the old east terracing that night, I did not know whether to admire Bremner for his skill or loathe him for the one-man barrier which he was so successfully erecting in front of the Leeds goal.

Try as they might, Hibs could not break Leeds down so we were into the lottery of a penalty shootout. 36,000 Hibs fans held their breath as Pat Stanton walked forward to take the first kick. Pat, of course, had told Alan Gordon after a previous spot kick miss that he was 'not to be trusted with penalties.' His words rang all too true this night. Our inspirational skipper, so loved by the fans, struck his shot from the spot against the post. All the other nine penalty takers were successful so Leeds completed the ultimate in smash and grab jobs and Hibs lost after one of their best ever European performances. Nobody held Pat's miss against him. We all loved him too much for that but, in truth, he should never have taken a penalty that night as his record from twelve yards was at best mixed. Pat tells of how he was given the nod to step forward for the vital first penalty that night. 'Eddie Turnbull pointed and said, "You take the first one". I looked behind me to see who he was talking to and then I realised that he was actually pointing at me. I wasn't confident but I went forward anyway. The rest is history.'

Turnbull's choice of Stanton to lead off the penalty shootout wasn't a good one but he was to take a far more significant decision in February 1974. He moved into the transfer market and signed the Everton centre forward Joe Harper for £120,000. This was a massive sum of money for Hibs to spend and it was a major gamble. Harper had been a prolific scorer for Turnbull when he had managed Aberdeen, but his spell on Merseyside had been less than successful. We fans were astounded at Hibs splashing out so much cash. We were pleased that the club had signed a player with the potential to deliver a hatful of goals but we were surprised that Turnbull had seen the need to buy a striker when he had, in Jimmy O'Rourke and Alan Gordon, two of the best goal thieves in the country.

Harper's signing coincided with a tragic time in our family. In early February, I was called from my classroom to receive a telephone call from Margaret's brother Terry. Terry had shocking news to impart. Arthur, Margaret's dad, had collapsed and died of a heart attack at his work that morning. I left school immediately and headed for home as I wanted to break this news to Margaret in person. As I walked up the road, I saw her pushing our two young children in their pushchair as she made her way to the shops. I then had to tell her that her fifty-one-year-old father whom she loved so deeply had sadly passed away. Arthur was a lifelong Hibs fan and had many friends in the Hibs supporting community. His funeral took place on the day of Joe Harper's debut.

Harper started his Hibs career at Falkirk. He was overweight and ineffectual. Eddie Turnbull left Alan Gordon and Jimmy O'Rourke on the bench and the match ended as a tame goalless draw. The following week, Hibs met St Johnstone at Perth in the Scottish Cup. The school staff trio of Carl Carney, Ian Mooney and myself were back on the road again. We joined many Hibs fans in the crowd at the old Muirton Park and the first surprise we got was when Turnbull's team selection was announced. There was no place for Harper and the old firm of Gordon and O'Rourke had been restored. Hibs played really well and achieved a very good 3–0 win over a St Johnstone team that was a match for anyone at that time. All of Hibs' goals were scored by a certain J. O'Rourke and as we drove home Carl, Ian and I continually asked each other 'Why does he continually leave out Jimmy O'Rourke and why in heaven's name did he need to sign Joe Harper?'

As the season progressed, Turnbull restored Harper to the

team and demoted O'Rourke once more. Harper failed to hit the high spots until a 3–1 victory at Dundee when he scored two goals and, for the first time, displayed the type of form which he had consistently demonstrated for Aberdeen. Roddy McKenzie, Gerry Adair, Derek Spalding, John Hazel, Willie Murray and Bobby Smith were all called into the Hibs team that night. There was no O'Rourke, no Schaedler, no Black, no Blackley and no Gordon. Most of these changes were to be of a temporary nature at this stage in Turnbull's reign but a clear signal had been given that things were starting to change.

In due course, events were to prove that the signing of Joe Harper was the beginning of the end of Turnbull's Tornadoes. A great team with its best years ahead of it was to be systematically dismantled on the whim of its manager. Now, looking back on the events of more than thirty years ago, I still feel a strong sense of frustration. A team with the ability to achieve many years of success was tampered with unnecessarily and individual players were treated poorly not knowing from one week to the next whether or not they would be selected for the next match, irrespective of their previous performances.

Season 1973–74 fizzled out for Hibs. We fell away in the league and lost in the Scottish Cup, after a replay, to Dundee. However, there was optimism around at the start of the next season and the early signs were encouraging. The Fairs Cup had now been renamed the UEFA Cup and Hibs opened their European campaign in majestic style. We beat the Norwegian side Rosenborg home and away. At Easter Road Hibs served up, in the words of the *Daily Record*, 'a dazzling, devastating display' to win 9–0. Harper, Munro, Stanton and Cropley all notched up doubles and our team proved just how much talent was in its ranks. I remember standing on the old terracing with my friends that night and all of us being of one mind. We genuinely felt that with consistency of selection and positive motivation, our team was capable of adding more trophies to the three which it had already garnered under Turnbull's management.

Publicly, at this time, there was unity in Hibs' ranks but behind the scenes things were not quite so harmonious. All the players regarded Eddie Turnbull's football knowledge and coaching prowess very highly. In fact, most of the players in Turnbull's great team will state to this day that he added new dimensions to their football knowledge. They will also tell you though that his man-management skills did not come close to matching his coaching attributes and that he was so sparing with praise that when he did issue a rare compliment, the team was completely taken aback.

The victory over Rosenborg sadly proved to be a false dawn. One fateful week in October administered the kiss of death to both Hibs' hopes in the league and their quest for European glory. On Saturday, 19 October, Hibs went to Parkhead and were humiliated 5–0. We just didn't turn up. Celtic were brilliant but Hibs were pusillanimous. A team with so many outstanding players just should not have surrendered as meekly as we did that day. For us fans, it was very depressing indeed. There was to be no respite either because on the following Wednesday, Juventus came to Easter Road on UEFA Cup business. We consoled ourselves that the Parkhead capitulation was a blip and that our beloved Hibees would roar back against Italy's finest.

For a time, it looked like our positivity was justified. In front of 28,000 fans, Hibs played really well and led 2–1 through goals from Stanton and Cropley with just twenty minutes left. Juventus, by this time, had introduced their veteran striker Altafini. In the words of Alex Cropley, Altafini was 'old, balding and podgy.' This may have been the case but there was no doubt that he could still play. He had run Hibs ragged in Naples six years earlier and now, he did so once again. He scored twice and created another and Juventus, who had been in trouble at 2–1 down after seventy minutes, ran out 4–2 winners.

Our depression now deepened but there was worse to come. On the Saturday, Hibs were due to travel to Glasgow to meet Celtic once more. This time we would contest the League Cup Final. We travelled in apprehension rather than hope and our worst fears were realised. Celtic blew us away 6–3 and despite a Joe Harper hat-trick, Hibs were again completely outplayed. In one short week, although at the time it seemed never-ending, Turnbull's Tornadoes had been transformed into Turnbull's Timorous Beasties by losing three major matches and conceding fifteen goals in the process.

It was all desperately disappointing and difficult to explain. Our team was talented beyond doubt but it seemed to lack backbone on big occasions. Yet this was not totally true because, in the space of only twelve months, we had defeated Celtic and Rangers three times each in semi-finals and finals. The team probably did require the infusion of a couple of harder players but most of all it needed to know that its manager still believed in it. This is where I think Eddie Turnbull went wrong. From the Hajduk Split match onwards, he made it clear to his players that he had lost faith in them. This resulted in the players beginning to doubt themselves and the consequences of this lack of self-belief were manifested in poor results and timid performances in big matches.

That cataclysmic week in October 1974 left Hibs with only the Scottish Cup to play for. Such was our luck at this time that we drew Celtic in the third round. The match was played in snowy weather and Hibs, with a young medical student

Hugh Whyte in goal, lost 2–0. I wasn't at Easter Road that day because, for once, I had more pressing priorities than supporting the Hibees. Margaret was pregnant again and when our son Dominic was born on Wednesday, 15 January 1975, which was the day when Radio Forth first took to the air, there was cause for concern. Dominic was born six weeks premature and spent the first week of his life in an incubator. We were frantic with worry but thankfully Dominic, whose middle name was Arthur after his recently deceased grand-father, pulled through. He now stands at well over six feet and is a formidable all-round sportsman and the father of two beautiful little girls.

By the time season 1975–76 got under way, our ever-increasing young family was blossoming and we could concentrate once more on matters Hibernian. It was our centenary season and all the bad memories of the previous campaign had been put to one side as we anticipated a return to flowing football and winning ways. We started brilliantly. Rangers were swept aside at Easter Road. They were flattered by a 3–1 defeat as Hibs played magnificently and opened their historic season with a majestic display. Next came Hearts and they were beaten 1–0 thanks to a wonder goal by Joe Harper who rifled a twenty-five yard shot high into Jim Cruickshank's net.

Once again, we supporters were beginning to feel hopeful. Once again our optimism, like Dominic's birth, was to be premature. Liverpool came to Easter Road in the UEFA Cup and were beaten 1–0. Hibs' margin should have been twice as much. Joe Harper had given us a first half lead with an excellent goal after a great run and cross by Arthur Duncan. With ten minutes to go, Duncan, who was in fine form that night, was brought down in the box and the Dutch referee pointed to the spot. By this time, John Brownlie had become Hibs' regular penalty taker and he had proved to be completely reliable in this role. Sadly on this occasion, he was more fallible and Ray Clemence dived to his right to save the full back's weakly-struck shot.

The big worry for the return leg at Anfield was Liverpool's twin strike force of John Toshack and Kevin Keegan. In particular we feared the big Welshman's exceptional aerial ability. A tremendous Hibs support travelled by car, bus and train to Merseyside and helped to swell the crowd to just under 30,000. All the discussion on the way down was centred around who would be the best player to mark Toshack. The consensus was that Pat Stanton, with his ability to read the game and his strong heading power, was undoubtedly the right person. Everyone thought this except for one man and that man was the one who counted most. Incredibly and unaccountably, Eddie Turnbull took the decision to omit Stanton from the team. Despite a fine Hibs performance, which included a superb goal from Alex Edwards, Hibs lost 3–1 and went out by one tantalising goal on aggregate. All of Liverpool's goals were scored by Toshack and all three of them were headers. Imagine the chagrin of the large Hibs support as we saw all this unfold while our brilliant captain sat on the bench. If we had conceded one less goal, we would have achieved a momentous victory on the away goals rule. Would Stanton have allowed the towering Toshack those three free headers? I think not but once again the team had suffered due to managerial team selection which did not make sense to the majority of supporters.

This proved to be the last hurrah for Turnbull's once-great team. He now began to wield the axe with increasing ferocity. Players who still had a great deal to offer and who were much loved by the fans were moved on. There were good signings but these were outnumbered by poor decisions in the transfer market and the quality of the team was needlessly reduced.

By the end of the '70s only Arthur Duncan remained from the team which had won the 1972 League Cup. Herriot and Black had been released, Brownlie and Blackley had been transferred to Newcastle, Erich Schaedler and Alan Gordon had gone to Dundee, Alex Cropley had been sold to Arsenal and Alex Edwards had been shipped out to Arbroath. Jimmy O'Rourke had continued to score goals but now he was hitting the net first for St Johnstone and then Motherwell. Jimmy had in fact been the second member of the great exodus after Jim Herriot. Even Joe Harper, who had been the original catalyst for change, was allowed to return to Aberdeen for a fraction of what Hibs had paid Everton for him. Harper had eventually proved himself to be a great goalscorer but he was never fully accepted by the Hibs support. The only mistake he really made was to replace one of the fans biggest favourites, Jimmy O'Rourke. When he was signed Hibs were riding high, didn't need him and couldn't afford him. By the time he left, Hibs were inexorably on the slide.

Worst of all, in the eyes of the supporters, Pat Stanton had been allowed to move to Celtic in a swap deal for Jackie MacNamara. Pat was a Hibs man through and through and did not deserve to be pushed out of the club that he had served with such distinction. His heart never left Easter Road. He told me that when he won the league with Celtic at Tannadice, the players' coach interrupted its return journey to Glasgow to drop him and the rest of the Edinburgh Celtic contingent at the Barnton Hotel to collect their cars. As Pat passed Jock Stein on his way off the bus, the great man said to him, 'Are you going out to celebrate winning the league tonight?'

Pat replied, 'Probably.'

Stein rejoined, 'With your Hibs pals, no doubt.'

'Probably,' said Pat again.

'Aye,' said Stein with a sigh, 'we've only got a wee loan of you.'

Much of Turnbull's managerial hatchet work was accompanied by unnecessary acrimony. O'Rourke and Cropley would have been more than happy to have stayed with Hibs, Gordon was made to train with the young players and Stanton was given the cold shoulder by his manager before reluctantly making his way to Parkhead. This left all Hibs fans, not least myself, in a state of despair and disillusionment. Only a few short years before, Tom Hart our chairman, had said that none of the trophy-winning team would be sold. Now all but one had been moved out.

Turnbull's Tornadoes were a magnificent team. They won three trophies and could have won many more. The team was cruelly broken up by a manager whose anger at a couple of defeats in major matches was such that he wrote off a golden generation of Hibernian greats when they were still in their prime. Turnbull later admitted that he may have been too hasty in breaking his team up. If anyone ever drew up a list of the fifty greatest understatements of all time, that remark of Eddie Turnbull's would be a challenger for the top spot on the list.

9

BEST OF TIMES, WORST OF TIMES

As he broke up his great team, Eddie Turnbull sought to replace the players he no longer had use for with new men who, one presumes, he considered would do better than those he had let go. He singularly failed to achieve this. He did make some good signings but he also brought in players who, frankly, were not Hibs class.

He did a good piece of business in signing Jackie McNamara from Celtic. This was a swap deal for Pat Stanton. Jock Stein was looking to move McNamara on so Hibs could have signed him without losing our great skipper. In the event, McNamara proved to be an excellent acquisition. He initially struggled as he was played out of position at right back but once he switched to sweeper, he didn't look back. Jackie Mac was to go on to give Hibs many years of great service and is a popular man with the fans to this day.

Another good move was the signing of George Stewart from Dundee. Big George was a lifelong Hibee and just the centre half that Hibs needed. Indeed if he had been purchased earlier, he would have provided exactly the physical presence in central defence which Jim Black had been unable to supply for Turnbull's Tornadoes.

Probably the best deal which Turnbull brokered was to take Ally McLeod from Southampton for a mere £30,000.

McLeod was a maverick but a very talented one. He had great close control and dribbling skills and a real eye for goal. He was arrogant and possessed of a sharp tongue which he used with equal effect towards team mates and opposition alike. His main drawback was his laziness. When Ally wasn't on the ball, he wasn't in the game. Off the ball running or foraging most definitely did not feature in his game plan. For Turnbull's final years as Hibs Manager though, Ally McLeod was definitely the main man.

Turnbull also procured the signature of Ralph Callachan from Newcastle United as part of the deal which took John Brownlie to St James Park. Callachan had been at Hearts before heading for the north-east but Hibs fans never held his past against him as they recognised his talent and his commitment to our club; a commitment which he maintains to this day as he still attends matches with Jackie McNamara. Although not as good a player as McLeod, he had similar characteristics inasmuch as he was skilful but very laid-back and not the most industrious of players. By 1977, I had become a primary school Head Teacher. One summer, I contacted Hibs to ask if they could send a player down to present the trophies at the school badminton competition. Ralph Callachan was the man who came to represent the club. He turned up dressed very smartly in a jacket, trousers, shirt and tie. As we chatted in my office, he asked if I would like him to take the school football team for a training session in the playground before the badminton competition started. I was delighted to accept his offer and told him that I would go and round up the members of the team while he was getting changed. 'Och, I'm not going to bother getting changed,' said the bold Ralph and proceeded to tuck his beautifully-pressed trousers into his socks. He then went out and, without removing his jacket, provided the school footballers with a perfectly executed demonstration of a series of ball-control exercises using his newly polished, highly fashionable shoes.

A player for whom Turnbull did not pay a fee was Gordon Rae who hailed from close to Eric Stevenson in Bonnyrigg. He signed the big fellow as a seventeen-year-old striker from Whitehill Welfare in the East of Scotland League and handed him a first-team jersey at Ibrox only a short time later. Rae's debut was in the dream-like category as Hibs won 2–0 and he scored the first goal. As his career developed, Gordon Rae became a midfield player and then finally an excellent centre half. George Stewart takes the credit for persuading Pat Stanton to convert Rae into a centre half during Pat's time as manager. It was an inspired move and the man mountain from Midlothian became the bulwark of Hibs' defence and went on to earn a well-deserved testimonial match against Manchester United. Gordon Rae was a big man with a big heart and not a little skill.

Turnbull also made some poor signings at this time. Players like centre half Rikki Fleming from Ayr, Pat Carroll and Willie Temperley, who came through the ranks, and Ally Scott and Graham Fyfe, who were acquired from Rangers, were simply not good enough. Turnbull exchanged Iain Munro for Scott and Fyfe. He had originally signed Munro, who was a fine player, as cover for Alex Cropley. Now, having sold Cropley, he let Munro go. At the time, this did not strike the supporters as the most of logical of moves. It seems no more logical thirty years on. Scott was a tall, balding, workman-like centre forward. Fyfe was a skilled but slow midfield player. Neither made the grade.

Then there was Duncan Lambie, brother of the legendary Partick Thistle Manager and pigeon fancier supreme, John Lambie. Duncan Lambie was signed as a left winger and converted into a left back. During his time at Hibs, he was very poor in both positions. Years later, I was part of the editorial committee for the Hibs fanzine, *Mass Hibsteria*. The magazine ran a series which was ironically titled 'Hibs Grates.' For many fans, Duncan Lambie was a candidate for inclusion.

Another very poor player that Turnbull brought in at this time was Bobby Hutchinson, a centre forward from Dundee. Incredibly our manager swapped Erich Schaedler for this mediocre striker. Hutchinson was busy and hard-working and known to the fans as 'the striker who can do everything but score.' Another striker who didn't score regularly was Joe Ward. Ward had been signed by Aston Villa from Clyde. By this time, Des Bremner was part of the backbone of the Hibs team in the holding midfield role which he had perfected. Following what seems to be the never-ending Hibs pattern of selling their best players, Bremner was allowed to move to Villa and Ward came to Easter Road as a makeweight in the deal. He never looked like being a success.

Finally, there was Ally Brazil, or 'Benny' as he was known owing to his resemblance to a hapless character in the television soap opera *Crossroads*. The only thing remotely Brazilian about Benny was his surname. With his mop of curly hair, gangly frame and non-stop effort, Brazil held down a regular starting place throughout most of the latter years of Eddie Turnbull's reign. Sadly, his talent did not match his work rate and he should never have been selected. Poor Benny suffered a lot of abuse from the supporters, who, while recognising his commitment, became exasperated by his inefficiencies. Turnbull later justified his continued selection of Brazil by claiming that he was a players' player and stating that other managers had also picked him regularly.

This then was the team which Eddie Turnbull guided into the late '70s. Yes, there were good players but there were also players who were nowhere near up to standard. In terms of ability, they did not come within a country mile of matching Turnbull's Tornadoes. Why our manager was prepared to settle for so much less than he had previously had is a complete mystery. George Stewart was exactly right when he said that Hibs had some skilful players but were only half a team.

The 'half team' could still produce the occasional excellent result but the fans were becoming disillusioned. We had seen a magnificent team gratuitously dismantled and we didn't like watching what had been put in its place. A good example of the growing resentment among Hibs supporters at that time was the league derby against Hearts at Easter Road in 1977. Hibs won 3–1 but the game was played in front of only 13,625 fans. The *Daily Record* confirmed that this was 'the poorest Edinburgh derby gate since the war.' The press reports of the match also made the point that 'Hearts were no match for a Hibs side which itself was no world-beater.' Hearts were really struggling and not far from relegation at this time but if results like this helped Turnbull to paper over the cracks, they did little more than that. You can't fool Hibs fans and, at that time, we knew that things were deteriorating and we did not particularly like what we considered the future might hold for us.

Our concerns for the future were to be borne out, but not in the short-term. Amazingly, in season 1978–79, despite their obvious weaknesses, Hibs embarked upon a Scottish Cup run that took them all the way to the final. Dunfermline and Meadowbank Thistle were beaten in the early rounds. Indeed, Meadowbank, who were later to undertake a metamorphosis into Livingston, were dispatched to the tune of 6–0. Since, by mid-March, Hibs had only scored twenty-five goals in twenty-three league games, this was extraordinary and obviously a sign that this season's Scottish Cup campaign might be a little special.

The quarter-final draw paired Hibs with Hearts at Easter Road. Both teams were near the bottom of the league but, as always, a derby was a derby and the match was eagerly antici-pated. It was not eagerly anticipated by anyone more than my good self. I had won a newspaper competition, the prize for which was a crate of beer and two tickets for the cup tie. My oldest son Patrick was coming up for seven now so I decided that he would have the honour of accompanying me. I had been taking Patrick to games for some time but he had never yet sat in the centre stand. Come to think of it, I had only been able to afford centre-stand tickets a few times myself in my years of watching Hibs. I had now been going to games for twenty-two years. Anyway, Saturday, 10 March 1979 saw us take our places in the best seats in the house. We saw a great game and a superb Hibs victory. George Stewart gave Hibs the lead with a towering header then Gordon Rae crashed home a rocket shot to double our advantage before half-time.

Needless to say with Hibs, the second half wasn't as comfortable as it might have been. Hearts pulled a goal back and put Hibs under late pressure. Thankfully we held out and I was able to go home and make a dent in my newly-won box of beers. By this time, I was a Head Teacher in South Queensferry and we were living in the shadow of the Forth Bridges. We travelled home by train and most of our fellow passengers were disappointed Hearts fans making their disgruntled homeward journey. Patrick and I kept our counsel but our silence was a happy one and we had even begun to entertain slight hopes that this could, at last, be Hibs' year for the Scottish Cup.

The semi-final saw Hibs take on Alex Ferguson's Aberdeen. Ferguson had just started to make his mark at Pittodrie. The

Dons weren't yet the massive force which they were to become under Ferguson's stewardship, but they were still a very strong side. Certainly, on paper, they were a vastly superior team to the Hibs outfit of that time In their lack of wisdom, the SFA decreed that the match should be played at Hampden on a Wednesday night. This ludicrous decision, at a time when Hampden was even less accessible than it is now, resulted in an attendance of only 9,837 on what was a cold, wet, miserable April night.

Despite the trying circumstances, Hibs achieved a famous victory. Due to my work commitments, I was one of the many supporters who weren't able to make it through to Hampden. Full of tension and no little apprehension, I decided that I would take a bath and listen to the radio while doing so. I filled the tub to the very top and prepared for a long soak in the hope that the healing powers of the hot water would soothe my tingling nerves. Steve Archibald, whom Hibs fans would come to know and love at a later date, put Aberdeen ahead and things did not look too good. Then in a seven-minute spell just before half-time, Hibs turned the game round completely. First, Gordon Rae slid home a Ralph Callachan cross and then Ally McLeod converted a penalty, which he himself had earned, to give Hibs the lead. When McLeod scored, I was informed by my family that I wasn't even to consider getting out of the bath until the end of the match. To do so, I was told, 'would break Hibs' luck.'

So I stayed put getting gradually chilled as, by this time, I had run off all the hot water. I shivered with cold and anxiety in equal measure as Aberdeen mounted a last twenty-minute siege on the Hibs goal. Somehow we survived and I was able to rise at last, drookit but delirious, from my freezing bath. That night we sat as a family round the fire planning our trip to the final. We ate warm buttered toast and drank hot tea and entertained hopes that the Holy Grail might, at last, be ours.

Playing for Hibs at centre forward that night was Colin Campbell. Campbell had recently graduated from Edinburgh University and had been handed the task of filling Alan Gordon's shoes by Eddie Turnbull. Colin never quite managed to achieve this but he was a good player. He later opened sports shops in Edinburgh and by the early '90s had taken over as Player-Manager of the Edinburgh University football team in the East of Scotland League. He was in his mid thirties by then but, at that level, still an excellent performer. He led the University team to promotion and to victory in the British Universities Championship. I know all this because the centre forward in Campbell's Edinburgh University side was none other than my son Dominic. The less than robust baby, who had given his parents such cause for concern, had now developed into a six-foot-plus striker, who was a handful for any centre half. Our son made us proud by scoring goals all the way through Edinburgh's successful progress towards securing the British title. Back in 1979, we were wondering whether Colin Campbell could find the winning goal for Hibs in the Scottish Cup Final.

This time we were not playing Celtic. Instead we were facing the other half of the Old Firm. Rangers, at that time, had a very strong team featuring players such as Sandy Jardine, Derek Johnstone, Tommy McLean, Derek Parlane and Davie Cooper, so Hibs started the final as clear second favourites. As always, we Hibs fans headed for Hampden with a mixture of hope and fear, and confidence in short supply. It was a dour match with little in the way of goalmouth action until the closing minutes when Colin Campbell went round the Rangers goalkeeper Peter McCloy. McCloy sent Campbell crashing to the turf. It was the most obvious penalty imaginable. The Hibs fans roared in anticipation of the spot kick which would allow Hibs to win the game and the cup. The Rangers fans prepared themselves for the inevitable as they waited for the referee to point to the spot. Incredibly, the official in question, Ian Foote, chose to wave play on. There was a shocked silence at the Hibs end, followed by complete and utter disbelief. After the game Eddie Turnbull stated that McCloy had 'crucified' Campbell. This rare religious reference by our manager might have been slightly hyperbolic, but he was undoubtedly correct in his contention that Hibs should have been awarded what would have been a trophy-winning penalty kick. Speaking to Colin Campbell years later, he referred to this incident in less graphic terms than his former boss, but was equally adamant that Hibs had been denied the most clear cut of decisions in that 1979 final.

So, it was back to Hampden for a replay and again we had a tightly contested struggle, which once more ended goal-less. The second replay was scheduled for Monday, 28 May. This time I was unable to go. I had to attend an educational meeting that would end too late to allow me to reach Hampden in time for the match. On this occasion, I came up with a different tactic to combat my stress. When I got home just before kick-off time, I decided to go for a long jog. My intention was to run backwards and forwards across the Forth Road Bridge until the match was over and then go back and find out the score. It was a wet but warm night and I was soon into my stride. I was very fit in those days and the running was not too difficult. What was extremely difficult was keeping my mind off what might, or might not, be happening at Hampden. The game was not being televised but I knew that the family would be gathered round the radio in the house, hanging on to every word uttered by the inimitable David Francey who was still in charge of the Radio Scotland microphone for big matches.

As my watch told me that half-time was approaching, I gave in and headed for home. On arrival, I joined the family group in the living room and parked myself, still in my running gear, on the floor to hear if Hibs could, at long last, break their Scottish Cup hoodoo, which now stretched to seventy-seven years. It was 1–1 at half-time with Tony Higgins having given Hibs the lead and Derek Johnstone having found a forty-second minute equaliser for Rangers. The second half provided all the drama which the first two matches had lacked. Jim McArthur was still in goal for Hibs and his error had led to Johnstone's goal. The goal had given Rangers confidence and they took control of the match in the second half. Johnstone scored again to give them the lead and they increased the pressure on Hibs.

Then, after seventy-eight minutes, the game took another twist. Eddie Turnbull had introduced Bobby Hutchison as a substitute and the centre forward went down in the box after a tackle by Rangers centre half Colin Jackson. This time, even though the decision was much more arguable, Mr Foote gave the penalty. The tension in our Queensferry living room was now at boiling point. My daughter Lisa, who was almost six by this time, said, 'I am so nervous that I can't look.' Despite my own sky high anxiety level, I retained the wherewithal to reply, 'You don't need to look because the game's on the radio!'

Our worries were unfounded because the super-confident Ally McLeod did his usual immaculate job from the spot and sent the game into extra time. As half-time in the additional period approached, Mr Foote took a hand again. He awarded Rangers a penalty after an Arthur Duncan tackle on Derek Parlane. The next day's press reports described Hibs penalty as 'controversial.' They were less equivocal about the spot kick which Rangers were given. Even the *Daily Record* had to admit that the award was 'soft.' The man who stepped forward to take the kick was none other than Alex Miller, a man who was to play a significant part in Hibs' history in years to come. Miller may not have been universally popular with Hibs fans during his ten-year tenure as manager but he went straight to the top of the popularity charts on this occasion. He struck his shot to McArthur's right but did not hit the ball with sufficient power. Our keeper dived to make a fine save. This was typical Jim McArthur. As a goalkeeper, he could be prone to unforced errors but was also capable of brilliance.

So the drama raged on. We all began to wonder if the final would go a third replay, which would be the first Scottish Cup Final to be played in June. However, fate had one more twist in store and sadly it was to be a tragic one for Hibs and one of their finest servants. Arthur Duncan was the only member of Turnbull's Tornadoes who remained at the club. He was now playing left back and used his pace to overlap with great effect. It was to be at his own end of the park though that Arthur would make the decisive contribution to this marathon final. Davie Cooper made a great run down the left touchline and fired his cross across the Hibs goal. Derek Johnstone and Gordon Smith, later to become SFA Chief Executive, waited to make contact. They didn't get the opportunity because Arthur Duncan threw himself at the ball in an attempt to head it for a corner. All he succeeded in doing was diverting it into his own net.

There were still ten minutes to go but we all knew the game was up. Duncan was in tears at the end of the match and some of the fans were fairly moist in the ocular area themselves. My children headed off to bed saying, 'Don't worry, Dad, we'll win it soon.' Still in my sweaty running gear, I trudged disconsolately to the shower. I thought of my own dad telling me in 1958 after the Cup Final against Clyde that we would win the cup the following year. I remembered the 6–1 rout against Celtic in 1972 and I began to wonder if Hibs would ever win the Scottish Cup again.

During the return coach journey after the final, Eddie Turnbull, who normally kept his distance from his players, broke with tradition and went to the back of the bus to speak to his younger players. He told them that they had done the club proud and that they were the future of Hibs. Clearly Turnbull was optimistic about the future. As a fan I did not share his optimism. The 1978–79 Cup run had been great but Hibs' form in the league had given serious cause for concern. There was nothing to suggest that the new campaign would be any better. Indeed, the team was further weakened when Des Bremner was sold to Aston Villa. It was a good move for Des because he went on to win the league and the European Cup with the Midlands club but it was a disastrous move for Hibs. Bremner had been one of Hibs' mainstays in his midfield role. His work rate was prodigious and he would cover miles in his protection of the back four. He was also able to use the ball skilfully and initiate attacks. Although not a prolific scorer, he was also capable of getting on the score sheet. Unusually for him, he had scored four goals in five games in early 1979. Now all of these attributes were lost to Hibs and the consequences were to be cataclysmic.

Season 1979–80 was a total disaster for Hibs. We plunged from the highs of the previous season's run to the Scottish Cup Final to the depths of a battle against relegation which began right from the beginning of the campaign. After six matches we had only two points and were bottom of the league. By mid January 1980, we were even more firmly rooted at the foot of the table. We had only ten points from twenty games and were seven points adrift of the team above us. This was at a time, remember, when a win was worth only two points. Relegation had seemed a certainty for most of the season and that depressing demotion duly came to pass. It was a dreadful season from start to finish with only one major event to lift the gloom.

In November, with Hibs in dire trouble, Stewart Brown, the chief football reporter of the *Evening News* floated the idea that Hibs could move for George Best. We fans treated Brown's idea as a bit of a joke. It would have been fantastic to have the legendary former Manchester United genius sign up for Hibs, but we just couldn't see it happening. To one man, however, Brown's suggestion was something to be taken seriously. That man was our chairman Tom Hart. When Hibs met Kilmarnock in early November at Easter Road, a rumour swept the crowd that George Best was in the centre stand. I have heard quite a few rumours go round Easter Road in my time of supporting Hibs. Once before a New Year derby match against Hearts, everyone was saying that the Hearts Manager Tommy Walker had died. When Walker strolled up the tunnel at the start of the match, the lack of veracity in that particular story was well and truly established. Another time, when Hibs were struggling under the ultra cautious stewardship of Kenny Waugh, the word was out that Rod Stewart had bought Hibs. Sadly he hadn't. So like most folk at the match that day, I treated the talk about Best being at Easter Road as no more than a flight of fans' fantasy.

However, the next day's papers were full of photographs of Best and his glamorous wife Angie making their way into Easter Road. This was fantastic news. As the week progressed, the news got better still. Best had actually signed for Hibs. Apparently Tom Hart had promised to pay him £2,000 per week out of his own pocket. We fans were delirious. A season which was dying on its feet now had new life breathed into it. After leaving Manchester United at a ridiculously early age, owing to his problems controlling a lifestyle that gave more prominence to drinking and womanising than to playing and training, Best had played intermittently in America and with Fulham. Now he was a Hibee. To put this in perspective, it was a bit like Cristiano Ronaldo deciding to leave Manchester United, spending a couple of years in the footballing wilderness, then making a comeback with Hibs. That was how big a story it was at the time.

Best made his debut at Paisley against St Mirren. I was determined that all of my growing family would be present on this momentous occasion. Patrick was now seven, Lisa had just turned six and Dominic was coming up for five. My mum had come out to Queensferry to visit us on the morning of the match. As we readied ourselves to go, she announced that Dominic wouldn't be coming with us because he was going to stay with her and have a tea party. To this day, we rib Dominic mercilessly about his decision to pass up the chance to see George Best's debut so that he could have a tea party with his granny. He points out in his defence that he was only four at the time.

Hibs took a massive support to Paisley and George Best, although clearly lacking fitness, was magnificent. Unfortunately his team mates weren't quite so good and we lost 2–1. Hibs' goal came from none other than Georgie boy himself and it was a masterly effort. The following Saturday he made his home debut against Partick Thistle. Hibs last home match had been watched by 5,000 fans. 21,000 rolled up to see the little Irish superstar.

Hibs won 2–1 to achieve only their second league victory of the season although we were now into December and Best was again inspirational. Ally McLeod scored one of Hibs' goals from the penalty spot. When the penalty was awarded, everyone looked towards Best but Ally was having none of it. Super confident as ever, he strolled forward, placed the ball on the spot and dispatched it with aplomb. He was said to be furious that Best was being paid so much money and is alleged to have told his team mates that if George was worth £2,000 per week, then he was worth double that!

The signing of Best gave Hibs a temporary lift and there were a couple of really good performances. On the Saturday before Christmas, Rangers were beaten 2–1 at Easter Road. Tony Higgins and Colin Campbell were the scorers and Bestie was again to the fore. In goal for Rangers that day was George Young. George lived in Leith and had been signed by Rangers as cover for Peter McCloy, after a long and distinguished career between the posts for Stirling Albion. He was Margaret's sister's brother-in-law and a popular member of our family circle. Although he was blameless for either of Hibs' goals, it can be easily imagined the kind of stick which he had to endure from friends and family over the Christmas season. I had first encountered George Young back in the mid 1960s when I was playing secondary juvenile football At that time, the top Edinburgh under-eighteen team was Melbourne Thistle. George was the goalkeeper and Erich Schaedler was the left back. Playing against Melbourne one day at Drumbrae, I hit a tremendous twenty-five yard shot. I struck the ball perfectly and was convinced I had scored. As the ball headed for the top left-hand corner of the net, George sailed across his goal and tipped the ball to safety. It was clear to me that day that he was a goalkeeper who was going to make it at professional level. He did indeed and enjoyed a very successful career. His pre-Christmas debut for Rangers at Easter Road, though, was not one of George's more successful days. His son Keith is now a committed Hibs fan and a regular at Easter Road.

Best's outstanding performance was against Celtic at Easter Road in January 1980. The visit of the league leaders seemed to rekindle his old fire and he gave the crowd a master class in the footballing arts. He ran Celtic ragged and scored a magnificent goal. His scoring shot was hit with such force that Peter Latchford, the Celtic goalkeeper, was knocked over the line trying to keep it out. The match ended 1–1 but Hibs could have, and should have, won as we also missed a penalty.

With Georgie, of course, things were not always straight-forward. Hibs were due to play Ayr in the Scottish Cup on a Sunday afternoon. He was staying in the North British Hotel (now the Balmoral) and, on the Saturday evening, joined the French rugby team, who had played Scotland at Murrayfield that day, in their post-match celebrations. The celebrations became rather prolonged and no one participated in them more enthusiastically than G. Best Esquire. Next day, Eddie Turnbull sent two of his coaches, John Fraser and John Lambie, up to the hotel to collect Best. When they got there around lunchtime, he was still in bed and in an utterly comatose state. They shook him into consciousness and he uttered the classic remark, 'I'm sorry boys, but you've wakened the wrong man.' Fraser and Lambie's attempts to resuscitate our intoxicated main man were doomed to failure and when his absence through 'indisposition' was announced before the match that afternoon, the wave of disappointment which swept through the large crowd was palpable. Hibs still managed to win the match 2–0 and, thanks to a favourable draw, made their way to the semi-final where they met Celtic at Hampden. At that point, reality kicked in and we suffered an ignominious 5–0 defeat.

Despite Best's efforts and because of his periodic unavailability due to sporadic relapses into 'playboy mode', Hibs were relegated. It had looked inevitable all season and, without the George Best factor, would probably have happened much earlier than it did. This completed Eddie Turnbull's self-inflicted fall from grace.

Only eight short years earlier, Hibs had had three recently-won trophies in their sideboard. They had also had a superb team with its best years still ahead of it. Eddie Turnbull, for reasons known only to himself, had decided to break that team up. The team which succeeded it was not nearly good enough and decline had been certain. None of us had ever imagined that the team would go down hill as dramatically or as quickly as it did. The predictable consequence was that Turnbull stepped down. There was great sadness among the fans as he had served Hibs wonderfully as both player and manager but there was no little anger too. None of us could understand why this ultra-talented coach had so brutally destroyed something which was so good and then lost the managerial plot so completely afterwards.

Almost every player who played under Eddie Turnbull sings his praise. Pat Stanton, Alan Gordon, Alex Cropley, and Jackie McNamara, among others, will all tell you that he widened the horizons of their footballing knowledge and taught them a huge amount about the game. McNamara, in fact, is on record as stating that he rates Turnbull as a coach more highly than Jock Stein, under whom he played at Celtic. These same players, however, will also tell you that Turnbull's man-management skills were sadly lacking. Jackie Mac is on record as describing him as someone who bullied his staff and players.

Hibs fans have a lot to be grateful to Eddie Turnbull for. As a player, he was part of a world-class forward line which won three league titles. As a manager, he delivered three trophies and the 'best brand of football the world's ever seen.' Sadly his time at Easter Road ended in an anticlimax which he brought upon himself. These days, he is an honoured elder statesman in the Hibs community. He attends every match and is treated with the respect, and accorded the admiration, that his distinguished career merits. We must always, though, see the whole picture. Eddie Turnbull is a great Hibee but the healing powers of time and the warm glow of rose-tinted recollection should not allow us to forget that he, for reasons only he can explain, systematically undid all the excellent work which he had undertaken in his early years as manager of our club, and led Hibs from regal heights to relegation.

10

EARLY '80s AUSTERITY

Eddie Turnbull was replaced as manager by one of his Famous Five colleagues, Willie Ormond. Willie had managed St Johnstone and led them into Europe. He had then taken Scotland to the 1974 World Cup Finals where they remained unbeaten. He was a very different person from his predecessor. Where Turnbull was dictatorial and confrontational, Ormond was genial and conciliatory. He started well at Hibs and soon had his team at the top of the First Division. Most of the good players from Turnbull's latter days like McNamara, Rae, Callachan and McLeod were still at the club and Craig Paterson had emerged as a commanding young centre half. To this mix, Willie Ormond added John Connolly from Everton. Connolly was a splendid creative player who had worked with our new manager at St Johnstone. We fans were pleased that the team was top of the league but we were under no illusion that a predominantly mediocre group of players had been transformed into a set of world-beaters overnight. When Hibs met Ayr in the League Cup in September 1980, only 4,000 supporters turned out and those faithful few diehard Hibees were rewarded for their loyalty by seeing their team lose 2–0. Unfortunately, Ormond was not able to build upon the good start which he had made because he had to relinquish his post halfway through the season due to ill health.

Tom Hart appointed Partick Thistle Manager Bertie Auld to succeed Ormond. Auld had been a member of Celtic's European Cup winning team and like Pat Quinn, who he appointed as his assistant, he had also played for Hibs. They had both been gifted, creative players. As a manager, Auld adopted a flamboyant persona. He wore a huge flat cap and a sheepskin coat and smoked large cigars. He was a bit like Del Boy Trotter without the laughs. This was because in complete contrast to their playing styles, Auld and Quinn's approach to management was negative in the extreme and under their control Hibs were dire to watch.

At that point, I had started to take my three children to most matches. They loved Hibs and even idolised some of the very ordinary players who plied their trade under Auld and Quinn. Their particular favourite though was one of the better players, Craig Paterson. I had met Paterson once when I had been with Jim McArthur and found him to be an impressive and articulate young man. His father John had played in Hibs' Famous Five team and Craig seemed destined for success both on and off the field. He now puts his articulacy to good use as a pundit for BBC Scotland. His footballing success arrived much earlier when Rangers paid Hibs £225,000 for his services. In early 1981 though, that move was in the future and Paterson was doing a splendid job of replacing George Stewart.

Bertie Auld maintained Willie Ormond's momentum and guided Hibs to the First Division title. Promotion was assured with a victory over Raith Rovers at Easter Road. A bumper crowd rolled up for this vital game and indulged in huge celebrations at the end. I just could not understand this. Yes, I was pleased that we had returned to the Premier League at the first time of asking, but I was embarrassed that we had found ourselves in the First Division in the first place. To me promotion was the least we should have expected and it was an essential return to respectability rather than a reason for jubilation.

During the close season, Jim McArthur invited me to a celebration to mark the birth of his first child. Most of Hibs team were there. They were all very excited about a summer tour which the club was about to undertake to Haiti. At that time, one of the most popular light entertainment programmes on television was *The Comedians,* a half-hour quick-fire gag show, featuring some of the country's most popular funny men. When we were talking about Haiti, I mentioned the famous book by Graham Greene which was set in that country. 'If you want to find out all about Haiti,' I said, 'you should read Graham Greene's book *The Comedians.*' One of the players replied, 'I dinnae need to read it because I've seen it on the telly.'

Benny Brazil was at McArthur's celebratory gathering and I asked him if he was looking forward to returning to playing in the Premier League again. He told me that he was. I asked him what would be the best thing about being back among the big clubs. Without hesitation, he answered, 'The big crowds.' I wondered if this was because the larger crowds meant more atmosphere and this brought the best out in him. 'Oh no,' said Benny, 'with the big crowds, I just get general abuse. With the smaller crowds in the First Division, I could make out every word that was shouted at me.' This enjoyable evening was held in Erich Schaedler's pub in Leith. The host himself was present and was tremendous company. No one watching him mingling and bantering so cheerfully that night would ever have expected him to take his own life, as he did so tragically, just a few short years later.

The early '80s was an austere period in British social history. Margaret Thatcher was at the beginning of her premiership (the English football league of the same name hadn't even been thought of) and inflation was at an extremely high level. I had just been appointed Head Teacher at St John's Primary School in Portobello and we had bought a house back in Edinburgh. At the time our offer for the house was accepted, the mortgage rate stood at twelve per cent. When we received our keys two months later, the interest rate on our repayments had risen to fifteen per cent. We were so hard up that our weekly treat was a Chinese carry-out and a bottle of wine on a Saturday. With a growing family and a major mortgage, we couldn't afford any other luxuries, except watching Hibs of course.

Not that watching Hibs at that time was any kind of treat. Bertie Auld had been given money to consolidate Hibs' position in the top flight and he had spent reasonably large sums of money to bring in right back Alan Sneddon from Celtic, striker Gary Murray from Alloa and centre half Peter Welsh from Leicester City. None of these players proved to be a lasting success but they did enough in the 1981–82 season to ensure that Hibs stayed in the top league. Sadly the team's football was cautious and utilitarian and this did not attract big attendances. The Specials were high in the music charts at the time with 'Ghost Town' and that was what Easter Road resembled most Saturdays. Back then, we used to stand in the top tier of the old east terracing. Such were the gaps in the crowd that my children used to spot some of their friends standing twenty yards or so away from us and conduct shouted conversations across the empty spaces which punctuated the assembled home support.

However, Bertie Auld did manage to unite his players. They were united in their dislike of the way in which he was asking them to play. He even took exception to Jackie McNamara moving out of defence to link with his midfield.

One day at training, he twice stopped a practice match to tell Jackie to stop coming forward and to stay at the back. To someone like Jackie Mac, who had been schooled in pure football by Eddie Turnbull, such an approach to the game was anathema so he kept playing the only way he knew how. Infuriated, Auld told him to leave the field and walk the three miles from the training ground back to Easter Road.

Auld was sacked early in season 1982–83 by the new chairman Kenny Waugh. Waugh owned betting shops and pubs and had once tried to buy Hearts. His decision to sack Bertie Auld was well received by the fans but was apparently even more popular with the Hibs team. When their manager's departure was announced to them, the players were rumoured to have sung a lusty chorus of 'Happy Days are Here Again'. The sacking of Auld and his assistants Pat Quinn and John Lambie came at a price. When the club published its accounts, the expenditure included around £40,000 in compensation for the previous management team. This was at a time when the club's weekly wage bill was only £5,000.

Waugh now appointed Pat Stanton as manager, a move which earned him great praise from us supporters. We were delighted too by Pat's choice of assistants. In Jimmy O'Rourke and George Stewart he could not have selected two more dedicated or well-liked Hibees.

Pat Stanton had served his managerial apprenticeship. After a successful spell as Assistant Manager at Aberdeen where he played 'good cop' to Alex Ferguson's 'bad cop', he struck out on his own, first at Cowdenbeath and then Dunfermline. Easter Road had been a depressing place during the reign of Bertie Auld but now the feel-good factor had returned. Sadly though, goodwill, no matter how strongly expressed, is not enough to win football matches. Pat had, without doubt, inherited a poor team.

I had attended Holy Cross Academy with Pat and Jimmy O'Rourke and had watched them display their tremendous skills during bounce games in nearby Victoria Park at lunchtime. I had also watched them tear other school teams apart in league and cup matches on Saturday mornings. Now by coincidence Pat's and my paths crossed once again. Pat's children attended the school where I was the Head Teacher and his older son, Patrick, played for the school team. I enjoyed many conversations with Pat during his time in charge of Hibs. His playing pool was limited and the funds he received from his chairman were even more limited. Pat had the misfortune to manage players like Stewart Turnbull, Alan Sneddon and Benny Brazil. These players gave their all but their all amounted to much less than Hibs fans had become used to. Pat would tell me how Kenny Waugh would promise him money for signings on a Saturday evening then disclaim all knowledge of such discussions on the Monday morning. It was like a variation on the title of Alan's Sillitoe's famous novel *Saturday Night and Sunday Morning*. In Pat's case it was Saturday Night and Monday Morning. Pat also used to tell me of his frustrations at working with players who couldn't replicate the moves he demonstrated to them on the training ground, and who frequently fell short on the field of play. They never fell short in terms of effort though and being the gentleman he is, Pat always bore that in mind. Every Saturday morning at the school games, Pat would take time out from watching his boy to vow that today would be the day when he would really rip into some of his players for their inadequacies. When I met him the following week and asked him if he had followed through on his intentions, he would shrug his shoulders and say:

No, not really. I was going to bawl them out for their mistakes but when they came in at the end of the match they had tried their hearts out and were drenched in sweat. It's not their fault that they're not all that good.

To be fair to Kenny Waugh, times were hard at Easter Road and crowds were low. As chairman, he was doing his best to run the club efficiently. He did allow Pat some money to spend and our manager used it wisely. He bought midfield player Mike Conroy from Celtic. Pat used to refer to him as 'The boy Conroy' with the emphasis on the second syllable of his name. Conroy scored a fantastic goal against St Mirren from what had seemed an impossible angle until he struck the ball and he was always industrious, but he didn't really set the heather on fire. Pat's major signing was also a major success. He paid £65,000 to Partick Thistle for Alan Rough and never was money better spent. Rough was outstandingly consistent and consistently outstanding. It is no exaggeration to say that his form was probably the main reason why Hibs managed to escape relegation in the early '80s.

Another great signing Pat made was that of Willie Irvine. Irvine was a lanky centre forward who wouldn't have recognised style if he had met it in the street, but he certainly knew where the goals were. He came to Hibs as part of a swap deal for Bobby Flavell and didn't get off to the most impressive of starts. He did not cut an imposing figure at first sight. His hair was unruly, his top was inevitably hanging out of his shorts and his socks were always down round the ankles of his stick-thin legs. His early displays were not encouraging either as he failed to score in his first eleven games. In his second season however, he was a revelation, banging in goals galore and becoming a real favourite with the fans.

Money was so tight at Easter Road that Pat Stanton sometimes had to employ desperate measures to strengthen his squad. One day he bumped into the former Hearts winger Malcolm Robertson at Waverley Station. When Pat asked Robertson what club he was currently with, he was told that the player was not attached to any club at that time. Pat immediately invited Robertson to sign up for a three-month trial period with Hibs. Robertson was a talented player but due to his penchant for a pint he was lacking in the fitness stakes. Although he did not do badly during his trial period, his contract was not extended.

At that time, I managed the Edinburgh Primary Schools football team. Coincidentally, at the time that Malcolm Robertson was playing for Hibs, his son Sandy was in my Edinburgh team. He was a centre forward and a good one and went on to play for Rangers although they used him in a midfield role. As a schoolboy centre forward though, Sandy Robertson did not come close to another young striker who had represented Edinburgh during my time as a manager. The 1975–76 Edinburgh Schools team won the Scottish Cup in style beating Dundee 8–2 on aggregate in the two-legged Cup Final. In the first leg at Tannadice, an eleven-year-old red-haired lad from Greendykes Primary School scored a superb hat-trick. His name was Keith Wright and he loved Hibs then as much as does now. He was a wonderful young player and I recommended him to Hibs when he was sixteen and banging in the goals for Edina Hibs. They sent a scout to watch Keith score two goals in a 4–2 defeat and the verdict was that he was 'good but not good enough.' This meant that Keith had to start his career at Raith Rovers before moving on to Dundee. After making a major impact at Dens Park, he was able, at last, to join the club he had supported all his life. Unfortunately, Hibs had to pay £500,000 to secure his services when they could have had him for nothing ten years earlier. One of Keith Wright's colleagues in the Edinburgh schools side was Calum Milne who also went on to play for Hibs. Calum played in a range of different positions for Hibs but they never used him in the sweeper role at which he excelled during his schoolboy days. He read the game superbly and played like a primary-school version of Franco Baresi.

Jimmy O'Rourke and George Stewart did not stay long in their support roles to Pat Stanton but in the short time they were there, they helped Pat to instil the true Hibernian values in their players. Once again, despite our limitations, we were trying to play attacking football and an outstanding young group of players was beginning to emerge for the future. This group included Brian Rice, Paul Kane, Gordon Hunter, Mickey Weir and John Collins. That summer, I worked as a coach at a children's coaching course, which was sponsored by Nike and led by Ian St John. On the last day, there were to be a series of games involving the youngsters attending the course, the coaches and some of the young players at Easter Road and Tynecastle who wore Nike boots. Paul Kane and Brian Rice came along from Hibs, and John Robertson and Davie Bowman flew the flag for Hearts. As the players arrived, the Hibs duo and the Hearts twosome circled each other warily. It was like the preliminaries for the gunfight at the OK Corral. Eventually Kane broke the silence. He gave the merest nod in the direction of the Hearts midfielder and intoned 'Bowman.' The response of 'Kano' was equally monosyllabic and that was the extent of the conversation. The game was great though. My sons Patrick and Dominic played and did well. Dominic, in fact, launched his seven-year-old frame at a rebound from a Brian Rice shot and scored with a fine header.

One game which gave Pat Stanton particular satisfaction that season was a 1–0 win over Motherwell at Fir Park on the Saturday before Christmas. The two teams were locked together near the foot of the league table and the outcome of the match was likely to be crucial. It was a cold day and, before Hibs left Easter Road, Pat telephoned Jock Wallace, the former Rangers manager who was then in charge of Motherwell, to ask him about the condition of the pitch. Wallace told him that the ground was fine so Hibs did not pack alternative footwear.

When the team got to Motherwell, it was clear that the playing surface was anything but fine. It was hard after an overnight frost and Motherwell were kitted out in appropriate boots. Pat asked Wallace if he had any spare hard-ground studs and received a resoundingly negative response. This inspired our normally mild-mannered manager to really fire up his team for the contest ahead. Hibs, despite their un-suitable footwear, won and won well through a goal by Gary Murray. Pat was able to enjoy an important victory and enjoy his post-match handshake with Wallace even more. This was a doubly good day for my family as my brother John got married. John, who my parents had fostered when he was eighteen months old, had played for Falkirk and Meadowbank Thistle. He had also played for Scotland Schoolboys in the same team as Roy Aitken. He had left Edinburgh on the day of Elvis Presley's death to take up a soccer scholarship at a university in the United States. Now he was marrying in Long Island. We all gathered round our dining room table to toast the health of John and his new wife Holly and when he tele-phoned us, just before he left for the church, we were able to let him hear the Hibs-Motherwell post-match radio report over the phone.

Pat Stanton brought in John Blackley, his old colleague from Turnbull's Tornadoes, as his assistant manager after Jimmy O'Rourke and George Stewart left. Pat's plight was so pronounced as season 1983–84 developed that he was forced to play Blackley as sweeper. Such was the paucity of Hibs' resources at that time that Blackley, in his mid-thirties, was as often as not our best player. He had great skill and arrogance and was as hard as they come. He liked to beat Hearts and was at his most determined when they paid Hibs a visit. At that time John Robertson, Gary Mackay and Davie Bowman had established themselves in the Hearts team as three young players with great futures. The story goes that before a derby match at Easter Road, one of the younger Hibs players spoke up to Pat Stanton in the dressing room. He said, 'We'll need to watch that Bowman, Boss.' Pat is reported to have replied, 'Don't worry, son. John will stiffen him early doors!' Blackley was as good as his manager's word. Bowman, who had entered the fray exuding arrogance, left it before half-time clutching broken ribs which were the result of a crunching challenge from the Hibs assistant manager. As Bowman made his painful return journey to the dressing room, he was sent on his way by a resounding chant of 'cheerio, cheerio, cheerio' from the Hibs support.

Pat had a difficult time as manager of Hibs but he never lost his personal touch. One summer at my school, we decided to stage a match between the school football team and the parents. Pat was good enough to referee the game. At half-time, the parents were well ahead so Pat decided that he would play for the boys in the second half. This was agreed on condition, that he wasn't allowed to score. He proceeded to give a masterly exhibition of skill and ball retention. The pupils fought back to earn a draw and luxuriated in the experience of playing alongside one of Hibs greatest-ever players. The parents also had a night to remember as Pat took them back to the hotel he owned at that time, provided sandwiches and put on a video of Hibs beating Hearts 7–0!

At the first derby match of that season, I renewed my

acquaintance with my schoolboy friend Walter Easton. Hibs were 1–0 up at half-time at Tynecastle through an excellent Ralph Callachan goal against his old club. I had my children with me and we had all just agreed that the second half was going to be a nerve-wracking affair. At that point, Waldo came past. I hadn't seen him for years but he hadn't changed. With commendable confidence, he informed Patrick, Lisa and Dominic that there was no way in which Hibs could lose. The game, he declared was 'in the bag.' Unfortunately his prediction was not correct. Hearts fought back to win 3–2 with John Robertson as always scoring a vital goal. It has to be said that Hearts' comeback was helped in no small measure by a contribution from Ally Brazil. With Hibs 2–1 up, the whole-hearted but hapless Benny misdirected a pass back and changed the course of the game. The lack of accuracy in his touch reminded me of the remark attributed to George Best that Benny Brazil thought a lay-off was a week in his bed.

Hibs' best display of the season was against Aberdeen in October. Ferguson's team was, by that time, undeniably the best team in the country. They were less than a year away from winning the European Cup Winners Cup against Real Madrid. John Blackley marshalled Hibs' defence superbly, Willie Irvine scored twice and Hibs won 2–1. The level of belief which existed in the Hibs support at that time is shown by the fact that only 7,000 fans witnessed this notable victory.

Blackley had a less successful day against Celtic in December when he scored an own goal. The next match was against Hearts and their supporters serenaded our player/assistant manager with a sarcastic chorus of 'Blackley, Blackley, give us a goal.' Sloop John B gave them not a goal but an expansive V-sign!

The frustrations of managing a weak Hibs squad began to catch up on Pat Stanton. While Hibs were at this low ebb in their history, it is fair to say that referees did the club no favours. Some of the refereeing performances we endured were enough to stretch the patience of even one of nature's gentlemen like Pat. He began to incur the wrath of the officials on a more frequent basis than he would have liked. I remember Pat's wife Margaret telling me that at one match against Celtic, she saw the referee head for the Hibs bench. He then pointed towards the stand and she thought 'Oh no, not again.' Much to her relief however, it was John Blackley's turn to be ordered from the dugout this time. Ironically, he was only there because he was serving a playing suspension.

Pat did not feel that he always received justice on his visits to Park Gardens. On one occasion he attended a SFA hearing to defend a charge from a referee of the time called Bob Valentine. Valentine had accused Pat of becoming agitated and using profane language. Pat vehemently denied both charges and continues to do so to this day. Even though there was no independent witness to verify either party's version of events, the SFA backed the referee. Pat, quite rightly, did not consider this to be true justice.

Early in season 1984–85 with the team continuing to struggle, Pat was sent to the stand again at Aberdeen and fined by the SFA. Once again our manager had reacted to what he perceived to be injustice to Hibs on the part of the referee. This time, Pat decided that enough was enough. The SFA told him that if he returned to football management, he would have to pay his fine. Pat never did return and he never did pay that fine. His time as manager had been difficult but he could look back with pride on the fact that he had retained his dignity at all times despite having to deal with many trying situations. He had also left the club the legacy of a talented group of young players.

11

COMING ALIVE IN '85

Pat Stanton was succeeded by John Blackley. Blackley decided to concentrate fully on management and brought to an end his brief but successful return to playing under Stanton. The new manager was given money which had not been available to his predecessor. His initial signings were of a high order. He brought in a skilful and exciting teenage striker from East Fife, Gordon Durie, and a talented young left winger, Joe McBride. McBride was the son of the goalscoring centre forward who had done so well for Hibs in the late '60s and early '70s. Blackley also brought in Tommy Craig as Player Coach. Craig was a cultured midfield player. He had been the first teenage £100,000 player when he had moved from Aberdeen to Sheffield Wednesday. He joined Hibs from Newcastle where he had been a popular and successful player.

Early in Blackley's reign, my son Dominic was invited to be Hibs mascot for the game against Hearts at Tynecastle. Tom O'Malley, later to be Hibs Chairman and a Head Teacher colleague of mine, organised the mascots at that time and was kind enough to offer Dominic the opportunity. We arranged to meet Tom outside the stand at 2p.m. and while we were waiting for him to appear, a plainclothes police officer hustled by with an aggressively struggling, less than sober Hearts fan in an armlock. The officer in question was my cousin Alex

Stout who was a fanatical Jambo. As he carried out his legal duty, he turned round and spoke to us in passing: 'Hi, Ted. Sorry I can't stop but as you can see, I'm a wee bit busy.' He then added, 'I told you I wasn't biased.'

Dominic was disappointed that day because Tom O'Malley eventually joined us and explained that there had been a mix up and that the mascot slot had been double-booked. He asked if Dominic would mind being mascot at the next home game instead and gave us two complimentary tickets for the centre stand, which brightened up our day. It brightened up even more when Hibs managed to achieve a fighting goalless draw.

Two weeks later we were at Easter Road for a match against Rangers and it turned out to be a great day for the Brack family. Not only was Dominic the mascot but Patrick was asked to be a ball boy. Even better, their father was told that he could join them for their adventure. Margaret and Lisa weren't best pleased that there was no place for them in the day's events. However, Margaret had just learned that she was pregnant again and was under orders to take things easy. Lisa, who by this time was a regular at every game, reluctantly agreed to stay home and keep her mum company.

Before the game, John Blackley and Tommy Craig were really nice to Dominic and Gordon Rae, who was the captain at that time, was even nicer. Dominic got to meet all the players and then came his big moment when he ran on to the field with the team. I got some great photographs including one of my nine-year-old son firing a shot past Alan Rough in the pre-match warm-up. I also got an excellent picture of Patrick sprinting onto the pitch in his ball boy kit which, at that time, was a Hibs tank-top jumper and a pair of green tracksuit bottoms. His wage was a pie and a cup of tea at half-time but he loved the experience.

Dominic changed quickly and we raced upstairs to take

© SNS GROUP

A very young Pat Stanton, all time Hibernian great, struts his stuff in front of the old Easter Road terracing

Patrick Joseph Brack in his first Hibs strip. Aren't the '70s curtains wonderful?

© SNS GROUP

The Baker Boy is back! Joe Baker shows the Rangers defence a clean pair of heels during his second spell with Hibs

We've won the cup! Turnbull's Tornadoes display the Drybrough Cup which they won in both 1972 and 1973, defeating Jock Stein's Celtic on each occasion

Fifty years and counting but still happy to be on the Hibee highway - Ted at Easter Road in early 2009

New Year's Day 1973 - Jimmy O'Rourke (right) has just scored his sixth goal. As Jimmy is congratulated by Pat Stanton who set the goal up, Jim Jefferies looks on in disbelief

We've won the cup 2! Goalscorers Keith Wright and Tommy McIntyre hold aloft the 1991 Skol Cup after beating Dunfermline 2-0 in the final

Simply the Best! Georgie boy displays his class in Hibernian green

Dominic and Gordon Rae lead out the team for the 2-2 draw with Rangers in 1986

Ted, Margaret and Kevin in the shadow of the South Stand shortly after its completion

Spot on! Darren Jackson coolly converts a penalty kick in the 1997 relegation play-off win against Airdrie. Sadly, only one year later, Hibs found themselves in the First Division

Head Teacher and pupils welcome Darren Jackson and community coach John Ritchie to the school

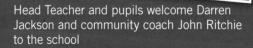

Two blasts from the past - Michael O'Neill and a double-breasted suit

Lisa, her cousin James and her great-aunt Margaret at a family Hibs night

Margaret and I show the goals tally on our return home after the 6-2 victory over Hearts in October 2000

The Hibees are back! Captain courageous John Hughes with the First Division trophy in 1999 after Hibs' shortlived but successful 'great adventure' sees the club restored to the SPL

Cheer up, Jimmy Jefferies. JJ and his assistants look suitably downcast as Hibs crush Hearts 6-2 in October 2000

C'est magnifique! Franck Sauzée, Hibs' Gallic God, runs the full length of Tynecastle to celebrate with Hibs fans after his memorable goal in the Millennium Derby

Margaret, Dominic, Lisa and Ted say 'au revoir' to the great Franck Sauzée

Dominic, Ted and Kevin before setting out for another Hampden disappointment. This time the 2004 League Cup Final with Livingston

The scourge of Rangers, Ivan Sproule. The electrifying Irish winger always reserved his best for the Light Blues

Double delight! Garry O'Connor and Dean Shiels take great pleasure in beating Hearts at Tynecastle in April 2005

© SNS GROUP

© SNS GROUP

The crying game. John Collins, who had recently lost his father, shows his emotions in the aftermath of Hibs' 2007 CIS Cup triumph over Kilmarnock

Patrick flies the Hibee flag at Hampden before the 2001 Scottish Cup Final

advantage of our second consecutive pair of free centre-stand tickets – these were happy days indeed! It was a great match and finished 2–2. Hibs again played well with Craig influential in midfield and Ralph Callachan and Willie Irvine scoring two fine goals. Our afternoon was slightly marred by an unsavoury incident which erupted just along from where we were sitting. Some Rangers fans had bought seats for the Hibs section of the stand and celebrated enthusiastically when their team scored. This provoked a belligerent reaction from some of the Hibs supporters in the vicinity and a major fight broke out. Fights may look spectacular in action movies but in reality they are very unpleasant events to observe. However, the police were quick to restore order and we were able to enjoy the rest of the game.

After the game, our day was made complete. We went across to the Fifties Club opposite the back of the stand for a snack and drinks as guests of Hibs. We were joined by the players including Alan Rough. Our incredibly laid-back goal-keeper had just faced extreme pressure for ninety minutes and had done magnificently in defying the Rangers attack with a series of tremendous saves, but you would never have known it from his demeanour. He was totally relaxed as he sipped a pint of lager and munched a packet of crisps. He spotted Dominic and shouted over 'Hey son, what were you doing embarrassing me before the game. I recommended you to the boss as a signing. We could do with another striker!'

Despite these two spirited draws, Blackley's Hibs were struggling and relegation looked a real possibility. When Hibs went to Ibrox on Saturday, 12 January 1985, no one gave them a chance. They had played twenty-two games and won only three. I, for one, had written the game and the season off. Eddie Cumming, the lollipop man at my school who was much loved by all the pupils, was seriously ill in the old Royal

Infirmary. I thought that it might cheer him up if I took the children to visit him. I did so and he really enjoyed their cheery chatter. As we were leaving, he said, 'You've made my day.' I took the kids on from the hospital to Murrayfield where the Scotland rugby team was playing an international trial match. The children had seen a lot of Gavin Hastings and Co. on television but they had never seen them in the flesh and really enjoyed their experience. As we left the ground, I saw a man with a transistor radio clamped to his ear. I asked him if he had heard the Hibs score. He told me that they had won 2–1. I answered, like Mr Cumming the lollipop man before me, 'Thanks very much. You've made my day.' Goals by Brian Rice and Colin 'Bomber' Harris and a wonder display of goal-keeping by Alan Rough had combined to create the upset of the season. We floated home on a wave of new-found optimism because now there was some hope that we could overhaul Dumbarton who were above us in the league.

We met them at Easter Road the following week and won 3–1. The following week, we played a friendly against Celtic and amazingly beat them 6–3. Even more amazingly, Benny Brazil scored a hat-trick. At the start of the match, the crowd was quite small but as word of Hibs display and Benny's exploits spread, the ground filled up rapidly. A late arrival next to us said, 'I was in bed with a hangover but when I heard on the radio that Brazil had scored two, I just had to get down here in case he got a hat-trick because that's one thing that'll never happen twice.' As we left the ground, the fans sang 'The Hibees are back' over and over again. On the Monday morning after Benny's great triumph, the club coined the slogan 'Coming alive in '85' and it seemed like the corner had been turned.

This was not quite the case though and a sequence of poor results followed. By the time we met Hearts at Tynecastle on the evening of Tuesday, 6 April, our season was well and truly on the line. With two minutes to go, Hearts led 2–0 and relegation looked all but a certainty. Miraculously (and in the circumstances I don't think that using that word is an exaggeration), Joe McBride scored two goals in the time that was left to salvage a draw which felt like a win. This Lazarus-like comeback set the next match up perfectly because Hibs' next fixture was a trip west to play Dumbarton, their rivals in the fight to stay in the Premier League.

Hibs took a massive support to the aptly named Boghead. The club organised a fleet of buses and the Brack family travelled through on one of them. To say that this vehicle contained a wide range of basic characters would be a major understatement. Much alcohol was imbibed, a great deal of cursing took place and my children's view of the world was considerably widened. On arrival at the ground, we decided that we wanted to move round behind the goals that Hibs were lining up to attack. Most fans had the same idea and soon the perimeter wall had been scaled and a phalanx of Hibees was making its way along the track towards the terracing behind the Dumbarton goalkeeper. A loud chorus of 'Oan the park, oan the park, oan the park' rent the air as we undertook our journey. The singing was led in lusty fashion by none other than Hibs reserve goalkeeper Robin Rae, who to put it mildly, was quite a character.

Pat Stanton told me that once when the team travelled to an away match on Boxing Day, young Rae, who should have been going out of his way to impress his manager with his dedication, got on the team coach carrying a large box. When Pat asked him what it was, he was told that it was a crate of beer. When Pat looked taken aback, the Hibs goalkeeper in waiting exclaimed, 'Oh come on boss. It is Christmas, ye ken.' This day at Dumbarton, Rae had appointed himself cheerleader-in-chief and he didn't have to wait long before he had something to cheer. Two early goals by Brian Rice and Willie Irvine set up a comfortable victory and this victory proved to be the catalyst for a strong finish to the season by Hibs and a decline from Dumbarton. In the end, we stayed up reasonably comfortably and we were all able to embark on the close season feeling some optimism about the season ahead. The close season saw me become a father for the fourth time as Margaret gave birth to our third son Kevin. Margaret entered hospital on Wednesday, 29 May as the doctors planned to induce the baby's birth next day. The rest of us settled down at home to watch the European Cup Final between Liverpool and Juventus at the Heysel Stadium in Brussels on television. The horrors of that sad night when football came a distant second to tragedy are etched on all our minds forever. So too, for happier reasons, are the events of the next day. Kevin came into the world happy and healthy and it wasn't just Hibs who were coming alive in '85.

At the start of season 1985-86, John Blackley moved into the market again. He signed Aberdeen striker Steve Cowan, midfielder Gordon Chishom from Sunderland and centre half Mark Fulton from St Mirren. Hibs made a poor start in the league, not winning a game before 28 September when they beat Motherwell 1–0. In the League Cup however, they were flying with Gordon Durie and Steve Cowan forming a formidable partnership up front. Cowdenbeath were thrashed 6–0 and then Motherwell were taken apart to the tune of 6–1. Durie and Cowan shared ten goals in these two games. The quarter-final against Celtic was a classic. Cowan and Durie were again on target as the match finished 3–3. Both teams scored again in extra time so it was on to the dreaded penalty kicks. Alan Rough made two brilliant saves and when each team had one penalty left, Hibs led 3–2. If we scored with our next kick, we were through to the semi-final to face Rangers. We all looked to see who would take the potentially decisive penalty. There was a gasp of disbelief when Ally Brazil stepped forward. Thousands of Hibs fans mouthed the same involuntary question simultaneously: 'Why is he taking it?' The inevitable happened and Brazil missed which allowed Tommy Burns to equalise for Celtic and the shoot-out now moved into sudden death. Steve Cowan, who should have taken the previous penalty, came forward to score and the spotlight switched to Celtic centre half Pierce O'Leary. The Irishman made himself into an instant Easter Road folk hero by sending his shot high over the crossbar.

The Rangers semi-final was a two-legged affair with the first game at Easter Road. Hibs again rose to the occasion with goals from Durie and Chisholm. Rough continued to save penalties by superbly turning aside an Ally McCoist spot kick which unsurprisingly had been awarded in controversial circumstances. Our goalkeeper's heroics enabled us to take a 2–0 lead to Ibrox. The second leg was a nerve-wracking night from start to finish. First, like many Hibs fans we were held up in roadworks on the motorway. We arrived late to see Davie Cooper pull one back for Rangers with a supersonic strike from a twenty-yard free kick. The rest of the match was a siege but yet another inspired performance by the incomparable Roughie saw us through.

My children were in a state of huge excitement over the prospect of going to the League Cup Final. Our opponents were the now all-conquering Aberdeen, who were still, for the moment at least, led by Alex Ferguson. Dominic now played for Hutchison Vale where he was a prolific scorer. One one occasion, he managed eight goals in one Scottish Cup game in Lanarkshire. He had a match on the morning of the League Cup Final so it was going to be a bit of a mad rush for us to make it through to Hampden in time. Thankfully we did but unfortunately that was where the good news stopped.

Hibs froze and Fergie's Dons brushed us aside. We badly missed Gordon Rae who was suspended and even Rough could do nothing to stop Aberdeen taking a two-goal lead within twelve minutes. The final score was 3–0 and two of Aberdeen's heroes were Jim Leighton, a future Hibs goal-keeper, and Alex McLeish, a Hibs Manager-to-be. Hibs took a tremendous support to the match and comfortably provided more than half of the 40,000 crowd.

We also did well in the Scottish Cup and made it all the way to the semi-final, which was played at Dens Park, Dundee. Again Hibs met Aberdeen, again we took a huge support and again Aberdeen were too good for us. Ferguson would not be around to make us suffer much longer as a year later he would move to Manchester United where, I think it is fair to say, he has done quite well! But the size of Hibs' following for these two Aberdeen games demonstrated just how much potential the club had. Although our league performances had been of the ordinary variety, the young players brought through by Pat Stanton were now starting to establish themselves. John Collins, Paul Kane, Gordon Hunter, Mickey Weir and Eddie May now all featured regularly. That combined with our Cup exploits gave us hope for the future.

Things didn't look quite so bright at the beginning of the next season. Gordon Durie was sold to Chelsea for more than £400,000. John Blackley was given the money to spend and bought five players. He signed George McCluskey from Leeds United. McCluskey while short of pace, was still a skilful player and proved a good signing. The other four did not. Billy Kirkwood and Stuart Beedie came from Dundee United but should have stayed there. Hibs signed another centre forward called Willie Irvine, but he couldn't make the transition from scoring freely in the First Division to scoring regularly in the Premier League. The original Willie Irvine was still at the club but had fallen out of favour with his manager. Just like Jimmy O'Rourke with Eddie Turnbull twelve years earlier, Irvine's fall from grace was never explained and he never regained the status of first-team regular. The fifth summer signing was Mark Caughey, a winger from Northern Ireland who proved to be a major disappointment.

Kenny Waugh had gone all the way to Mexico to sign Caughey at the Northern Ireland World Cup base. I'm not sure why he bothered. Caughey never broke through and like the other players mentioned, proved to be a poor signing. There was a story doing the rounds at the time which is almost certainly apocryphal. Frustrated with Caughey's performances, Blackley is alleged to have said to him, 'Mark, since you're not doing much else, will you give my car a service?'

Caughey replied, 'I don't know the first thing about cars, Boss.'

Blackley responded by saying 'I thought that you were once an RAC man.'

'No, Boss.' said Caughey in his broad Ulster accent, 'I was an RUC man.'

Hibs started the season brilliantly beating Rangers 2–1 at Easter Road. This game was Graeme Souness' debut as Rangers' Player-Manager. He marked it by inflicting a deep cut on George McCluskey's shin which caused him to be sent off and sparked a free for all in the centre circle involving every player on the field except the laid-back Alan Rough in goal.

Things deteriorated for Blackley and results went from

161

bad to worse. It was sad for those of us who had watched him at his imperious '70s heights to hear the fans singing 'Blackley must go.' But in the autumn of 1986, John Blackley did indeed go.

12

TEN YEARS OF MILLER TIME

Blackley had the integrity to recognise that Hibs were struggling under his control and did the honourable thing by resigning his post. As usual, the great guessing game as to the identity of the new manager was soon in full swing. Blackley's assistant Tommy Craig wasted no time in throwing his hat into the ring. His first game in charge was a home match against Hamilton Academicals, who were enjoying one of their rare spells in the upper echelons of Scottish football. They weren't actually enjoying things that much since they had failed to win a league match all season. So desperate was their plight and so keen was Hamilton's manager John Lambie to motivate his players that he had declared publicly that he would not make love to his wife until that elusive first victory was achieved.

On Saturday, 29 November 1986, Hamilton came to Easter Road. The team was still winless and their manager remained celibate. It was my thirty-ninth birthday and the day hadn't started well. Through my Londoner father, I had gained a great love of cricket at an early age and was a passionate supporter of the England Cricket Team. They were currently involved in an Ashes Test Match against Australia in Perth. When I got up, I switched on the radio to discover that my favourite player, Ian Botham, had been dismissed for nought.

163

If the news from Western Australia got the day off to a less than auspicious start, things took a turn for the worse at Easter Road that afternoon.

Tommy Craig's team was extraordinarily ordinary and embarrassingly lost 3–1. One of Hamilton's goals was scored by Graham Mitchell. Mitchell would join Hibs before the end of the year. Hibs' consolation goal came from John Collins. Collins and Craig would combine again at Easter Road to much more significant effect more than twenty years later. This dismal performance effectively ended Craig's chances of succeeding John Blackley. When asked by the media on the day after the match if he had enjoyed his Saturday night after at last securing his first win, John Lambie replied that he had but unfortunately not all his celebration plans had come to fruition as his wife had had a headache.

The spotlight now turned to other candidates to manage Hibs. Initially it looked like Kenny Waugh was going to appoint Terry Christie as manager. A local secondary Head Teacher, who had enjoyed great success managing in the lower divisions, Christie was all set to give up his post in education to take over at Easter Road. He had been successful all his life. As a senior secondary pupil at Holy Cross Academy, Terry had been the dux of the school due to his academic excellence. As well as achieving a university degree, he had gone on to play successfully for Dundee and Stirling Albion. By the mid '80s, his playing career was confined to school staff football. I had played against him on several occasions and his skill was complemented by a sharp tongue that ensured his team mates followed instructions and played to their maximum level. He had clearly carried this approach into his management of Meadowbank Thistle and Stenhousemuir. I had also come across Terry's son Max who had played for me in the Edinburgh Schools football team

and had been good enough to go on and play profession-
ally.

Just when it seemed that Kenny Waugh was poised to
appoint Terry Christie, he had a change of heart. He plumped
instead for former Rangers stalwart Alex Miller who was
at that time managing St Mirren. Miller had done well at
Love Street and had taken Saints into Europe. He had done
less well in one fixture though. On the last day of season
1985–86, Hearts went to Dundee needing only to draw to
win the Premier League. Even if Hearts lost, Celtic had to
win 5–0 at Paisley to deprive them of the title. It turned out
not to be one of Miller's more successful days in management
as David Hay's Celtic did indeed embarrass St Mirren by
five clear goals on their home territory. Over at Dundee
goals were proving harder to come by.

I had taken the family out for the day as I couldn't possibly
have sat and watched my television if the screen had been
displaying scenes of Jambo jubilation. We came in around
4.30p.m. I turned on the telly and tuned into *Sportscene*. Hearts
were drawing 0–0 and on course to be champions. I reached
over to switch the set off. As I was in the process of doing
so, word came through from Dens Park that Albert Kidd had
scored for the home side. I ran from room to room rounding
up Margaret and the children. 'You'll have to come through
to the living room and watch *Sportscene*,' I said. 'Dundee are
one up on Hearts.' As I was uttering these words, Patrick
chipped in to tell me, 'Your information is out of date, Dad.
Look, it's just come up that Dundee are winning 2–0. Albert
Kidd's got another one.' Dundee were indeed now two goals
to the good and that was how the game finished.

Albert Kidd became a Hibs cult figure overnight. Grown
men dressed in maroon sat and wept on the terraces of Dens
Park, Dundee and in the living room of a bungalow in East

Edinburgh, six people called Brack celebrated with unconfined joy. That night, I took pleasure in asking Hearts fans if
they had really blown the league or were they just *kidding*. I
also enquired to a few Jambo acquaintances of mine if they
were planning to hold their next supporters club rally in the
Albert Hall. All of this was extremely childish, I know. It was
also very enjoyable indeed. Schadenfreude is not the most
positive of human emotions but I have to say that I, and many
other Hibs supporters, took the greatest amount of pleasure
imaginable from Hearts' sufferings on that unforgettable day
in May.

Alex Miller may not have succeeded in keeping Celtic at
bay on the day that decided the Premier League title but he
was the successful candidate in the race to replace John
Blackley. His appointment was not universally popular. He
was seen as a dour pragmatist who put industry before flair.
Many Hibs fans never altered their original perception of
Miller but he was to defy his critics at every turn and remain
in charge of Hibs for ten years.

He marked the start of his reign by signing three players
on Hogmanay. Dougie Bell, Graham Mitchell and Tommy
McIntyre all proved to be good signings. They made their
debut in an excellent 3–1 win over Falkirk at Brockville. Next
up was a home derby against Hearts. The game ended 2–2
and the new signings again did well. Hibs should really have
won but were prevented from doing so by two goals from
John Colquhoun. Usually it was John Robertson who spoiled
the party for Hibs but this time it was his striking partner. If
you thought that Colquhoun was annoying as he sat in the
Scotsport studio extolling the virtues of Hearts and picking
holes in Hibs, you should have seen him that night. He scored
with two long-range strikes, a feat which I don't recall him
replicating against any other team, and celebrated each in a

triumphalist fashion. He was aided by Alan Rough who had an uncharacteristic off-night.

Miller like his predecessors was initially restricted by his chairman's caution with money. However when Waugh sold out to the flamboyant David Duff, things changed dramatically. Duff was a young lawyer who was based in England but had attended school in Edinburgh and claimed to be a lifelong Hibs supporter. His first act upon acquiring Hibs was to appoint his brother-in-law Jim Gray as Chief Executive. With their dark hair and matching moustaches, Duff and Gray looked like a footballing version of the comedy duo Cannon and Ball. In due course, their reign was to prove more tragic than comedic. Duff launched his period of control of Hibs by organising a shares issue to raise money. Having succeeded in that aim, he proceeded to throw caution to the wind. He bought a chain of pubs and hotels in England and told Hibs fans that they would generate income for the club. Because we were excited by his big talk and lavish promises, we believed him. He also made substantial transfer funds available to his manager. Miller was able to spend big money to bring in players of the calibre of Oldham's outstanding goalkeeper Andy Goram, the haughty but gifted Barcelona striker Steve Archibald and centre forward Keith Houchen, who had scored a historic FA Cup-winning goal for Coventry City. He also signed a speedy centre forward called Gareth Evans from Rotherham for a bargain fee.

Goram was quite a character. He was reputed to have a penchant for gambling, drinking and womanising. Certainly, as his career progressed, he was no stranger to the front pages of tabloid newspapers. When he could, he found some time for goalkeeping and despite being less than dedicated in his preparation, he proved to be a master of the custodian's art. The writer and broadcaster Simon Pia told me that when he was collaborating with Goram on the writing of his auto-biography, the goalkeeper would insist that they met in the Elm Bar at lunchtime on a Friday. By closing time, Simon would be desperate to escape. Goram, after several sorties to the adjoining betting shop and several more drinks would be keen to carry the evening on somewhere else. The next day, while his ghostwriter sat nursing a severe hangover in the press box, the Hibs goalkeeper would perform heroics and give every impression of having retired to bed early with a glass of milk the night before. Mind you, Alex Miller was fortunate in terms of signing the man who became known simply as 'The Goalie.' He had originally tried to sign Ian Andrews from Birmingham City. Andrews turned Hibs down and signed for Celtic instead. One of his first games for Celtic was a 5–1 thrashing from Rangers during which he did not cover himself in glory. Andrews turned out to be a poor buy and Miller could easily have wasted a great deal of Hibs money if he had signed him rather than Goram.

Archibald was a class act. Off the field, he sported a fedora and drove a Rolls Royce. On the pitch, he held the ball up brilliantly, possessed excellent all-round skills and finished with confidence and certainty. He also exuded arrogance which, in his case, was well justified. Houchen was once described in the Hibs fanzine as a 'raw boned squadron leader type.' He was tall, handsome and well built and could play when he was in the mood. Unfortunately, he quite often gave the impression of seeming disinterested. Evans had pace and commitment and if he had been able to finish with half of the composure which Archibald displayed, he would have been a world-beater.

1987–88 was Miller's first full season in charge of Hibs and he started well. A thrilling 3–3 draw at Dunfermline opened the season and Hibs would have won this game comfortably if Alan Rough hadn't experienced a rare bad day at the office. Our next game was at home to Graeme Souness' expensively assembled Rangers outfit. We won 1–0 with a fine goal from John Collins. The crop of young players which Pat Stanton had gathered was now maturing nicely. All the members of the so called 'Kane Gang' – Paul Kane himself, John Collins, Mickey Weir, Gordon Hunter and Eddie May – were really starting to make their mark. Weir started the season so well that Luton Town bought him for £100,000. Much to the relief of all Hibs fans, little Mickey failed to settle at Kenilworth Road and Hibs re-signed him within a year.

With the help of David Duff's transfer kitty, Miller was building a good squad and achieving some impressive results. He was also dividing the opinions of the fans. Those in the pro-Miller camp saw our manager as being dedicated, methodical and appropriately serious about his work. The anti-Miller brigade saw him as being lugubrious, dull and defensive. Some of his early victories crystallised this dichotomy. Hibs beat Hearts 1–0 at Easter Road in front of a 27,000 crowd. For this match, he chose to leave Mickey Weir and John Collins on the bench. Hibs dominated the first half and should have led by more than 1–0 at the interval. After Eddie May's goal, Paul Kane had missed an absolute sitter. In the second half, Miller pulled ten players back behind the ball and held on to what he had. Hibs won the game but didn't do so with style. That was the problem which a lot of us Hibs fans had with our manager. He was too negative for the liking of a support which had been brought up on a tradition of free-flowing football. His acolytes though, and there was no shortage of them, pointed to the result and claimed that it didn't matter how you beat Hearts as long as you beat them. I was able to observe Alex Miller from close quarters from time to time because my son Dominic was now training with Hibs and we would go and watch him playing in matches against other team's junior squads. Miller was usually around on these occasions.

Dominic was also invited to play a trial match for Hearts. In the dressing room before the match, Alex McDonald the Hearts Manager finished his team talk by asking if there were any questions. Dominic pointed to his maroon jersey and said 'Do I really have to wear this?' All his training was making Dominic a fit lad and I was working hard on my own fitness at that time too. I had given up playing staff football because of a recurring hamstring injury and this had caused me to gain some weight. Just how much weight I had put on was brought home to me quite dramatically on a visit to the fitness centre at the Royal Commonwealth Pool. A head teacher friend of mine, Paul Deponio, and I had gone along to work on the weights and run on the treadmill. I was wearing a distinctive football strip which my brother John had sent me from America. John had led his university team to victory in the National Competition and was now a professional player for Denver. He had seen this strip on one of his trips to an away game and sent me it as a gift. As Paul and I walked up the stairs at the Commonwealth Pool, there was a mirror straight ahead of us. I didn't realise this and thought that I saw someone coming in my direction. I said to Paul, 'That fat bloke who's coming towards us has got exactly the same strip as the one John sent me.'

Paul replied, 'I hate to tell you but that fat bloke is you!' This was not good news but it did provide me with the incentive to get fit again and to lose some weight. I started playing football at the Quarry Park. This is a park in Joppa where a crowd of friends gather to have a game of football every Saturday morning. They also play on Boxing Day and 2 January. The games are competitive but sporting. A wide range of players come along, ranging from teenagers to men in their seventies, and the standard of play is usually very good. I quickly made new friends from my visits to the park and as a result also became involved in weekly five-a-side games at Meadowbank on a Sunday and at the Jack Kane Centre on a Wednesday. Very quickly I went from being thirteen stone to eleven stone. People had been saying to Margaret, 'Ted's getting very heavy, isn't he?' Now because I had become so thin so quickly, they were asking her if I was ill.

One of my new Quarry Park friends, Raymond Abbott, gave Patrick, Dominic and me a lift to a Hibs v Motherwell League Cup quarter-final at Fir Park. He had taken delivery of a new upmarket sports car that day and was keen to give it a run. We were held up for a time in roadworks and, when we cleared them, Raymond put his foot down. I suggested to him that he should be taking it easy as new cars had to go through a 'running in' period but he ignored my advice and gave his new set of wheels its head. We got there in time only to see another idiosyncratic Miller selection cost Hibs dearly. He chose Mickey Weir at centre forward where he was pitted against former Hibee Craig Paterson. Paterson towered over the diminutive Weir and mopped up all the high balls that Hibs illogically continued to fire in the little man's direction. Hibs never looked like scoring and lost a game they should have won comfortably.

Raymond, by the way, could be an amusing character. He was a successful accountant with a big house in Barnton and a zest for living life to the full. One day in one of our Quarry Park games, he took strong exception to the over-robust tackling of one of the other players. The group who played at the park was a cosmopolitan one. We had locals, Spaniards, Frenchmen and even Brazilians playing at one time or another. People would regularly bring along friends or workmates which is what had happened this day. The newcomer was a fairly rough and ready character; very ready to tackle and very rough when he did so. He had caught Raymond late on a few occasions. Eventually the urbane man of figures had had enough. He snapped, 'Make that the last time you tackle me like that, you troglodyte.' Our new arrival looked at him for a few moments and then said in all seriousness, 'Ah dinnae ken what that means but ah dinnae like the sound of it.'

Early in season 1989-90, Hibs beat Rangers 2–0 at Easter Road with a highly convincing display through goals from Weir and Houchen. This game again demonstrated Miller's paradoxical qualities. We fans were delighted with our team and prepared to give the manager every credit for his success. We were also starting to get optimistic about the future. However Alex Miller's post-match comments summed up the pessimistic side of his nature which drove so many of us mad. When asked to reflect on Hibs' triumph, he answered by stating, 'The league runs for thirty-six games and I would not bet against Rangers finishing top again.' Thanks Alex, that's just what all Hibs fans wanted to hear!

My son Dominic was fourteen now and playing for Hutchison Vale Boys Club. As I have mentioned, he was also training with Hibs. Margaret and I were very proud parents as we sat in the Easter Road stand one night and watched our boy play a great game for a Hibs' training squad select and score a magnificent diving header. Dominic was impressed by Alex Miller. He told us that Miller knew every young player who trained with Hibs by name, whereas his assistant Peter Cormack didn't have anything like the same familiarity with the youngsters in his charge.

Alex Miller also took Hibs into Europe in 1989. Our first UEFA Cup opponents were Videoton from Hungary. A Graham

Mitchell header gave us a narrow lead to take into the second leg. The return match, which had looked like a difficult hurdle, turned into one of Hibs' greatest nights in Europe. We achieved a marvellous 3–0 victory despite rough on-field tactics from the Hungarians and bottle-throwing from the crowd. A huge Hibs support travelled with the team and gave them tremendous backing. I was not able to go due to work commitments and listened to the match on Radio Forth. Former Radio Scotland commentator David Francey was behind the microphone. Francey could make a wake sound exciting but this evening he didn't need to hype things up at all. The match had everything and he brought it to life brilliantly. We celebrated at home with a couple of quiet drinks. The Hibs players' post-match celebration was rather more zealous. Andy Goram, in fact, introduced Gordon Hunter to the joys of the demon drink. Hunter had a great champagne-laced evening but did not feel quite so good next day when he woke with his first ever hangover.

We met the Belgian club Liège next. The first leg was at home and Keith Houchen missed a penalty. Hibs played well but couldn't score and travelled to Belgium as clear second favourites. A great display almost saw us through but Andy Goram, who had been immense, was finally beaten by a forty-yard wonder strike in extra time and Hibs went out. Goram's display earned him the soubriquet 'The Lion of Liège' in the next day's newspapers. Despite his consistent brilliance, he was still not a regular choice for Scotland. One Hibs supporter phoned Radio Scotland in high dudgeon to press his claim. It is fair to say that the caller's passion outweighed his articulacy. When the presenter asked him with some exasperation to say exactly why Goram should be Scotland's number one, the Hibee replied, 'Because he's cried the Lion of Liège.' He pronounced the last word as 'Leege.'

The man whose goals had taken Hibs into Europe was Steve Archibald. 'Archiegoals' as the fans had christened him was outstanding. He reserved his best performance for Tynecastle in early 1989. Paul Kane put Hibs ahead in the first half. He was later cautioned by the police for celebrating in front of the Hearts support. Gordon Rae, who was still doing a superb job as centre half, then got sent off and we were well and truly on the rack. The second half seemed interminable as Hibs hung on to their lead with extreme difficulty and Hearts pressed continuously. Then came a moment of pure magic. In a rare Hibs break, Archibald fastened on to a Kane overhead kick. He took the ball past Dave McPherson and drove an unstoppable twenty-yard shot past Henry Smith with his left foot from a challenging angle. This happened in front of the Hibs end of the ground. The whole area duly erupted into a sea of green and white. Archibald stood imperiously in front of us Hibbies with his arm aloft and a look on his face which seemed to say, 'Am I or am I not absolutely brilliant?'

Absolutely brilliant he certainly was and that magnificent goal helped Hibs to hang on for a rare but sweet victory at Tynecastle. For some reason Alex Miller fell out with Archibald and the superstar striker moved on when he still had much to offer Hibs. Archibald made his exit with characteristic panache. Hibs were playing Motherwell at Fir Park. When Miller read out the team in the dressing room, Archibald's name was conspicuous by its absence. Archie knew his worth so he did not indulge in any histrionics. That was not his style. The story goes that he simply took out his prototype mobile phone (needless to say he had a mobile long before anyone else) and called a taxi to take him back to Edinburgh. When the cab arrived, he got up without fuss, wished his team mates well in the forthcoming game and left. His colleagues were impressed, his manager was embarrassed and Archibald had once again demonstrated his class.

Hibs under Alex Miller were having some good times but there were unsuccessful days too. We beat Clydebank 4–1 at Easter Road in the league one Saturday and completely outclassed them. The following Saturday we met the same team in the quarter-final of the Scottish Cup and lost 1–0. In early 1990 Miller had again spent big. He had signed striker Paul Wright for nearly £300,000 from Queens Park Rangers. Wright's first match was a home game against Aberdeen. Miller left him on the bench until late in the game and the striker made the perfect start by scoring the winning goal shortly after taking the field. The following week Hibs met Dundee United at Tannadice in another Scottish Cup quarter-final. This was the day of the Scotland rugby team's famous Grand Slam win over England when David Sole led the team onto the field in a slow march of grim determination. Hibs didn't exhibit too much grim determination in Dundee and exited the Scottish Cup once more in disappointing fashion. Even more disappointingly, Alex Miller again left Paul Wright on the bench for most of the match. That night, while most of the nation celebrated the making of rugby history, the Brack family drove home in silent despair.

Another recent big-money Miller signing was that of midfield player Brian Hamilton from St Mirren. Hamilton worked hard but was anonymous in most matches. He was chosen regularly however and there were rumours that he was a relative of his manager. Miller was always quick to defend Hamilton saying that he was a 'players' player.' Most fans took this to be managerial speak for 'He doesn't do anything but I signed him so I have to defend him.' When the media gave Alf Ramsey a hard time about Martin Peters' peripheral performances for England, Ramsey dismissed them by saying that although they couldn't see it, Peters was 'ten years ahead of his time.' If that criterion had been applied to Hamilton, he would have had to be described as 'half a century ahead of his time.'

So as Hibs entered the '90s, our manager continued to split the fans. There were plenty who said that Hibs under Alex Miller were much better than they had been under Pat Stanton and John Blackley. Others argued that there would have been something wrong if this hadn't been the case because Miller had been given far more money to spend than his predecessors. The biggest debate though was over the way in which the team was playing. Fans of the manager said that Hibs were now much more 'compact.' Detractors considered the team to be boring and negative.

By the summer of 1990, however, there wasn't just concern with the style of football which Hibs were playing. There was major anxiety on the money front. David Duff had over-stretched himself. He was involved with a financier called David Rowland and through this relationship he had bought into a chain of ailing hotels and restaurants in England. This had not proved a good investment and Hibs were financially vulnerable. Little did we realise just how vulnerable we were. June 1990 brought an absolute bombshell. The Hearts chairman Wallace Mercer moved to take over Hibs.

I woke to this news one week after the death of my mother. It seemed like a second death in the family. That Monday will forever be etched in my memory. Like a lot of Hibs fans I did the natural thing at the end of my working day and headed for Easter Road. I met a lot of people I knew that night and we were all of like mind. We were terrified that we would lose our beloved team, but were also defiant and determined to fight to the end to save our club from the predator from across the city.

Mercer was an arrogant man who understood money but clearly did not understand what made football supporters tick. He claimed that he would merge Hibs and Hearts and enable Edinburgh to mount a real challenge to the Old Firm. What Hibs fans feared he had in mind was to buy Hibs, sell off their assets and make Hearts the only show in town. Hibs were in real danger of going out of existence at the hands of the figurehead of our bitterest rivals. The Saturday after Mercer's takeover bid was announced, a massive rally was held at Easter Road. My youngest son, who had just turned five, was in my group that day and so was my mother-in-law who at nearly seventy had insisted on going along to represent her late husband Arthur who had, of course, been a lifelong Hibee. 'I just had to be there,' she said. 'Arthur would have expected me to go on his behalf.'

The late and much lamented Kenny McLean was beginning to emerge as the leading figure in what had now become known as the 'Hands off Hibs' campaign. I knew Kenny because his grandson and my son had played in the same team at Hutchison Vale Boys Club. I knew Kenny to be a good man but over the next few weeks, he proved himself to be a great man.

The rally at Easter Road featured emotional speeches from Joe Baker and Pat Stanton. Joe spoke about what it meant to belong to what he called 'the Hibernian family.' Pat asked those present to imagine what Christmas Day would be like for a child if there was no new Hibs strip for a present. The music of the Proclaimers filled the Easter Road air and the Hibs support filled the Easter Road terracing and stands. There was an atmosphere of complete unity and total commitment to the future of Hibs.

The rally at the ground was followed a week or so later by another gathering of the Hibernian faithful at the Usher

Hall. Again a capacity crowd was present. Kenny McLean thanked the fans 'from the bottom of his heart' and promised them that 'Hibs would rise like a phoenix from the ashes.' In truth we should have been thanking him. That same rally saw John Robertson, who was then the main man at Hearts, speak out and oppose his chairman's bid to buy Hibs. Tom Farmer also came forward that night to declare his commitment to ensuring the survival of Hibs and the tide began to turn against Mercer. He had made the correct pecuniary calculations but he had totally misjudged the public mood. What he thought was 'tribalism' was in fact loyalty to a club and love for a team. Hibs fans did not want to watch some cobbled together Edinburgh Select playing in a soulless out of town stadium, which was apparently Mercer's vision. We wanted to watch our beloved Hibees irrespective of their ability to challenge the Old Firm or otherwise. They were our team and they were the only team we wanted.

Despite claiming, with typical insensitivity, that he 'had Hibs in the palm of his hand', Mercer was eventually forced to call off his bid. He had completely missed the point but one Sunday not long after the failure of his attempt to buy Hibs, Mercer had some facts pointed out to him in no uncertain fashion. I was browsing in HMV in Princes Street with my daughter Lisa when Mercer came into the shop. You would have thought that after the trauma he had caused, he would have been keeping a low profile but oh no, not the bold Wallace. He entered the record store wearing a Hearts blazer and tie and looking around to see if anyone had recognised him.

Lisa, who was seventeen at the time, most certainly had. She strode across to the cocksure Hearts chairman and poked her forefinger into his corpulent midriff. 'You, Mr Mercer,' she said, 'are an absolute disgrace.' For probably the only time in his life Wallace Mercer was rendered speechless. I have always been proud of my children but I was particularly proud of my daughter that day.

Having seen off Mercer's hostile bid, Hibs moved from crisis off the field to crisis on the field. The 1990–91 season was not a successful one and for a time all those fans who had claimed during the takeover saga that they would be happy to watch Hibs in the First Division as long as they survived looked like they might get their wish. However, in the summer of 1991, things began to change for the better. Tom Farmer restructured the club's finances and appointed Douglas Cromb as Chairman. There was also a place on the board for Kenny McLean. When Dominic and Kenny's grandson Mark had gathered at the McLean residence for lunch one Saturday, they were told to eat up because they were going through to Dens Park to watch Hibs play Dundee. Dominic was surprised to hear this because it was nearly two o'clock. A family dispute then ensued between Kenny and his son of the same name. Young Kenny wanted to drive the group through in his Porsche. His dad wanted to take his Mercedes. In the end, Kenny senior prevailed and the party set out for Tayside just before 2.15p.m. Amazingly they were in the ground before the kick-off. They didn't enjoy the game though because Dundee, inspired by a certain Keith Wright, proved too good for Hibs. It seems that when Kenny McLean set out to achieve something, he usually succeeded. He certainly succeeded in his fight to ensure the survival of Hibernian Football Club. He deserves great credit for doing so.

I think that most Hibs fans expected Alex Miller to be sacked during the summer of 1991. Hibs had only just escaped relegation at the end of the previous season and an *Evening News* supporters' poll had shown the majority of Hibees wanted a change in the Easter Road hot seat. Even Renton in

Irvine Welsh's novel *Trainspotting* had vowed, 'Ah'm no gaun back until there's a new cat in the manager's basket.'

The new chairman did not agree with the fans and made it clear very early in his tenure that he was standing by Alex Miller. Miller himself had never lost his self-belief as he regularly proclaimed his two favourite mantras of 'quality players' and 'I am a winner.' He brought in a couple of quality players that summer and was very soon to prove that on at least one occasion, he was indeed a winner.

Miller paid Dundee £500,000 for Keith Wright. This pleased me a great deal. As I mentioned earlier in this book, I had managed the Edinburgh Schools football team in the 1970s and our star player by a long way had been Keith Wright. For as long as I could remember I had been telling anyone who would listen that Hibs should sign Keith. Now we had signed the lifelong Hibee from Greendykes and what a signing he was to turn out to be. We had also signed John Burridge to replace Andy Goram who had gone the way of so many Hibs stars before him and since by travelling along the M8 to sign for Rangers. Burridge was a revelation and quite a character. He organised his defence superbly, kept goal immaculately and formed a great relationship with the Hibs fans. Every home game now finished with Budgie running the full length of what was then the east terracing to salute the fans. The fans had no difficulty reciprocating.

Hibs made a great start to the season. They were flying in both the league and the League Cup. In the first round of the latter competition, we travelled to McDiarmid Park in Perth to play Stirling Albion. This was a potential cup upset but as soon as the game started, all thoughts of a surprise outcome went out of the window as Hibs took total control. The whole team played well but one man stood out. That man was Keith Wright who ran the Albion defence ragged and capped his performance with a superb solo goal.

I had gone through to this game with another of my Quarry Park friends, Russell Mould. On the way back, we were drooling about Keith Wright's performance. I even went so far as to say that he was the fastest Hibs centre forward since the young Joe Baker. We both felt that something special was in the air and we made a pact to travel to every round of that season's League Cup competition.

Next up was a visit to Kilmarnock which looked a dangerous assignment. We travelled hopefully but cautiously to Rugby Park on a warm late August Wednesday evening. We had expected a hard game and we certainly got one. Kilmarnock played out of their skins but Hibs, with Wright and McGinlay both on the scoresheet and Murdo McLeod chipping in with a rare goal, prevailed 3–2. We had now been paired with Ayr United in the quarter-final and a genuine belief was growing that this could indeed be Hibs' year.

Alex Miller now had a settled team. In goal was the venerable and eccentric Burridge. At thirty-nine years of age, he was as fit and dedicated as he had ever been throughout his long and distinguished career which had been spent mainly in the higher echelons of English football. Apart from his goal-keeping prowess, Budgie was a superb organiser and from our seat behind the goal in what was to become the Famous Five Stand, we could clearly hear him telling his defenders where to go and what to do.

Willie Miller at right back was a local lad who had played for Portobello High School and Edina Hibs. He could tackle with steamroller force and came forward well to support the attack. Graham Mitchell was at left back after previously having been used by his manager as a central defender or a midfield player. With his carrot-coloured hair and thin white legs, Mitchell did not have an imposing physical presence. What he did have was a tremendous engine, an inbuilt will to win and not a little skill. His meandering forays up the left flank became known among the fans as 'Mitch's mazies' and he regularly complemented his quietly effective defensive work with exciting and telling attacking incursions.

Having signed Tommy McIntyre as a centre half, Alex Miller had used him mainly at full back. The best indicator that this hadn't worked out was the Scottish Cup semi-final against Celtic in 1989. After half an hour, Celtic were 3–0 up, a young Steve Fulton had run riot on their left flank and right back McIntyre had been substituted. Now reinstated in his proper position, big Tommy was strolling through games with coolness and confidence and forming a rock-like partnership with Gordon Hunter. Hunter tackled so hard that he made Willie Miller look gentle, which was no mean feat. His most memorable tackle was in the derby match at Tynecastle which Hearts won by the game's only goal from Husref Musemic. Hunter went through Scott Crabbe with such force that day that the Hearts player had to leave the field on a stretcher. If I had to choose a verb which best summed up what Hunter did to Crabbe, I would settle on 'decimate.' That is exactly the effect which Hunter's tackle had on the unfortunate Jambo.

Crabbe was someone else who had played for me during my time as Edinburgh Schools Manager. His father George provided an unforgettable piece of phraseology during that time. Edinburgh played Glasgow at Meadowbank on a beautiful sunny May day. The terracing side of the ground was bathed in warm, spring sunshine. The parents of the boys in the team, however, were directed to sit in the stand which was in the shade and much cooler. George Crabbe decided he wasn't having this and went to remonstrate with a steward.

The official proved unhelpful and inflexible in equal measure and a lively debate ensued. Eventually the 'jobsworth' tried to end the conversation by saying, 'Give me one good reason why you shouldn't all stay in that stand.' The retort may have lacked verbal elegance but was very much to the point: 'Because my wife's sitting there like a frozen snotter,' replied Mr Crabbe.

Gordon Hunter had earned the *nom de guerre* 'GBH' or 'Grievous Bodily Hunter' due to his destructive tackling style. The nickname later changed to 'Geebsie' and he was a player who could have won Scotland caps if he had displayed a little more dedication. Hunter was renowned as a player who was often unfit to train during the first part of a week but was amazingly sufficiently recovered to do some light work on a Friday and play on a Saturday, and that attitude did him few favours. He was an excellent central defender though and was probably at his peak in 1991.

By this time, my son was playing for a team in East Lothian called Lothian United. Lothian were formed as an under-twelve team and coached by John McGlynn who has since, of course, enjoyed success at Hearts and Raith Rovers. Within four years, McGlynn took Lothian from formation to success in the Scottish Cup at under-sixteen level. His nephew David played in the team and had become friendly with Dominic. The McGlynns lived close to Gordon Hunter in Wallyford and knew him well. One day Dominic and David were at Gullane beach. They met Geebsie and were engaged in some football chat with him about a recent injury he had sustained when they noticed that the centre half's eye was definitely wandering. Eventually it settled upon a highly attractive young lady who was sitting nearby. Hunter changed the conversation quickly from rehabilitation to romance but his choice of words would not have challenged Robert Burns in the field of writing love song lyrics. His request to young McGlynn was brief and basic – 'Davie, gaun tell that bird over there that ah fancy her.'

Miller's 1991 team employed a four-man midfield. Wide on the right was Mickey Weir. The little man had enjoyed a mixed relationship with his manager which had resulted in his often being left out of the team for inferior players. He was now fully back in favour and playing magnificently. Weir could dribble and cross and also had an eye for goal. He was the closest Hibs had come to finding a like for like replacement for Alex Edwards since the little Fifer had moved on in the late '70s. On the left was captain and assistant manager Murdo McLeod. McLeod had been signed from Borussia Dortmund for a large fee and was a vital presence in the team. Although not as dynamic as he had been in his Celtic and Scotland days, he read the game well and marshalled the team expertly. He was still a more than useful footballer and was able to use his battle-hardened approach to good effect to protect his less physical colleagues in the midfield area.

In central midfield was Pat McGinlay who had been signed on a free transfer from Blackpool. McGinlay had an all action style and the ability to achieve a double figure goal scoring tally each season. He was partnered centrally by Brian Hamilton. Hammy worked as hard as ever but continued to be largely anonymous in most games. He was clearly doing something right though because Alex Miller picked him for almost every match.

Three players vied for the striking positions. Newly signed and full of pace and goals, Keith Wright was the main man up front. At this stage of his career before injuries and age took their toll, Keith was on fire. His direct running at speed, skilful link play, deft headwork and composed finshing all made him more than a handful for every centre half he encountered. His original partner was Mark McGraw, the son of Morton manager and former Hibs stalwart Alan, who had been signed from his dad's club for a six-figure fee. Although young, he had come to Easter Road with a big reputation which he had found difficult to live up to. Undoubtedly skilful, he was also lightweight and not a natural in the goalscoring stakes. Our other main striker, Gareth Evans, had a big heart and the ability to run defences off their feet. He scored a few goals but missed more chances than he took. It was only this lack of composure in front of goal which prevented Gareth from being a top player.

These then were the men who carried Hibs' League Cup hopes to Somerset Park. Once more playing with authority and backed by an increasingly optimistic support, Hibs eased through 2–0. After Pat McGinlay's opener, Keith Wright administered the *coup de grâce* with a pinpoint diving header. During another happy return car journey, Russell and I again agreed that our good feeling about this League Cup competition was becoming ever stronger.

The draws for each succeeding round, however, were certainly not becoming any easier. The three teams who now remained in the competition with Hibs were Airdrie, Dunfermline and Rangers. We all knew which team Hibs would be paired against and we were all right. Alex Miller and Murdo McLeod made the usual positive noises saying that they were happy to play anyone and that they were sure that Hibs could take care of Rangers. We fans were not quite so sure but we did believe that we were in with a real chance. Russell and I, joined by my daughter Lisa, set out early for Hampden on semi-final day to make sure that parking wasn't a problem and that we were in the stadium in plenty time for the kick-off. Patrick and Dominic left later on a supporters' bus with their friends and did indeed miss the start of the match. Margaret stayed at home to listen to the radio and look after our youngest child Kevin, who was now six years old.

By the time everyone had arrived, there were just under 41,000 supporters in Hampden. This was a very strong Rangers team which included players like Andy Goram, recently signed from Hibs for £1 million, Mark Hateley, Maurice Johnston and Ally McCoist. Hibs, however, were very much in the mood. We started the game well, matching Rangers in midfield where Murdo McLeod was particularly prominent and causing Goram problems. Half an hour into the match, we scored a fine goal. Mark McGraw jumped with Goram for a high ball. The goalkeeper won the challenge and punched the ball as far as Mickey Weir on the edge of the penalty area. The little man controlled the ball, looked up and sent a superb cross on to the head of Keith Wright. Goram was still adrift but Rangers had two players guarding the goal line. This did not deter Keith whose perfectly directed header bisected the Rangers men and nestled in the back of the net.

Normally, this would have signalled another hour of nail biting tension with an inevitable Rangers equaliser at the end of it. Not this time though. Hibs continued to play with skill and composure and only once looked like losing a goal. A shot from Mo Johnston hit the bar and the post and rebounded to Ally McCoist. McCoist drove the ball towards the Hibs net but John Burridge displayed anticipation and agility which belied his years by changing direction and diving to clutch the ball. Indeed Hibs might have increased their lead as Gareth Evans came on to replace McGraw and provided an electrifying twenty-minute cameo. Twice Gareth might have scored but didn't. In the end it didn't matter. Hibs held on with some comfort and the large support, which had followed them to Glasgow, erupted as referee Douglas Hope blew the final whistle. The players ran to the Hibs end and celebrated as though they had already won the cup. We fans did likewise. Keith Wright, who had now scored in every round of the competition, recalled afterwards that the last time Hibs had been in a Cup Final, he had organised a supporters' bus to the match. This time was going to be a little bit different.

When we returned to Russell's car, the car park was still completely full. It was clear that we would not be going anywhere in a hurry. We had just sat back to bask in the glow of a famous victory when the sound of music rent the air. This was not Julie Andrews though. This music was much sweeter and much better. It was the sound of our very own Proclaimers. One of the fans had opened his car windows and turned his stereo on full blast. The strains of 'Sunshine on Leith' were all around us and the song had never sounded quite so good. Just over a year earlier this music had been the soundtrack for our club's desperate fight for survival. Now it was the overture to a Cup Final and the prospect of trophy-winning glory. As I sat in that car park, I am not ashamed to say that tears of joy and emotion streamed down my face.

During the drive home, we were held up in a traffic jam just outside Glasgow. At first we thought that the hold up had been caused purely and simply by the volume of traffic. This was not the case. A car containing five Rangers fans had broken down and was stuck, motionless, in the middle of the road. As the cars carrying Hibs fans passed them, the light blues received all sorts of stick. Rarely have I seen any group of football supporters look quite so woebegone.

The last time I had observed such misery had been looking at the television pictures of Hearts fans trooping dejectedly out of Dens Park in May 1986. The scene I was witnessing now therefore brought back some pleasant memories. By sheer coincidence the car in front of us was being driven by another Quarry Park friend, Roger Durkin. As we drove past the stranded and stunned Rangers contingent, Roger opened his window and shouted back to us, 'That's just made my night.' I think it is fair to say that we all shared his sentiments.

Hibs' opponents in the final were Dunfermline. The Fifers had beaten Airdrie at Tynecastle in the other semi-final in highly controversial circumstances. With three minutes to go, Airdrie led 1–0 and seemed destined to be Hibs' Hampden opponents. Then referee David Syme decided to step in. This was the same David Syme who had served up such a lamentable refereeing display when Hibs had played East Fife in 1973 just a few days after beating Hearts 7–0. We Hibs fans (and no doubt supporters of other clubs too) had suffered from some idiosyncratic performances from Mr Syme in the intervening eighteen years but now he surpassed himself. The ball struck Airdrie's Jimmy Sandison on the chest just inside his own penalty area. No one in the ground thought that Sandison had handled the ball – except for Mr Syme. He invoked a mini riot by pointing to the spot. Dunfermline equalised, took the game into extra time and then added further irony to the proceedings by qualifying for the final after a penalty shoot-out. Television pictures conclusively confirmed Syme's error but that was little consolation to Airdrie. In truth, all Hibs fans were happy to play Dunfermline. Airdrie under the management of Alex Miller's old Rangers colleague Alex McDonald were always troublesome opponents. As a player, McDonald had specialised in niggling and fouling Alex Edwards when Hibs met Rangers. Now as a manager, he had drilled his team in his own image. His Airdrie side, featuring such luminaries as Kenny Black, Sandy Stewart, Walter Kidd and the aforementioned Sandison snarled and kicked their way through matches. They also played some effective football at times and always presented Hibs with problems. For once then, David Syme, however unwittingly, had done Hibs a favour.

The League Cup Final was scheduled for Sunday, 27 October 1991 so we Hibees had to wait thirty-three days for our special occasion. For most of us, the time between semi-final and final seemed interminable. Hibs continued to play well though and, two weeks before the Hampden show-down, comfortably beat Dunfermline 3–0 at Easter Road to lay down a clear marker for the forthcoming contest.

Margaret's brother Terry had organised a coach for the journey to the final. He had decided that the bus would leave Edinburgh at 11a.m. This proved to be a very wise decision as the Scottish League had declined to make it an all-ticket game, a foolish decision which was to have serious implications for many Hibs supporters before Cup Final day was out. When the great day arrived, Terry's bus was packed with a combination of family, friends and people from the local St John's parish church. Not all of the people on the bus could truthfully call themselves Hibs fanatics. Quite a few were along for a day out and were Hibs sympathisers rather than supporters. There was a great atmosphere on the bus though as CDs of Hibs songs provided a musical backdrop and, for once, we travelled to Hampden for a Cup Final with confidence as well as hope. I am a pessimist by nature but ever since our victory over Rangers in the semi-final, I had been convinced that Hibs were destined to win the League Cup. I still felt this strongly as our coach headed westwards. Margaret and I had brought Kevin with us and he was really excited at the prospect of his first-ever Hibs game.

All of my family were on the bus except for oldest son Patrick. At the age of nineteen he had decided that travelling with a family group wasn't for him and had travelled through to the game via various watering holes with his friends. Young Kevin was having the time of his life. We had even bought him a ticket in the sweepstake to name the first goalscorer in the final. He had pulled the name of Tommy McIntyre out of the hat and was convinced that he was going to win the pot of money for the winner which was £27. He couldn't understand why the rest of us shook our heads and told him that he had no chance.

We arrived in plenty of time for the game and took up places in the old Hampden terracing opposite the players' tunnel. To that point, I had felt totally confident of victory. Now doubt began to creep in. As the time leading up to kick-off passed, I began to ponder the possibility of defeat. 'Surely,' I thought, 'we can't come through so much and get this far and then throw it all away by losing to Dunfermline.' As I consoled myself that I was being over negative, I couldn't quite erase all thoughts that if any team was capable of spectacular anticlimax it was our ever unpredictable Hibernian FC. While I was indulging in such sacrilegious thoughts, a significant number of our fellow Hibees were having anxiety problems of their own. The Glasgow police had decided that the Hibs end of the ground was full and that it wouldn't be safe to allow Hibs fans into the Dunfermline end. Sadly while the ground remained only three-quarters full, 2,000 Hibs fans were refused entry and had to find a pub to watch the game on television. Terry's decision to leave early for the match was well and truly vindicated. I would have hated to have been one of those Hibees who were turned away from one of the biggest occasions in the club's history through no fault of their own.

When the match started there were 40,000 supporters inside the ground. 30,000 of that number were bedecked in green and white but as the first half unfolded they were tensely silent. It was a sterile game. Dunfermline, with nothing to lose, were grittily competitive. Hibs, as favourites and in such an emotionally charged atmosphere, were taut and tentative. At half-time, Alex Miller made possibly his most telling contribution to Hibs history when he told his team simply but brilliantly, 'If you don't win this cup today, you will regret it for the rest of your lives.'

With their minds thus concentrated, Hibs came out for the second half a different team. Within four minutes of the restart, we were ahead. Mickey Weir, who had risen above big match nerves better than any of his colleagues to that point, was brought down by Ray Sharp and referee Brian McGinlay pointed to the spot. Who should come forward but Tommy McIntyre. I was a bag of nerves but Tommy was coolness personified. Andy Rhodes the Dunfermline goalkeeper was a cocky character with a reputation for saving penalties. He didn't save this one. Rhodes dived to one corner and McIntyre placed the ball in the other. Margaret and I hugged and shouted, 'We're going to win the cup.' Kevin leapt about and shouted, 'I'm a millionaire. I've won £27.'

Seven minutes from the end, Mickey Weir took a hand again. This time he sent Keith Wright clear with a slide-rule, defence-splitting pass. Keith drew Rhodes and slotted the ball past him. Hampden erupted. Keith had scored in every round of the League Cup, Hibs were two goals up and the trophy was ours. The pressure lifted from 30,000 sets of Hibernian shoulders inside Hampden and no doubt from 2,000 more outside and the celebrations began.

As Murdo McLeod went up to receive the cup and the players cavorted euphorically round the national stadium afterwards wearing Hibs scarves and hats, I took time out to think. Fifteen months earlier, our great club had been on the verge of extinction. Now we were alive and kicking and in possession of a national trophy. Life just didn't get any better than this. Even our usually reserved manager took part in the celebrations. As he was carried round Hampden by John Burridge, his normally serious face wore the widest of grins.

As we returned to our coach, we were talking excitedly about how much we were looking forward to the scenes in Princes Street when the team's open-topped bus brought the League Cup home. Almost everyone was back on board very quickly. There were, however, two exceptions. A couple of teenage girls who had come along with their father for 'the experience' had decided to widen that experience further by going for a walk. There was no little irritation on the coach and increasing concern that we would get back late and miss the victory parade. To a torrent of 'Where in God's name have you been?' the girls eventually turned up, blissfully unaware of the worry they had created and the driver pointed the bus in the direction of Edinburgh.

We needn't have worried. Back at the ground, man of the match Mickey Weir was still trying to provide the urine sample which had been asked of him as he had come out of the hat as the Hibs player to undergo a post-match drugs test. That was one more thing to thank Mickey for on this great day. When we reached Princes Street, we took up a spot at the East End outside Register House. There were Hibees every-where and the atmosphere was so highly charged that it would have operated a power station for a week. People sang, danced and drank from bottles and cans. Joy and good nature were everywhere. Even the statue of Sherlock Holmes at York Place was draped in Hibs regalia. We gave the team a euphoric welcome when their bus drove past and then got off our marks for our next port of call which was the Holy Ground itself. As the Hibs group snaked down Leith Walk, along

Duke Street and up Easter Road past thousands of delirious fans, we headed down Waterloo Place towards the stadium. We didn't want to be locked out and we didn't want to miss the team's arrival so speed was of the essence. I gave Kevin a 'high shoulders' carry and we all strode out for the ground. At six, Kevin probably represented a fair weight to carry for a distance of over a mile but I was so happy that I hardly even noticed that he was there. The boy himself was still on cloud nine after his sweepstake triumph and made his priority of the day clear by repeating endlessly, 'I'm rich. I've got £27.'

We found ourselves a place on the old east terracing and prepared for the latest highlight of this happiness filled day. We didn't have long to wait. A huge roar rent the air as Alex Miller and Murdo McLeod walked out arm in arm to hold the cup aloft. They were followed by their players and coaching staff. The players hugged, punched the air, waved to the crowd and joined in with the Hibs songs which were being played over the public address system. These were magical, unforgettable moments. Opposite us in the main stand was Margaret's mum. She was at Easter Road for the second time in her life. Just over a year earlier, she had represented her late husband at a rally organised to safeguard Hibs future. Now she was back to celebrate a triumph on his behalf.

Eventually, the team headed for their post-match banquet and we fans dispersed. We had left our car in Portobello when we had got on the bus that morning and now we walked back to it through Lochend. We walked with John Stewart, an old school friend of mine and a lifelong Hibee. We had bumped into John during the day and together we had savoured what we knew were historic happenings. Back in the car, we stopped off en route for home to collect fish suppers. By this time we were a group of four as Dominic had gone off to team up with his friends and celebrate late into the night. I had bought a 1.5 litre bottle of sparkling wine for the hoped-for celebration and I opened it as soon as we got in. We couldn't afford champagne but we didn't need it either. As we settled down to watch a video recording of the match, the fish and chips tasted wonderful and the wine went down like nectar. Having said that, Margaret and Lisa only managed one glass apiece as the emotions of the day caught up with them and they drifted off to sleep on the couch. That meant I was left with the onerous task of finishing off the wine. I didn't find this difficult and quaffed my way through more than a litre of poor man's champers while watching the game and the scenes which followed. I felt great.

I didn't feel quite so great next day. I woke with a thumping headache and a tired but elated feeling. It was my custom at school to start each day by taking in the pupils' lines and exchanging words with the children as they came in. That morning, as 400 or so youngsters chorused 'Good morning Mr Brack,' I responded cheerily and did my best to appear absolutely normal. In truth, I was more than a little hungover. It was a busy day and my sore head subsided as it progressed. At 5.30p.m. I set out for home, stopping along the way to pick up every Scottish newspaper. As I came through the door, a new dining room table was being delivered. The table immediately became known as the 'Skol Cup table.' I still think of it in that way now. It is overdue for replacement but that may never happen. Who cares if your table is scratched and scored, if it reminds you of one of the greatest days in the history of Hibernian FC.

That Sunday in October was undoubtedly a momentous day. Its significance was increased by the remarkable recovery Hibs had made from bankruptcy to breakthrough. A banner at Hampden which stated 'From oblivion to glory' had said it all. The author Jim Hossack described the Skol Cup winners as 'The team that wouldn't die.' Kenny McLean's prediction, that Hibs would rise 'like a phoenix from the ashes', had been proved correct.

Alex Miller had reason to be proud. He had been doubted and criticised and the fans had called for his head. Now he had proved that he was indeed a winner. He deserved great credit for delivering Hibs' first major trophy for nineteen years and I was more than happy to accord him the praise he was due. Interestingly, the Dunfermline team beaten by Hibs in that Cup Final contained no fewer than three successful managers of the future in the shape of David Moyes, Billy Davies and Ian McCall. For now though, the managerial spotlight was on Alex Miller. Having achieved the breakthough, could he build on it and lead Hibs to more success in future?

Hibs' first match after their Hampden triumph was a home derby. We outplayed Hearts but had to settle for a 1–1 draw thanks to a Keith Wright goal. This set the pattern for derbies to come. As often as not, we would match or better Hearts but always they would win or gain a fortunate draw. We drew with them again at New Year when a Tommy McIntyre penalty secured Hibs a point. A few weeks later we met Airdrie in the Scottish Cup. We were all optimistic about a cup double but this game was to prove a sad anticlimax. Airdrie performed their usual spoiling act and Hibs never looked like overcoming them. This time Tommy McIntyre missed a penalty and Mickey Weir went off injured. Neither were to be first team regulars again under Miller. Two late Owen Coyle goals put paid to Hibs' hopes of collecting a second piece of silverware.

In the summer of 1992, Alex Miller signed Darren Jackson to partner Keith Wright up front. Jackson's signing was to prove an excellent piece of business. Like Keith, he had played for me in the Edinburgh Schools team. In Darren's year, we had lost in the Scottish Cup Final to Glasgow. At that time,

Darren was on the small and slight side and I tended to use him as a substitute for that reason. On a number of occasions since, he has reminded me that my team selection skills were less than infallible. His own secondary head teacher Terry Christie had similar doubts about Darren's physical attributes. However, Terry overcame his doubts to sign him for Meadowbank Thistle. A move to Newcastle came next and Darren's spell at St James' Park led to a very successful career at both club and international level when he returned to Scotland.

Just after the 1991 Skol League Cup win, Keith Wright kept a promise to me. Keith had told me that he would bring the Cup to the school and show it to the pupils and he did in February 1992. Accompanied by director Tom O'Malley and reserve goalkeeper Chris Reid who was a former pupil of our school, Keith addressed a fully gathered throng at assembly and then he and his colleagues took the trophy round all the classes afterwards. Before they left, I made sure that I had my photograph taken with Keith, Chris and the League Cup.

This photograph has since been framed and hangs in my study between pictures of Gordon Smith scoring against Hearts in the 1950s and Joe Baker scoring against St Johnstone a decade later. As he was going out of the door, Keith made me another promise. 'If we ever reach another Cup Final,' he said, 'I will give you a couple of centre-stand tickets as a thank you for the help you gave me as a schoolboy footballer.'

The highlight of season 1992–93 was a titanic UEFA Cup tie against Anderlecht. In the home leg, Hibs played really well. Backed by a roaring, rowdy crowd, we took an early lead. The Anderlecht goalkeeper failed to hold a Darren Jackson shot and there to slot in the rebound was Dave Beaumont. Since signing Beaumont, Alex Miller had tried him at full back, centre half and in midfield. He had come up short in all of these positions and this close-range goal was probably his most significant contribution as a Hibs player. Anderlecht were a good side (they were to hold AC Milan to two draws in the group stages of the Champions League the following season) and they came back to claim the lead. A late Hibs surge down the slope which recalled European matches from days gone by saw first Pat McGinlay equalise for Hibs and then Keith Wright hit the underside of the bar when he might have scored. Hibs took a tremendous support to the away leg. The players said afterwards that they were proud of their following and inspired by them. The fans also had reason to be proud of their team who drew 1–1, with Darren Jackson scoring, and only went out to a top team on the away goals rule. It was Alex Miller's custom to give a team talk to his players before a match and carry out a post-match dressing room analysis with them as soon as the game finished. That night in Belgium, the fans roared for Hibs to come back out and take a bow. Miller eventually allowed the team to do so but only after he had completed his post-mortem.

Alex Miller made three outstanding signings in 1993. Kevin McAllister came from Falkirk and Michael O'Neill arrived from Dundee United. Both of these players were tricky, exciting dribblers with the ability both to cross and to score. They gave Hibs the width which the team had previously lacked and they went on to become firm favourites with the Hibs support. The third signing was to prove the best of all. Alex Miller had fallen out with John Burridge over, of all things, the jersey he should wear. He now moved for the former Aberdeen and Manchester United goalkeeper Jim Leighton. This was considered a gamble at the time. Leighton had followed Alex Ferguson from Pittodrie to Old Trafford in a big money move. He had failed to reproduce his Scottish form down south and this had culminated in Ferguson dropping him cruelly from United's team for the FA Cup replay against Crystal Palace at Wembley after the goalkeeper had let in three goals in the first match. Leighton had never recovered from this and he was languishing at Dundee when Miller gave him the opportunity to resurrect his career. He seized this chance (and many shots and crosses) with both hands in the years which followed. Hibs had had a procession of top goalkeepers during the '80s and '90s. The outstanding Alan Rough was followed by the supremely talented Andy Goram who in turn was succeeded by the eccentric but gifted John Burridge. Now came Leighton, and in my opinion, he was to prove the best of all. He gave Hibs tremendous service for four years, won back his place in the Scotland team and proved to be an acquisition *par excellence.*

Leighton and McAllister made an early mark in the League Cup. Hibs won a thrilling match at Firhill on penalties. McAllister contributed a goal and a tremendous performance. Leighton weighed in with two vital penalty saves. This took Hibs through to a semi-final with Dundee United at Tynecastle. We were watching Alex Miller's 'new Hibs', but this game recalled echoes of his previous approach. Darren Jackson shot Hibs into an early lead. With the attacking players we had, we should have been looking to score more goals. Miller, however, proved that old habits die hard. He pulled ten men back behind the ball and the rest of the match became an exercise in survival for Hibs. Survive we did though and another final had been reached. Due to the refurbishment of Hampden, the match would take place at Parkhead. Hibs' opponents were Rangers.

A couple of weeks before this final, Patrick, our oldest son, who was now a student at Edinburgh University, was at home working on an essay when the doorbell rang. When he answered the door, Keith Wright was standing on the doorstep. He handed Patrick an envelope: 'These are tickets for the centre stand for the Cup Final,' he said. 'I promised your dad that if we got to another final, I would give him a couple of tickets so here we are.'

When Margaret and I returned from work later that evening, we were met by a very excited number-one son who rushed out to say, 'You'll never guess who was here this afternoon.' I replied, 'Keith Wright.' 'How did you know that?' said Patrick, a little disappointed that his great announcement had created less impact than he had expected. 'Because he made a promise to me,' I said, 'and I knew that he would keep that promise.'

Margaret decided that for this final she was going to dress completely in green. She purchased an elegant all-green outfit right down to an emerald coloured handbag in which our prized centre-stand tickets were securely placed. Hibs played well that day but lost 2–1 due to an incredible overhead kick from Ally McCoist nine minutes from the end of the match. The referee was Jim McCluskey, a man believed by Celtic at least to have a soft spot for their greatest rivals. Just before half-time, Keith Wright took the ball past Ally Maxwell in the Rangers goal. Maxwell brought Keith down. It was a clear penalty but McCluskey refused to award it. Instead he booked Keith for diving. At half-time, I met Keith's dad Harry in the queue for the toilets. I asked him, 'Did you think that it was a penalty, Harry?' Mr Wright Senior's response was concise and unequivocal. 'Guaranteed' was his one word reply.

Hibs' team for that match summed up Alex Miller's strengths and weaknesses. Excellent players like Leighton, Hunter, Wright, Jackson, McAllister, O'Neill and the young centre half Steven Tweed who had replaced Tommy McIntyre were joined by such journeymen as Brian Hamilton, Dave

Beaumont and Davie Farrell. Players like Joe Tortolano, Graeme Love and Danny Lennon also featured regularly to the team's detriment at this time as well. If Miller had cleared out all the players who weren't good enough and replaced them with players of comparable quality to his stronger performers then Hibs would have been a formidable force indeed. He never took that step and I think that this, more than anything else, stopped him from gaining more success. A game against Rangers at Ibrox, not long after the 1991 League Cup win, illustrates the folly of Miller's persistence with players who were not of the requisite standard. Hibs led 2–1 well into the second half and looked capable of victory. At that point, Joe Tortolano quite unnecessarily headed the ball into his own net. The game turned round completely and Rangers went on to win 4–2. The same Tortolano was still being selected by Miller five years later.

The next few seasons saw Hibs achieve high league finishes and reach Scottish Cup semi-finals but we never looked like winning another trophy. At that time, Hibs had appointed a community coach called John Ritchie. Along with the club's directors, John had started a scheme for local schools called the Hibs Merit Award. Classes could earn points for hard work and good behaviour. The class with the most points at the end of the term received a trophy. The children then voted for the player whom they would most like to meet. The player chosen visited the school along with John Ritchie, answered the children's questions, signed autographs and posed for photographs. It was a great idea and motivated lots of pupils irrespective of which football team they supported. We had visits from a wide range of players including Keith Wright, Darren Jackson, Gareth Evans, Stephen Tweed, Michael O'Neill and Jim Leighton. I remember Leighton's visit because he was wearing a particularly crumpled sweater which looked like it hadn't seen the inside of a washing machine for quite some time. He was, however, excellent with the children, answering their questions intelligently and humorously. Michael O'Neill was another who provided good answers. When asked what his predominantly Loyalist home town of Portadown was like, he replied 'Like Musselburgh with fewer Catholics.' When asked for advice, O'Neill said, 'Never argue with referees.' This from a man who was no stranger to red or yellow cards.

For season 1994-95, Margaret and I were the proud possessors of season tickets for the first time. Hibs were collaborating with Lothian Region Education Department to produce an education pack for schools. The pack would contain a range of History, Geography, Science and Personal and Social Development activities for pupils based on Hibs' past and on current happenings at the club. I had been asked to write the pack in partnership with a head teacher colleague of mine, Maureen Crandles of St Ninian's Primary School. As a thank you for our efforts, we were each given a pair of season tickets for prime centre-stand seats. This meant a lot to Margaret and me as, due to our large family, we had never been able to afford our own season tickets up to that point. I am delighted to say that we enjoyed the season ticket experience so much that we have bought our own ever since and it is a source of pride to me that all of my now grown-up children also became season-ticket holders in due course.

Hibs started that season brilliantly, thrashing Dundee United 5–0 in their opening match. Two ex-Tannadice players, Darren Jackson and Michael O'Neill scored three of the goals and new star Kevin Harper notched his first ever Hibs goal. Two weeks later, Hibs travelled to Tynecastle for the latest derby match. These fixtures had become nightmares for us Hibs fans. We hadn't beaten Hearts for over five years and twenty-two matches had passed since we had last tasted success in the fixture which we most wanted to win. When asked on television during this nightmare run of results if he thought that Hibs would ever beat Hearts again, Pat McGinlay had replied with real feeling, 'It just has to be done!' To this point though, it hadn't yet been done.

There had been a succession of heartaches, none more so than a Scottish Cup match at Easter Road in early 1994. After a slow start when John Robertson did what he nearly always did in derbies and scored for Hearts, Hibs equalised through Keith Wright then took control. Kevin McAllister hit the post and there were a number of other near things. A replay looked certain when Hibs got a free kick at the halfway line in the last minute. We threw almost everyone forward but the ball was headed clear into the path of Wayne Foster who set off for Hibs' goal with Dave Beaumont in pursuit. Foster was fast but he was no finisher. It became clear that Beaumont was not going to catch him. Almost every Hibs fan implored big Dave to bring Foster down before he reached the penalty area. Our centre half put sportsmanship before expediency and declined to do so. This resulted in Foster finding himself one-on-one with Jim Leighton. Jim came out to narrow the angle and gave the Hearts player little space to aim for. Foster hit his shot straight at Leighton but such was Hibs' misfortune in derbies at that time that the ball went between Leighton's legs and into the net. If the ball had been to either side of the goalkeeper, as it ought to have been, Leighton would have saved it. Instead a misdirected shot put Hibs out of the cup.

I couldn't attend the upcoming Hearts match as I was with Dominic who was playing for Edinburgh University that day. As the match finished, word came through that Gordon Hunter had given Hibs the lead at Tynecastle. I hardly dared hope that the impossible was going to happen at last. Somebody turned on a radio and we all gathered round it. There were twenty-eight minutes to go and it seemed like they would never pass. Hunter revealed after the game that he had continuously asked Les Mottram, the referee, how much time was left. Eventually Mottram had said, 'Fifteen minutes and don't ask me again.' Gordon said that the fifteen minutes which followed were the longest of his life. Time was dragging for Alex Miller too. He declared that he was going to buy a new watch since his current one 'hadn't moved near the end of the match.' It was no less tense around the radio outside the Edinburgh University dressing room. Eventually a blast of Mr Mottram's whistle signalled that after a wait of 2,065 days, Hibs had finally defeated Hearts. I jumped nearly as high as Hunter had on scoring. There is a classic photograph of Geebsie leaping skywards in front of the massed ranks of Hibs fans seconds after scoring his mould-breaking goal. The Hibees were there in numbers as usual. A succession of derby defeats and disappointments hadn't stopped the most faithful fans in the world from turning out in support of their team. On Saturday, 27 August 1994, they got the reward their loyalty deserved.

Incidentally, Edinburgh University had won their match 5–1 and Dominic had scored two excellent goals. The match was fully reported in that evening's *Pink News* and I was a very proud man as I read about Hibs' victory on the front page and my son's goals on the back page. The ever upbeat Alex Miller, by the way, was quoted after this seminal derby as saying, 'Our passing was so bad in the first half that I was wondering why I call some of my team footballers.' He did concede that his team had improved in the second half.

Derby famine was followed by feast as Hibs went on to win two more of their encounters with Hearts during season 1994–95. On a day of torrential rain in late October, Darren Jackson and Michael O'Neill scored in the first fifteen minutes.

A rout seemed possible but Hearts weathered the storm and gave Hibs some anxiety in the last ten minutes after John Robertson had scored from a disputed penalty. As ever Jim Leighton was equal to the task of keeping their attacks at bay. The *Daily Record* summed up his performance perfectly when it stated, 'The only way Jim Leighton could have made his goal more safe would have been by boarding it up.' While their team had coped with the footballing storm on the park, the Hearts supporters were less successful in dealing with the storm of a meteorological variety which drenched them as they sat at the Dunbar end of the ground. This south part of the ground was the only area which remained uncovered and Hibs handed out yellow cagoules to their Gorgie visitors. They proved totally inadequate and the Jambos were absolutely saturated. The Hibs fans celebrated victory at the end of the game with a quick and hilarious chorus of 'Raindrops Keep Falling on Your Head.'

We gained local bragging rights again in May 1995, when an up-the-slope second-half surge saw Hibs score three times to overhaul a 1–0 interval deficit. Keith Wright, Mickey Weir and Kevin Harper all scored fine goals and this ended up the most conclusive of the campaign's three derby triumphs. In the Hearts team at Easter Road was long time Hibee Brian Hamilton. Astonishingly, Hearts manager Tommy McLean had paid £200,000 for the hardworking but limited midfielder in January. It was Hibs' best result of the season. Former Edinburgh councillor David Begg is a great Hibs fan. David used to hold a 'Hibs Night' at the start of every year. He would invite a few friends round and over snacks and drinks, everyone would choose their player of the year, goal of the season and favourite moment from the previous twelve months. This year, he invited Lisa and me along. We arrived to witness scenes of tremendous jollity. I honestly thought that someone had won the lottery. When we asked what the cause of the celebration was, our host told us that not only had Hearts signed Brian Hamilton, they had paid big money for him. He then collapsed into a paroxysm of uncontrollable laughter.

In 1995–96, Hibs followed an excellent season with a very poor one indeed. We went out of the League Cup early on at Airdrie. This was the third time in five years that Alex McDonald's bunch of bruisers had outmanoeuvred and outmuscled us in cup competitions. This time we went down without even a hint of fight. By this time, I had joined the editorial committee of the Hibs fanzine *Mass Hibsteria*. The magazine had been founded by Colin Leslie and Stevie Burns as secondary school pupils. Colin and Stevie were now finding their way in the world of work and hadn't as much time to devote to their editing duties. They remained on board but John Campbell and Sean Allan had stepped into the editorial hot seats. We were joined by two long-term talented contributors in Sandy McNair and Mike Burns. We were all passionate Hibees who wanted the best for the club. While we were prepared to give praise when it was deserved and regularly did so, we were not afraid to criticise constructively when we considered such an approach to be in the club's best interests.

The first meeting of the new committee took place immediately after the League Cup capitulation to Airdrie. I hobbled into the meeting on crutches. On the first morning of the new season, I had been playing football at the Quarry Park. Early in the game, I was tackled from behind. I sensed the imminent challenge and pulled the ball back with the sole of my boot. The tackler, Paul Jones, slid in, missed the ball and caught my leg instead.

Paul was a Hearts fan but apart from that he was as nice a person as you could meet. I knew immediately from the pain level in my lower leg that my injury was serious. Foolishly, I allowed myself to be persuaded to go in goal so that the teams remained even. After a short time, I realised that this was not a clever move and decided to go home. A few of the boys offered me a lift but I made my second error by declining their offers. I set off to hobble the half mile or so to my house. It's fair to say that I was struggling and was very much relieved when a neighbour who was driving past, pulled up, ordered me into his car and drove me home. I arrived back at the house at 11.30a.m. Margaret's wifely sympathy was expressed in her opening comment of 'I told you that you were too old to play football.' Fortunately Lisa was more favourably disposed to my plight and suggested that we get into the car and she would take me to the Royal Infirmary for an X-ray. We arrived at the hospital around noon to discover that the Accident and Emergency Unit was overflowing. Taking my courage in my hands and using all the charm which I could muster, I asked the nurse on the desk if I might jump the queue as I had to get to Easter Road for three o'clock to see Hibs playing Stenhousemuir. To my amazement, she acceded to my request. In a matter of minutes, I was told that I had broken my leg, encased in plaster, handed a pair of crutches and told that I was free to go. As luck would have it, we had to park further from the ground than usual that afternoon but I eventually managed to mount the stairs to my seat in the stand just in time for kick-off. As I did my Long John Silver impersonation towards where we sat, those around us gave me a sarcastic round of applause. An eventful day ended happily when Hibs won 3–1.

At the next editorial meeting there was split opinion. Some of the boys felt that Alex Miller had overstayed his welcome and should be replaced. Others, myself included, were at that point less certain that our long-term leader deserved dismissal.

He did nothing to strengthen his case for retention, however, when he took Hibs to Ibrox on the last Saturday of 1995. Hibs were humiliated to the tune of 7–0. This was usually our favourite score line but on that dark day it had an altogether different resonance. I had been watching Hibs since 1957 and this was the biggest defeat I had known in that time. It was very hard to take. This was the game when referee Doug Smith dropped his yellow card. Paul Gascoigne picked it up and booked him. Smith then showed that he completely lacked a sense of humour when he cut Gazza's mirth short by taking back his card and flashing it in the Geordie maverick's face. No Hibs supporter was in the mood for laughing that night either. I had booked cinema tickets to take Kevin, who was now ten, to see the film *Babe*. Although it was the last thing I felt like doing, I kept my promise and sat through the whole movie staring at the screen but taking nothing in. The eponymous hero of the film was a baby pig. I was simply pig sick.

Hibs' next match was the New Year's Day derby at Easter Road. Defeat might have meant the end of the road for the Hibs manager but Alex Miller, the great survivor, beat the drop again. We made the worst possible start, conceding a goal to Neil Pointon after only seven minutes. Miller turned to his coaches at that point and said, 'Now we will see if they are men.' He was to witness a response from his team which was as impressive as it was unexpected. By half-time, Hibs had equalised and gone ahead. First Michael O'Neill leapt prodigiously to bullet head a Kevin McAllister cross in at the near post. He celebrated with a frenzied touchline run which covered half the length of the park. Then came an all-time great goal. Darren Jackson chipped a free kick towards Keith Wright. Keith seemed to hang in mid air as he nodded the ball in the direction of Kevin Harper. Harper struck the most perfect volley from eighteen yards into the roof of the net.

The next day's papers called the goal 'An absolute wonder strike' and they were right. Only heroics from Giles Rousset and careless finishing on Hibs' part prevented an avalanche of second half goals as Hibs produced a second half blitz on the Hearts goal. Having lost seven goals two days earlier, Hibs have could easily have scored just as many on this first day of 1996 with better luck and increased composure. A 2–1 victory though was enough to lift the pressure on Miller for the moment. In his programme notes for the next home match, he described the defeat by Rangers as 'The most embarrassing day of my footballing life.' He added, 'Against Hearts, the players were on trial and knew that if they didn't perform, they were out of the club.'

In the same programme, there was an article covering the launch of the Hibs Education Pack which had just been been issued to schools. Scotland manager Craig Brown, a former teacher himself, helped with the launch and had kind words to say about the materials which we had produced. Alex Miller was a guest at the event and I had a chat with him in the course of the afternoon. He was very frank in discussing his team's recent performances and, it has to be said, less than complimentary about some of his players. Interestingly, when I spoke to the players any time they visited the school as part of the Hibs Merit Award programme, they were always completely loyal to their manager. They praised his dedication and attention to detail and never criticised him.

Miller's strong words weren't followed by equally strong action. The rest of the season petered out without any significant improvement and the close season was clearly going to be a crucial time for the beleaguered boss who simply had to sign what he himself would term 'quality players.' He didn't entirely succeed in doing so. In previous summers, players like Wright, O'Neill, Jackson, McAllister and Leighton had been brought to the club. These really were players of quality. This time, Miller brought in Ian Cameron, Brian Welsh and Barry Lavety. Cameron was skilful but lightweight, Welsh made a slow start but ultimately proved to be a good signing and Lavety, who was embarrassingly overweight on arrival, succumbed to a mystery virus within a few weeks of joining up at Easter Road.

Such was the intensity of feeling about our manager at this time that the fanzine was devoting most of its space to debates about his continued tenure in his post. Most of the boys were unequivocal. They were firmly of the opinion that 'Miller must go.' I was less sure. I think my mindset at the time is summed up by two articles I wrote. One was called 'Should he Stay or Should he Go? – The Case for and against Alex Miller.' I followed this up with another piece called 'Making my mind up on Miller.'

When Miller signed forty-year-old Ray Wilkins to make square passes in midfield, this was seen as a clear sign of lack of ambition and the pressure grew for a change at the top. Incredibly, Gerry McNee on *Scotsport* proclaimed that Miller was 'too big for a club like Hibs.' In Wilkins' debut, Hibs struggled to beat Raith Rovers 1–0 at home. The team was set up defensively and there was a real feeling of déjà vu for those of us who remembered the manager's early days. The signing of Wilkins finally convinced me that it was time for a change at the top. Eventually Miller resigned. I was working with groups of pupils at school when the news broke. My secretary came into the classroom and said, 'Your son's just phoned to ask me to tell you that somebody called Alex Miller has resigned. I don't know who he is but it sounds important!'

It was very important. A significant period in Hibs history had come to an end. A manager who had arrived to a lukewarm welcome had remained in post for almost ten years. After Hugh Shaw, he was Hibs' second longest-serving manager since the Second World War. He had outlasted Eddie Turnbull and achieved a reign which was more than twice as long as the combined tenures of Bertie Auld, Pat Stanton and John Blackley. Chairman Douglas Cromb had always been Miller's strongest supporter. Now he was broken-hearted at the departure of his blue-eyed boy. Cromb blamed certain sections of the Hibs support for hounding their manager out. That was simply not true. Alex Miller's tenure had run its course. He had had his successes but also his disasters and he had certainly had a more than fair crack of the managerial whip. Despite his constant claims to be so, I am not sure that he really was a winner. There again maybe he was. He is rumoured to have received a healthy pay-off when he left Hibs. His next manager's job was at Aberdeen. He failed there and was apparently healthily reimbursed for doing so. Next, he was an assistant to Rafa Benitez at Liverpool and acquired a Champions League medal. He was regularly seen on television seated next to the Spaniard on the bench looking older but no less tense or sober-sided. I am sure that his remuneration at Anfield was not insignificant. Alex Miller may or may not be a winner but he is undeniably a survivor.

13

THE DUFF WITH THE SMOOTH

Douglas Cromb asked Alex Miller's assistant Jocky Scott to take charge on a temporary basis after Miller's resignation. Scott's first match was a home game against Rangers. Hibs managed to win 2–1. I don't think that Hibs generally carry much luck and I can't remember coming home from too many of our games thinking 'We were lucky to win today.' This day, however, saw us have all the good fortune in the world. We made two chances and took them both. Rangers created a myriad opportunities and scorned all but one of them. Rangers even managed to miss a twice-taken Brian Laudrup penalty. Jim Leighton made a brilliant save from the Dane's first effort. The referee decided that Leighton had moved too early and offered Laudrup a second attempt. Leighton again made a tremendous save.

That was a good Saturday night, with a victory over the team which was then by far the best in Scotland to celebrate and the prospect of an exciting new manager to ponder. The feel-good factor was well and truly removed next day when the press reported Hibs' chairman as saying that Jocky Scott had done his chances of becoming Hibs Manager on a long-term basis no harm by achieving such an excellent result in his first game in charge. The following Saturday, we drew

1–1 at Motherwell and Cromb had seen enough. He appointed Jocky Scott as Manager for 'an indefinite period' and said that Scott would have money to spend. This was a classic piece of misguided and muddled thinking. Hibs fans had looked forward to a new and fresh start. Instead we had been given more of the same. We should have had promise followed by permanence, instead we had been given continued dullness coupled with uncertainty.

Scott wasted no time in spending the money which he had been promised. He brought in three thirty-somethings. The first arrival was an ageing full back in Rab Shannon. He followed this by signing Brian Grant who had lost his place in the Aberdeen midfield and completed his £400,000 spending spree by securing John Hughes from Celtic. Hughes was the only member of this trio of soccer senior citizens whose acquisition was welcomed by the fans. Sadly he spent most of the season injured or suspended. Shannon and Grant turned out to be exactly the type of ineffective journeymen we had expected them to be. Scott was managing in a utilitarian manner. The team was long on perspiration and short on inspiration and the manager struck some as being no more than a clone of his predecessor.

On the last Saturday in December, Scott produced one of his better results when he managed to return from Pittodrie with a point after a 1–1 draw. It did him no good. Two days later he was sacked. With as much haste and as little logic as he had been installed, 'Jocky the Janny' as the Hibs fanzine had nicknamed him, was summarily removed from his post. He reacted with typical ire and it's fair to say that he did not accept his dismissal graciously. He was replaced by the Dundee manager Jim Duffy who was welcomed with some enthusiasm by the fans. This enthusiasm was not unlimited and owed more to the fact that Duffy was not Alex Miller or Jocky Scott than any conviction on the part of the fans that he was going to be a roaring success. The new manager arrived for his initial press conference in Tom Farmer's Kwik Fit helicopter but he wasn't a high flyer for long.

Duffy's first match was the New Year derby against Hearts at Easter Road and he got off to the worst possible start by losing 4–0. Like Scott before him, he was presented with a transfer kitty and he made even worse use of Hibs' precious money than his predecessor had done. He raided the First Division for players like David Elliot, Jamie McQuilken, Paul Tosh, Lee Power and Shaun Dennis. Duffy's first few months at the helm were a constant battle against relegation. In the end we survived in a two legged play-off decider against Airdrie thanks to an inspired performance by Darren Jackson in the second match at Broadwood.

On the night before the first play-off match, a big group of us from the fanzine editorial committee went out for an Italian meal and a few drinks. I am not sure how it started but we convinced the waitress who was serving our table that we were the Hibs team and we were hitting the town the night before a vital match. Despite the fact that we ranged in age from twenty-five to fifty and that some of our physiques were more athletic than others, we had her believing our story. She had her doubts though because she kept staring across at us with a quizzical look on her face. Eventually she came back to our table and declared 'You're no fitba players!' 'Why do you say that?' we asked her. She pointed at the only one of our number who wasn't clean-shaven and said, 'because one of you has got a beard and fitba players dinnae have beards.' We didn't mention George Best to her.

By the time of the play-offs, John Hughes was fit at last and really it was just as well. Of all teams to face in this end of season nail biting nightmare, we had come up against the club which was our long-term nemesis – Airdrie. We scraped through the first game at Easter Road 1–0 despite having Gordon Hunter sent off. The second leg at Broadwood Stadium in Cumbernauld was held the following Thursday. Margaret and I had been reading Alan Lugton's first book, *The Making of Hibernian*, about the early years of Hibs. We had been particularly taken with the sections on Canon Edward Hannon, the saintly and inspiring parish priest of St Patrick's Church in the Cowgate who along with Michael Whelehan, a distant relative of Pat Stanton, had been instrumental in the formation of Hibs. We were very tense about the possible outcome of the play-off second leg and on the Monday holiday before this match, we took a trip to Grange Cemetery to visit the Canon's grave. We found it with some difficulty. It was a large but unprepossessing monument to a man without whom Hibernian Football Club would not exist. We spent a few peaceful minutes paying our respects then left, feeling much more at peace with the world and now confident that every-thing at Broadwood would be just fine.

So it proved – eventually! Within ninety seconds, the hapless McQuilken gifted Airdrie a goal. Things almost got worse. The referee was Willie Young and this idiosyncratic official chose this occasion for one of his most eccentric performances. After thirty-five minutes, he awarded Airdrie a highly debatable penalty. Thankfully Steve Cooper sent the ball high over the bar. Before he was finished, Young was to award three more penalties, send two players off and produce his yellow card on numerous occasions. He didn't get many things right but fortunately in the second half, Hibs did. We scored four goals after the break. Darren Jackson coolly converted two penalties under intense pressure, Paul Tosh bundled home a rebound after originally missing a simple one on one and Keith Wright in his last game for Hibs scored his last goal with a trademark header. In the end, we won 4–2 and sighs of relief were breathed all round. John Hughes and Brian Welsh who had improved hugely as the season had progressed were immense in the play-offs and we owed our survival in large part to their character and confidence in these final vital matches.

After the match, as we sat on our supporters coach in the packed Broadwood car park waiting for our turn to move out, we saw Paul Tosh emerge from the players' entrance. He was with two extremely attractive ladies who looked quite alike. Most of us assumed that one of the girls was Tosh's wife and the other was her sister. One of our number thought differently. Norrie Fraser, who, like many other fans, had been scathing about Tosh's performances since his move from Dundee, couldn't believe that someone, who he considered to be less than impressive, was in the fortunate position of being in the company of two good-looking women. 'How has he got two birds?' wailed Norrie. 'He's hopeless!'

He was not Hibs' class and the same could be said of quite a few of his team mates but Hibs had at least survived in the top flight. The travelling party which left Cumbernauld reflected on a campaign of three managers, two play-offs and one season-long disappointment. I wrote a fanzine article called 'All there is to tell about the Season from Hell' and that title pretty much summed up season 1996–97 for Hibs and their supporters.

As we drove home from Easter Road later that evening, having picked up our car from where we had left it when we had joined our coach at the ground, we passed Lochend Park. There was a crowd of people standing around at the park gates. Police cars, fire appliances and an ambulance were also in evidence. We drove on thinking that there had been some sort of incident but not giving too much consideration to what might have happened. The next morning, the previous evening's events at the park came much closer to home for us. It transpired that a teenage boy who had been playing on a home-made raft in the park had drowned in a tragic accident. Football and relegation play-off matches suddenly seemed a lot less important.

After the travails of the end-of-season relegation dogfight in which they had been engaged a couple of short months earlier, season 1997–98 started amazingly for Hibs. Jim Duffy had signed thirty-four-year-old Chic Charnley as part of the fight for survival. Charnley had always been a gifted play-maker but he had also always been troubled by a fiery temperament. He had missed the play-offs and the matches preceding them due to a five-match suspension but now he was back and firing on all cylinders. The season's opener was against Celtic at Easter Road. The Hibs team had a fresh look to it. Jim Leighton had returned to Aberdeen after giving Hibs four years of sterling service. I genuinely believe Leighton to be the best and most consistent Hibs goalkeeper it has been my pleasure to watch. His one weakness was his kicking, but otherwise he was the complete custodian and time and again he earned Hibs points by his brilliance. To replace Jim, Hibs had signed Icelandic goalkeeper Ólafur Gottskálksson for a sizeable fee. Olly the Goalie was not to prove himself a worthy successor to the man he replaced. Another man to have left Hibs in the summer was Darren Jackson. Celtic had paid Hibs £800,000 for the gifted Jacko and there was no doubt that he would also be sorely missed. Jackson had given Hibs his heart and soul for five years. He was that rare phenomenon – a supremely skilled player with a high work rate. No Hibs fan grudged Darren his big move. We were far too appreciative of his contribution to the club to do that. Jim Duffy had splashed out around £400,000 on former Raith

Rovers striker Stevie Crawford to fill the gaping hole in attack left by Jackson. Our manager had also brought in left back Jean-Marc Boco from Benin. With his flamboyant attacking style of play and flowing dreadlocks, Boco soon became a firm favourite with the fans who, in true Leith style, took the liberty of abbreviating his Christian names to the somewhat more prosaic appellation of 'Jimmy.' Duffy's final summer signing was the mercurial but talented Trinidadian winger Tony Rougier.

Hibs ripped into Celtic from the first whistle, sustained this level of commitment for the whole match and achieved a memorable 2–1 win. Charnley provided a virtuoso performance. He pulled all the strings and twice even came close to scoring from the halfway line. He was not to be denied however. A certain Henrik Larsson was making his Celtic debut and, on this occasion, he fell short of the sublime standards which he was to set in the seasons ahead. He came on as a late substitute and his only act of note was to misplace a pass straight to Charnley thirty yards from goal. The bold Chico did not hesitate. He swung his gifted left boot and fired a spectacular shot into the Celtic net. Game, set and match to Hibs. This was Margaret's mum's seventy-fifth birthday and the whole family got together at her brother's barbecue for a happy gathering after the match. The sun shone, the food tasted great, the drinks flowed and the woman who had not entered Easter Road until her sixty-ninth year was happy to join in the celebrations like the true Hibee she had now become.

Charnley continued his rich vein of form in the following weeks. He seemed intent on scoring from the centre circle. The closest I had seen anyone come to doing this before was Pelé's famous effort against Czechoslovakia in the 1970 World Cup. On that occasion, the great Brazilian's shot had flown through the rarefied Mexican air only to miss the target by inches. In a League Cup match against Stenhousemuir, Charnley achieved his ambition when he actually managed to lob the goalkeeper from inside his own half. Amazingly, Pat McGinlay replicated this feat against Kilmarnock in the league a couple of weeks later. I had watched Hibs for forty years and never seen anyone score from halfway. Now I had seen this feat achieved twice in a matter of weeks. Talking of Pelé, Charnley was playing so well at this time that the fanzine editors decided to go with a tongue in cheek cover in their next edition comparing the gallus Glaswegian with the South American superstar. Their biggest problem was whether to go with a photograph of Charnley captioned 'The White Pelé' or to run with a picture of the great man himself under the caption 'The Black Charnley.'

Hibs' coruscating start to the season couldn't last and it didn't. The squandering of a two goal home lead to Rangers burst our bubble and by Christmas Duffy's team was staring relegation in the face. I had celebrated my fiftieth birthday in November 1997. Hibs were playing Motherwell at Easter Road that day and of course the whole family was out in force hoping to see dad's milestone marked by a home win. It looked like happening too. Despite performing poorly, Hibs were holding on to a 1–0 lead as the game entered its final moments. Enter Olly Gottskálksson. The goalkeeper had already demonstrated his fallibility on a number of occasions but this time he surpassed himself. With the game and the points in the bag, he spilled a harmless, straight shot into the path of Owen Coyle who gratefully accepted the gift to deprive Hibs of two points and spoil my birthday.

Seconds later, the full time whistle sounded and the crowd burst into an angry chorus of 'Olly, Olly get to F***.' The big Icelander clearly thought that the supporters were singing his praises as he embarked on a Budgie style lap of honour down the length of the east terracing, acclaiming the fans who were simultaneously castigating him in language which was less than parliamentary. If you hadn't laughed, you would have cried. Jim Duffy had now added former Celtic striker and current media pundit Andy Walker to his cast of thousands. Walker scored twice, on debut in a 2–2 home draw with Aberdeen and then came up with another vital goal at Tynecastle on New Year's Day as Hibs fought back from being two goals down to draw with Hearts. Ever since we beat Hearts 7–0, I have feared that our greatest rivals will one day turn the tables on us and reverse that score line. I always consider that this is more likely to occur at Tynecastle. This day, Hearts scored two early goals and were in complete control. I truly feared the worst. Chris Reid was in goal and had one of his best ever games for Hibs. A combination of Chris' great saves and second half strikes from Walker and Pat McGinlay gave Hibs the unlikeliest of points.

The great escape at Tynecastle served only as a temporary reprieve however. Charnley was now out of favour with his manager and Jim Duffy's selections and tactics became ever more muddled and ever less successful. A shambolic home loss in the Scottish Cup to Raith Rovers was followed shortly afterwards by a heavy league defeat at Motherwell. This was too much for the fans and also enough for the Hibs board. Duffy's short but sorry tenure was terminated and in came Alex McLeish from Motherwell. It was a big ask for Big Eck to keep Hibs up. He signed a reliable goalkeeper in Bryan Gunn and a neat midfielder in Justin Skinner and performances and results began to improve.

As the relegation battle raged McLeish took Hibs to Parkhead for a vital game. He used the mind games techniques which he had learnt from his former mentor Sir Alex Ferguson to put the spotlight on the referee before the match.

It worked as the referee turned down a very strong Celtic penalty claim early in the game. He also got his players led by captain John Hughes to respond to the Celtic huddle by confronting the Celtic team with a Hibee Haka. That also worked because we got a valuable point from a 0–0 draw.

Our new manager also inspired Hibs to a magnificent victory over Hearts at Easter Road on a snowy day in April. Hearts were flying high at that time but were well beaten through great goals from Barry Lavety and Kevin Harper. This set the standard for derby matches during Alex McLeish's reign. He won far more than he lost and established a definite psychological advantage over our city rivals. However, despite McLeish's great efforts, Hibs were unable to beat the drop. A home defeat to Dundee United sealed our fate and a calamitous campaign ended in the ultimate humiliation. Season 1998–99 would see the launch of a new elite Scottish top league called the Scottish Premier League (SPL). Sadly and embarrassingly when the new, highly acclaimed SPL made its much-heralded bow, the once mighty Edinburgh Hibernian would be languishing within the lower reaches of the country's football echelons, keeping company with the likes of Stranraer and Clydebank in the First Division.

The 'Hibee Haka' got another outing during the close season. The Hibs fanzine entered a team for the Scottish fanzine seven-a-side championship at Forthbank in Stirling. We did well and reached the final where we lost to a Cowdenbeath team which contained more than a few 'ringers', but the highlight was the quarter-final clash with Hearts. When the teams lined up before kick-off, we produced our version of the Hibee Haka for our Jambo opponents. I don't know whether they were intimidated or bemused but we managed to beat them in a ferociously competitive contest which was as close as any of us would ever get to representing Hibs in a derby match.

After more than a few drinks in the Forthbank bar after the final, we piled into our minibus to head for home. As we headed through the west of Edinburgh en route for the city centre, one or two members of our team were overtaken by a very strident call of nature. Coincidentally we were passing close to Gorgie at the time. In no time at all, the driver had been prevailed upon to stop outside Tynecastle and a large group of Hibees piled off the bus and ceremonially relieved themselves against the gates of the Hearts stadium. Some of the more cautious members of our company, myself included, stayed on the bus and kept a low profile. Having done their deed, the roaring boys came back on board, described what had happened as one of their proudest moments and burst into a song which recalled the 7–0 beating of Hearts on New Year's Day 1973.

14

RESPECTABILITY RESTORED

Starting season 1998–99 in the First Division was an un-
thinkable position for a club of Hibs' size and stature. What
we had to remember, though, was that we did not find
ourselves in the position we were in by accident. Over the
course of Alex Miller's final year and during the reigns of
Jocky Scott and Jim Duffy, the quality of our playing staff had
markedly declined. Our then Chairman Tom O'Malley promised us fans that playing in the First Division would be a
'great adventure.' When he made this remark, he was roundly
mocked. However, ultimately, if not initially, he was to be
proved absolutely correct. Most fans kept the faith and bought
their season tickets as usual. The Brack family was no
exception. We all hoped that our stay in the lower leagues
would be for one season only but we were also aware that
for this to happen, Alex McLeish would have to take drastic
action. And take drastic action he certainly did. In the summer
and autumn of 1998 McLeish embarked upon a turnover of
players which made Barry Fry's transfer policy seem cautious.
Out went the dead wood and in came a procession of new
signings.

Big Eck's first forays into the market were not entirely
successful. Players like Barry Prendeville, Peter Guggi, Klaus
Dietrich, Paul Holsgrove and Stuart Lovell all came in and

made little or no impression. The team's early performances were not much better. We did win our first match which was an away fixture against Morton on a Wednesday evening. We decided to mark this significant, if inauspicious, occasion by travelling through to the game as a family. The journey to Greenock was remarkably straightforward as we were able to leave the motorway and park close to the ground with great ease. We even had time to visit a local restaurant and sample a sumptuous fish tea before making our way to the ground. It seemed that lots of Hibs fans had decided that the team needed their support and had turned out in numbers to provide the required backing. Morton raised their game, as we expected, and made life difficult for Hibs. There was a happy ending though when Barry Lavety, who was still on the scene, scored a fine goal in added time to secure a late win.

Things then took a turn for the worse. Our first home match was against Stranraer, a team who usually have the epithet 'lowly' attached to them. Incredibly and outrageously, we lost 2–1. I had never thought that I would find myself leaving Easter Road after a home defeat to Stranraer but here I was undergoing that very experience. I can tell you that it did not feel good. However, I had to push my dejection to one side. Our oldest son Patrick had just got engaged. Patrick's fiancée Sharon and her mother were coming to us for dinner that Saturday evening so Margaret and I had to rush home, put the finishing touches to the meal which Margaret had prepared earlier, place smiles on our faces and welcome and entertain our guests. A further complication was that Dominic had had a number of wisdom teeth removed that morning. This is a major and painful procedure and the dental consultant had insisted on providing our son with a cocktail of medication which would kill the pain, keep infection at bay and allow him to have some sleep. He was not to eat solid food for twenty-four hours. When Sharon and her mum – also Margaret – arrived, Dominic was in a sedated sleep upstairs. As the meal unfolded in a pleasant and relaxed fashion, our new in-laws-to-be received a surprise visit from the dental patient. Clearly affected by his medication, looking sleepy and dishev-elled and sporting a grossly-swollen cheek, our number-two son joined the dinner party. He stated that he was ravenously hungry and insisted on having something to eat. Since he had to observe the no solids advice which he had been given, Dominic sat down to a plate of baked beans that made an incongruous contrast with the gourmet food with which Margaret had served the rest of us. Sharon and Margaret thought that this was highly amusing. They were also highly entertained by Dominic's conversation, which lacked nothing in garrulousness but everything in coherence. The drugs which he had taken may not have made him delirious but they had certainly made him disorientated. The impromptu cabaret act provided by the man with no wisdom teeth ensured that a day, which had begun disappointingly, ended happily.

The season did not improve. Our next away trip took us to Boghead to play Clydebank. To say that the facilities at this ground (you most certainly couldn't call it a stadium) were basic would be an understatement. Hibs' football that day was also of low quality. In injury time at the end of the match, Stevie Crawford gave Hibs an undeserved lead. Just as I was turning to warn everyone around me to take nothing for granted because this was Hibs we were dealing with, Clydebank equalised. If I had felt down after the Stranraer defeat, which most of us had optimistically put down to a blip, I was utterly depressed after this. In the car coming back, we asked ourselves why we were travelling long distances and paying good money to go to places like this and watch football of the lowest common denominator variety. Were we displaying faithful support or were we exhibiting blind loyalty? It certainly felt much more like the latter. What was supposed to be a 'great adventure' was turning into an awful nightmare. There was more disappointment when we lost to St Mirren at Paisley. Hibs were in the process of receiving a rude awakening. There were some competitive teams in the First Division, not least Airdrie, St Mirren and Falkirk. Every team in the league had Hibs in their sights. There were going to be no easy games and, if the early indications were anything to go by, we shouldn't expect any favours from referees either.

At this pivotal point of the season, our manager took a crucial hand. He signed Mixu Paatelainen from Wolverhampton Wanderers for £75,000 and Mixu proved to be the initial catalyst for recovery. Big, strong and equipped with experience, know-how and not a little ability, the big Finn brought a new dimension to the team. He also brought an aura of confidence and determination which had a positive impact upon his colleagues. McLeish next produced a masterstroke. He had just sold the talented, but underachieving, Tony Rougier to Reading. Before he left, Tony, casual as always, happened to mention that a player he had played with in the Trinidad and Tobago team was available and that he might be interested in coming to Hibs. The player was none other than Russell Latapy. McLeish invited him to Easter Road so that he could 'take a look at him.' One look was enough. Big Eck had found a wee gem and wasted no time in signing him up. Latapy made his debut at Ayr as autumn turned to winter. Hibs, 3–1 down with seven minutes to go, fought back to draw 3–3 with the help of two goals from John Hughes. This was the turning point. The team began to hit form. Latapy was exactly the sort of gifted playmaker which we had lacked and his influence was immediate and significant. Stuart Lovell, who had arrived as a striker and struggled to score, had now switched to midfield and was regularly on target. The ever-green Pat McGinlay was still going strong nearly ten years after joining Hibs and was doing what he had done all his career, providing a steady stream of goals from the middle of the park. The Rougier money had been used to sign Paul Hartley from Raith Rovers. Hartley at that time was a short-haired, clean-shaven, tricky winger. He was to play a significant part in Hibs' promotion push and no one then would have envisaged his later move to Hearts or the level of misery which he would inflict on Hibs on a regular basis. Two competent full backs in Derek Collins and Paul Lovering were also added to the mix and they joined Shaun Dennis and John Hughes in a defence which was becoming more miserly by the week. Up front Mixu and Stevie Crawford's contrasting styles complemented each other well.

Hibs had a cluster of five matches coming up starting in the pre-Christmas period and running through to just after New Year. Without making a fuss or making their intentions public, Alex McLeish and his players set themselves a target of winning all five games. To their credit, they achieved this aim and did so in some style. The two festive fixtures at Easter Road proved particularly memorable. On Boxing Day and 2 January respectively, Hibs comfortably disposed of Ayr United and Raith Rovers in front of near capacity crowds. The football flowed, the goals came in abundance. There was a feel-good factor in the packed stadium and Hibs' title push was well and truly up and running. This season now did indeed feel like a great adventure and it was becoming greater by the week. The momentum gathered over the turn of the year proved unstoppable and we embarked on a twenty-five match unbeaten run.

It was now clear that the First Division Championship would be won by either Falkirk or Hibs. The Brockville club, as they were then, had a strong squad and a formidable home record, and were determined to fight Hibs every step of the way for promotion. The crunch clash between the teams came in February. The weather that day could only be accurately described by one word – 'dreich.' Heavy cloud and rain hung over Falkirk's fortress of a ground as we Hibees made our way into what we knew would be a seminal contest. Prior to the match, McLeish had pulled another rabbit out of the hat and this time, it was a very big bunny indeed. To our amazement and delight, Hibs had signed the great Franck Sauzée. We all knew Sauzée through his European Cup-winning exploits with Marseille and his distinguished international career with France. He was in his thirties now and winding down his career but had responded to the overtures of Hibs' boss, whom he knew through international football, and had agreed to come to Edinburgh. Sauzée must have wondered what he had let himself in for when he ran out at Brockville for his debut. The dilapidated stadium was closed on one side and jam-packed on the other three. It was virtually dark at three o'clock and Hibs were having to cope with an intimidating atmosphere and a referee whose decisions were a constant source of puzzlement.

Kevin Toner, son of former Hibs centre half Willie Toner, was the man in the middle and, for most of the match, he was in the middle of controversy of his own making. He sent off Paul Hartley (the previous time he had officiated in a Hibs match, he had shown the red card to Mixu Paatelainen) and awarded Falkirk a never-ending stream of free kicks for offences which, to most of those watching, were less than obvious. Despite this, Hartley, not long before his dismissal, had put Hibs ahead by fastening on to an exquisite Latapy pass and sliding the ball low past the goalkeeper's right hand. Hibs' ten men fought hard in the second half but were forced to concede an equaliser when, from yet another Falkirk free kick on the edge of our penalty area, Scott Crabbe struck the bar and Marino Keith netted the rebound. The large Hibs support now got behind their team and Sauzée, who to this point had looked classy but short of match fitness, took a decisive hand. Making a crossfield run thirty-five yards from goal, he completely deceived the Falkirk defenders by sublimely back-heeling the ball into the path of Derek Collins. The right back, not a man noted for prolific goal scoring, let fly with a first-time shot which deflected into the Falkirk net. This goal, from an unlikely source, sealed a famous victory and there would be no stopping Hibs now. Going into the ground before the match, I had bumped into Pat Stanton and his family. Pat had stressed how difficult a game was in prospect and had reminded us that even in the days of Turnbull's Tornadoes, Hibs had quite often left Brockville without points. On this occasion though, all three points were safely garnered and the title was now well and truly in Hibs' sights.

Promotion and the championship were clinched against Hamilton Academicals at Firhill on Saturday, 3 April. Russell Latapy again provided the inspiration. The little magician scored two magnificent goals and controlled the game. Latapy was so good (despite a missed penalty which deprived him of a well deserved hat-trick) that the *Daily Record* compared him with Paul Gascoigne and Brian Laudrup. In terms of natural talent, they were not far wrong. Russell's goals and a compact performance from his team mates were enough to achieve a comfortable 2–0 win. The team ran to their fans at the end and the massive Hibs following responded with songs and chants which acclaimed the team's success over a testing but triumphant season. As the players left the field, the Brack family joined the rest of the Hibs fans spilling on to the pitch to celebrate with them. Lisa, now twenty-five, was as fanatical as ever. Paul Hartley had become a particular favourite of hers and she congratulated him on his performance as she passed him. After Hartley joined Hearts, Lisa took tremendous stick from her brothers for what they described as her 'Hartley worship.' Her embarrassment was compounded by the fact that she was now married and her husband Derrick, a lifelong Jambo and an all-round good guy, took gentle pleasure from winding her up every time the now bearded and long-haired Hartley appeared on screen in a televised match. 'There's your man Hartley', Derrick would say. It is fair to say that Lisa did not find such banter the least bit amusing.

The season ended on a tremendous high. The First Division Championship trophy was presented after the final game against Hibs' nearest challengers Falkirk. The Bairns came to Easter Road determined to spoil our party but didn't come close to succeeding. They were awarded an early and highly debatable penalty but Olly Gottskálksson rose to the occasion by diving to his right and pushing Scott Crabbe's spot kick to safety. After that Hibs didn't look back. Franck Sauzée, whose form had improved with every passing week as his fitness levels had increased, struck a stunning free kick from twenty-five yards to give us the lead, and Paul Hartley nipped in for a neatly headed goal early in the second half. The final whistle was the signal for mass celebrations among the sell out crowd. John Hughes proudly held the trophy aloft and Alex McLeish addressed the fans. Acknowledging that the supporters could have turned against the team earlier in the season and stressing how important their continued loyalty had been, he pledged his immediate future to Hibs. Press speculation had linked McLeish with a move north to manage Aberdeen. Now he roared to the fans, 'I want you all back here again next season and I can promise you that I will be here with you.'

This was great news as our manager had done a tremendous job. So too had the board of directors who had made funds available when times were tough, and by doing so had enabled the team to move to a higher level. This had ensured that the 'great adventure' was both successful and shortlived. It had been great to watch winning football in front of packed houses at Easter Road. It had also been enjoyable to travel to away grounds and outnumber the home supporters. It gave us an inkling of what it must be like for Old Firm fans in the top league week in, week out. The main thing though was to win promotion in one season and to return Hibs to the top flight where they belonged. When we had returned to the Premier League in 1981, I had been mildy embarrassed by the celebrations as I knew that the team we had then would struggle against better opposition and that we could only look forward to watching a fight for survival. This time it was different. Big Eck's team had class and the capacity to succeed in the SPL. Being the sentimental character that I am, I shed a quiet tear or two as I watched the title-winning party unfold. We were back and the new season was a genuinely exciting prospect which for me at least couldn't come quickly enough.

The close season flew by and, as always, Alex McLeish was active in the transfer market. During the previous season's campaign, the players' entrance at Easter Road had resembled a revolving door as players came and went with bewildering frequency. McLeish's transactions in the summer of 1999 were more restrained. He brought in Tom Smith from Clydebank, goalkeeper Nick Colgan from Chelsea, a rugged centre half from Germany in Matthias Jack and another

German, the Fulham centre forward Dirk Lehmann. Smith, a small combative player with a shock of black hair had impressed when playing against Hibs in the First Division while Colgan had been at Chelsea for some time but had never managed a first team appearance. There was no doubt however that the goalkeeper in possession, Olly Gottskálksson, although capable of occasional brilliance, was not a man to rely on for the long-term. Jack came with a fiery reputation but as a footballer, he was an unknown quantity. Lehmann had had his moments for Kevin Keegan's Fulham but he hadn't been a prolific scorer. He hadn't been offered a new contract either.

The fixtures computer presented Hibs with an opening match against Motherwell at Easter Road. Guarding the Motherwell goal was none other than old Hibs favourite Andy Goram. Since leaving Hibs, Goram had starred for Rangers and Scotland and managed to make almost as many headlines on the front pages of the newspapers as he had created in the sports sections at the back. Despite his penchant for extra-curricular activities, 'The Goalie' had achieved longevity in his career and was still a goalkeeper to be reckoned with. A bumper crowd rolled up on a beautiful day to welcome Hibs back to the big time. As we fans gathered in the ground, there was a palpable air of excitement and anticipation. Someone asked me what I was hoping for in the season ahead. My answer was to say that I wanted my team to be consistent, competitive and occasionally captivating. That turned out to be a not too inaccurate summary of the months which followed.

This first game back in the higher footballing echelons reminded us of all we had been missing over the previous twelve months. Played at a high tempo, in a packed stadium, the game flowed from end to end and finished as a 2–2 draw.

Hibs could, and should, have won. Goram made some excellent saves and we missed a host of chances. Lehmann marked his debut with an impressive double. This was deceptive though. He proved to be a player who always worked hard and occasionally scored excellent goals but he was not the out-and-out goal scorer that Alex McLeish had been looking for.

Our next game at Dundee was televised live on Sky Television and was even more exciting than the Motherwell game. This time we won 4–3 with Kenny Miller securing the points with an excellent goal in the last minute. A couple of years earlier I had attended a Hibs Youth Cup match with the intention of identifying 'stars of the future.' Hibs had won 8–1 and centre forward John Martin had scored four goals. Stuart McCaffrey at the back had strolled through the game in imperious fashion. I had written an article for the fanzine extolling the virtues of these two players. My article had not pinpointed Kenny Miller as a future prospect though. This was because Miller had displayed splendid lead-up work during the match but had failed to convert any of the chances which he had created for himself. I had concluded that Miller was a clever, pacy, industrious player who wasn't deadly enough in front of goal. This evaluation may have been borne out since then but there can be no denying that Miller has enjoyed a very successful career. Neither Martin nor McCaffrey made the big time. Miller most certainly did.

Alex McLeish soon had his chequebook out again. He signed Grant Brebner from Reading for £200,000. Brebner, a lifelong Hibs fan from Midlothian, had been loaned to Hibs by Manchester United in McLeish's early months at the club, to support our unsuccessful struggle against relegation. He had impressed everyone by his neat, thoughtful midfield play. Alex Ferguson made it clear that he would not stand in

Brebner's way if he wanted to make his move permanent, a prospect which delighted all Hibs fans, but the player decided instead on a move to Reading. This really disappointed us Hibees who couldn't understand why someone would choose not to sign for a club he professed to love when he was offered the opportunity to do so. Our feelings, if understandable at the time, now seem naive. Clearly, Brebner had chosen Reading purely for financial reasons. As we all now know only too well, in the world of football transfers when it comes down to a choice between sentiment and hard cash, there is only one winner and that winner is not sentiment. Brebner had initially done well at Reading but he was now ready to come home. While resentment at his original decision still lingered with a section of the Hibs support, most of us were delighted to see such a talented player committing himself, albeit belatedly, to the Hibernian cause.

Another bonus of being back in the big time was that derby matches against Hearts were once more on the fixture schedule. Hearts came to Easter Road in September and we Hibs fans faced this prospect with a mixture of excitement and trepidation. We wanted to play Hearts and beat them but the twenty-two games without a win sequence, which we had endured in contests for local bragging rights under Alex Miller, was still fresh enough in our memories to introduce an element of caution. In the event, we shouldn't have worried. Russell Latapy and Franck Sauzée had made a seamless transition from being the previous season's lower league main men to the current campaign's SPL superstars. Russell and Franck were class acts and revelled in the more competitive environment of the top league. There was no doubt that performing at a higher level was bringing out the considerable best in them. Russell gave Hibs a derby lead from the penalty spot but Hearts escaped with a flattering point when

Gottskálksson, who had played really well in goal, made a costly second-half error.

I think it is fair to say that Hibs supporters did not approach the next derby with a great deal of confidence. Hibs travelled to Tynecastle for the game which would be the last capital match-up of the twentieth century after defeats by both members of the Old Firm. Alex McLeish had been less than impressed with his players' performances at Ibrox and Parkhead. He had, in fact, branded them 'wimps.' Hearts had just received a massive injection of finance from the Scottish Media Group and their manager Jim Jefferies had already used some of this newly acquired capital to sign Antti Niemi, Fitzroy Simpson and Gordan Petric. However, the forebodings of manager and fans about the Millennium Derby were seriously misplaced. There was nothing remotely wimpish about the Hibs team which took the field on the evening of Sunday, 19 December 1999.

I was not there. I was with the rest of my family in the living room of Margaret's brother Terry seated in front of his television watching Sky's coverage of the match. After Wallace Mercer's abortive attempt to take over Hibs in 1990, I had vowed that I would never set foot inside Hearts' ground for a derby game ever again. On a point of principle, I would not allow a penny of my hard-earned money to find its way into Hearts coffers. My family shared my feelings on this matter so instead of being seated in the stand at Tynecastle, we were gathered in a front room in Portobello.

Every Hibs player was well and truly up for this match but no one was as highly motivated as the captain John Hughes. 'Yogi' had impressed upon his team mates before the game just how important victory in this fixture was to the club's supporters. He had reinforced this point in his own inimitable way as the players made their way out of the dressing rooms. What followed was a historic performance. Dirk Lehmann had been going through a lean spell and had actually lost his place up front to Kenny Miller. On this occasion, Alex McLeish opted for experience and, Lehmann, despite running a temperature on the morning of the game, rose from his sick bed to play. After twenty minutes, we were glad that Dirk had made the effort. Russell Latapy picked him out on the edge of the Hearts penalty area and he dispatched a sweetly struck shot past Niemi into the corner of the Hearts net. Terry's lounge erupted and his wife Pat, a Hearts sympathiser rather than supporter, quietly left the room to busy herself in another part of the house.

When Lehmann had first signed for Hibs, some fans had nicknamed him the 'porn star' on the flimsy premise that a recent film *Boogie Nights* had featured a porn king called Dirk Diggler. A father and son duo sat in front of us in the Famous Five Stand. The senior member of this family partnership looked like he was in his seventies and dressed accordingly. His normal match-day outfit was a cloth cap, anorak and muffler. His offspring was an altogether livelier character. During one match he shouted at Lehmann, 'Come on the porn star.' His father turned to him and said, 'What's a pop star doing playing for Hibs?' 'He's no a pop star. He's a porn star.' replied junior. The older man came back, 'What's a porn star?' His son shook his head and said, 'Dinnae worry, Dad. It's no something you really need to know.' On this December day however, Dirk Lehmann was performing like an authentic footballing star and his colleagues were doing likewise.

Seven minutes after Lehmann's goal, we witnessed an immortal Hibee moment. The great Franck Sauzée ran on to a mishit Steven Pressley clearance and from twenty-five yards out unleashed a bombshell of a shot which ripped past Niemi to double Hibs' lead. The shot was unstoppable and so was Sauzée. Frank turned on his heel and ran the full length of the field to celebrate his goal at the other end of the ground with the Hibs supporters in the McLeod Street Stand. As the players had danced and sung on the field at the First Division Championship celebrations in May, Sauzée had looked into the camera and shouted with great feeling 'Vive La France, Vive L'Ecosse, Vive Les Hibs!' Here was a man who had bought into the Hibernian culture in a very big way. The fans loved his play and they also loved his unmistakeable commitment to our club and all it stood for. His goal was memorable but his celebration was unforgettable.

In Portobello, the celebrations gathered momentum. We were surprised and delighted to be two goals ahead at half-time but knowing Hibs as we did, we were taking nothing for granted. The anticipated Hearts second half onslaught did not fully materialise. Nick Colgan, who by this time had displaced Gottskálksson as first choice goalkeeper, dealt admirably with everything the Jambos threw at him. In fact, Hibs, with Russell Latapy at his beguiling best, looked more likely to score and that is exactly what they did. Kenny Miller had come on to replace Lehmann and he fastened on to a Pat McGinlay header to draw Niemi from his goal and slot the ball past him with a composure which belied his teenage years.

Terry's son-in-law-to-be Kevin had been watching the game with us. Kevin was a dyed-in-the-wool Hearts fan and he had been happy to watch the match in Hibee company because he had been completely confident of victory. He had greeted Hibs' first goal by sitting motionless and expressionless as if nothing had happened. When Sauzée scored, Kevin looked at us leaping about and shook his head with an air of contempt. When Miller sealed victory, my son Patrick, now a twenty-seven-year-old married man, leapt from the sofa, slid across the floor on his knees and kissed the television screen. This uninhibited display of euphoria was too much for Kevin who rose from his chair and left the room and the house without uttering a word. Patrick had married into a Hearts supporting family but this had not diluted his passion for all things Hibernian in any way. His wife Sharon's three brothers were all regulars at Tynecastle. During the wedding speeches, Sharon's oldest brother Alex had presented Patrick with a Hearts top with 'Brack' printed on the back. This caused great hilarity amongst the guests of a maroon persuasion. Patrick's response was to pause, look the strip up and down and say, 'Thanks very much. If I ever run out of toilet paper, I will put it to good use.'

The Millennium derby had ended in a famous Hibs victory. After the game, Franck Sauzée was quick to praise the contribution made by our captain. Big Yogi had defended heroically throughout the ninety minutes of the game. He had also led the post-match celebrations in front of the Hibs support with his usual gusto. According to Sauzée though, his most important act had been the stirring talk he had delivered to his team prior to the match. Showing no little understanding of the nuances of the English language, Franck put it very succinctly indeed when he declared that Hibs had won the match in the tunnel.

Alex McLeish was proving himself a master of the art of winning derby games, a crucial skill which had seriously eluded his long time predecessor Alex Miller. When the sides met again in March at Easter Road, Big Eck wove his magic once more. Hibs went into the game on the back of a home win against Celtic in which Kenny Miller had scored a superb winning goal. However, we fell behind to an outstanding early goal from Darren Jackson who had now joined up at Tynecastle. Darren had scored many goals at Easter Road which had been rapturously received. This particular effort, despite its quality, was greeted in silence. That was as bad as things got for Hibs. Russell Latapy, who loved playing against Hearts, restored parity with a virtuoso counter of his own and then Franck Sauzée rose at the back post to loop a header past Niemi into the far corner of the net. In doing so, Franck clashed heads with a Hearts defender. This collision cost him four of his front teeth but he refused to leave the field and completed the match holding a blood-soaked handkerchief to his mouth. In showing such courage, our Gallic god proved that he was not only a player of significance but also a man of substance. Mixu Paatelainen, another Hibee who thrived on the derby atmosphere, added a third and conclusive goal five minutes from time. Hibs had now compiled a run of five derby matches without defeat under Alex McLeish. This may have fallen well short of Hearts' recent record in the fixture but it was a welcome turn of events nonetheless.

In early February 2000, Inverness Caley Thistle shocked the football world by knocking Celtic out of the Scottish Cup at Parkhead. On the same day, Margaret's family received earth shattering news of their own when their mum, Liz, was diagnosed as having terminal cancer. This indomitable lady had lost her husband at a tragically early age but had bravely got on with the business of supporting and enriching the lives of her five grown-up children, sixteen grandchildren and three great-grandchildren.

Hibs had qualified for the Scottish Cup semi-final against Aberdeen. To accommodate television coverage, the match took place at Hampden on a Sunday evening. By the time the game came round, Liz's condition had worsened. Margaret did not travel to the semi-final but stayed at her mum's bedside. She insisted that the rest of us should go as that is what her mum (and dad for that matter) would have wanted us to do.

We made the journey to the match but for obvious reasons we did not feel anything like the usual excitement and we weren't able to fully focus on the game. Russell Latapy scored a marvellous solo goal to put Hibs ahead in the second half. We began to realise that it was not going to be Hibs' night when Andy Dow, an ordinary player when at Hibs who would only use his left foot, equalised for the Dons with a block-buster of a right-foot volley. This was confirmed when Aberdeen scored a late winner. Once again massed ranks of Hibs supporters made their dejected way from the national stadium after their team had let them down by losing to an inferior team. As we stood in long queues for the train at Queen Street Station, our mood was bleak. When we got home our depression worsened as Margaret told us that her mum's health had deteriorated further. On Thursday, 13 April, Liz lost her courageous fight for life. Hibs' semi-final capitulation did not seem the least bit important to us as we reflected on the life and times of a 'bonny fechter' whose span of almost eighty years had come to an end.

That semi-final defeat convinced Alex McLeish that some of his players were not of the required standard. Derek Collins, who had gone into the game claiming that he had recovered from a hamstring injury, broke down again before half-time. McLeish moved him on. He also released John Hughes considering the Leither to have his best years behind him. This difficult but brave decision was probably right. Hibs' manager then determined to bring in a range of top quality players for season 2000–2001. However, before he got to work on identifying new signings, he made an important discovery about one of the players he already had.

Matthias Jack had struggled at centre half but in an end-of-season match at Parkhead, he played in midfield and was a revelation. Skilful for a big man, he proved to be a natural as a midfield anchorman and he was to play this role to perfection when the new season started. The Celtic game in which Jack piloted his new position ended in a 1–1 draw with Stuart Lovell scoring with a diving header for Hibs. I was there with three friends from the teaching profession – John Dames and Jim Langan, the former head teacher and depute head teacher of St Thomas' High School, and Kevin McCormick the principal teacher of guidance in the same school. John and Kevin are Celtic men through and through while Jim, like me, is a Hibee. We had inaugurated a tradition of going to Celtic Park together when Hibs were the visitors a few years earlier, Both John and Kevin had two season tickets each for the main stand and when Hibs were in town they were good enough to take Jim and me along as their guests. To that point, Hibs hadn't managed to secure victory in the games which we had attended but on that sunny spring day in the first year of the new millennium, there were clear indications that Alex McLeish was continuing to build a quality side and that good times might be just round the corner.

New players were certainly round the corner. McLeish had never been reticent in strengthening his squad and now he really went to town in the recruiting stakes. The defence was completely restructured. Two new centre backs came in in the shape of Gary Smith and Paul Fenwick and the left back that Hibs desperately required arrived in the shape of the tall, blond Dane Ulrik Laursen.

Smith had been an excellent player for Aberdeen before moving to the French club Rennes. He was now back in Scotland as a free agent and McLeish used his Pittodrie connections to secure his signature. Fenwick, a Canadian international, had been a calm presence in the Morton defence for a number of years and he brought much needed height to Hibs' central defence. The Dons' old boy network had proved effective again when Steve Archibald had tipped his former colleague off about Laursen. McLeish went over to Denmark to watch the left back in action. Within minutes, he knew that he had unearthed a gem. He described Laursen as 'an athlete who could play' and wasted no time in snapping him up.

The midfield was greatly enhanced by the signing of John O'Neil from St Johnstone. O'Neil had been a tireless and tricky wide player for the Perth club for a number of years but he was to show that he had hidden depths when he came to Easter Road where he adopted a central role. O'Neil's running power and passing ability proved the perfect complement for Jack's rugged artistry and their partnership freed up Russell Latapy to weave his intricate patterns closer to the opposition goal. McLeish also acquired a new striker in the shape of Frenchman Didier Agathe whose contract at Raith Rovers had expired. He clearly wasn't certain that Agathe was the right man for Hibs as he only signed him on a three-month deal. This was to prove a serious and expensive error.

The new season started at Tynecastle. Hibs fans were looking forward to seeing their new players in action. Initially they had problems identifying them as seven members of the team had shaved their heads before the game as part of a bonding exercise. They certainly gave Hearts a few hair-raising moments and Agathe, in particular, proved to be quite a handful for the home team's defenders. Unfortunately his finishing did not match his leading up work and he missed a couple of eminently convertible chances. Hearts were glad to escape with a goalless draw but they wouldn't be quite so fortunate a few months down the road.

There was nothing wrong with Agathe's finishing in Hibs next match. The team put in an exhilarating performance to beat Dundee 5–1 and the Frenchman, showing phenomenal pace and power and no little skill, scored two magnificent individual goals. Celtic manager Martin O'Neill was sitting in the Easter Road stand and obviously liked what he saw. The next day we discovered that Agathe had agreed to sign for Celtic when his short-term contract ran out. Hibs had no option but to accept a £50,000 bid and release him immediately. The only alternative would have been to keep a discontented player for two more months and then lose him without recompense. It wasn't like Alex McLeish to take a safety-first approach but on this occasion his caution cost Hibs dearly. O'Neill converted Agathe into a rampaging right back and the player gave Celtic great service both at home and in Europe. All we Hibs fans could do was to watch him on television and reflect that the skills which we were witnessing could have been on long-term display at Easter Road.

Our manager didn't let the grass grow under his feet. He replaced one French striker with another. In came David Zitelli. Zitelli was a friend of Franck Sauzée. He had attended Hibs First Division Championship celebrations as a guest of 'Le God.' Now he was available and happy to join up at Easter Road. We were just as happy to have him. Zitelli opened his account at McDiarmid Park on the day of my son Dominic's wedding. As the photographer organised an endless series of group and individual poses, we took turns to run to our cars in the hotel car park to check the Hibs score. Sauzée and Latapy added to the new striker's debut goal and Hibs achieved a stylish and comfortable victory which further enhanced a great family day. By now Sauzée was playing sweeper. He sat behind Smith and Fenwick and mopped up opposition attacks with panache and ease. He used his passing skills to initiate free flowing counter attacks and still managed to come up with the occasional goal from free kicks.

Zitelli was on target again in Hibs' next match at home to Rangers. His early strike was enough to ensure a 1–0 win which was much more comfortable than the narrow score line suggests. Hibs were really playing well now and we all looked forward to the next home match against Hearts. Dominic and his new wife Angie returned from their honeymoon in Spain on the day of the derby. They were tired and had spent most of their money. When they collected their car, they discovered that they had two punctures. After a visit to a tyre depot, their finances were even more severely depleted. Angie headed back to their new home in Fife and Dominic made his way to Easter Road in a less than cheerful frame of mind. His day, though, was to finish much more brightly than it had started because Hibs chose to make Sunday, 22 October 2000 an unforgettable occasion in the pantheon of Hibernian history.

The respective receptions accorded to the two teams as they came out for this seminal match were to prove prophetic. Hearts ran towards the Dunbar End to find it two-thirds empty. The Hearts fans obviously weren't confident in advance of this encounter. Hibs, in contrast, took the field to a standing ovation. It was the Gorgie team who scored first though. After only five minutes, one-time Hibee Gordon Durie, who had made his way to Tynecastle via Chelsea, Tottenham and Rangers, ignored the opprobrium which was being heaped upon him by his former supporters, to lay on a close-range goal for Andy Kirk.

Hibs stormed back. During the Alex McLeish reign, as players had joined and left Hibs with bewildering rapidity, Mixu Paatelainen had been a constant. The big Finn was never spectacular or particularly eye-catching but he was always dependable and consistently excellent. Tonight was to be Mixu's night. He headed home a corner from John O'Neil but referee Hugh Dallas surprised no one by chalking off the goal. Not to be deterred, Mixu had notched a double before half-time. He drove home a Latapy cross and then bundled a head-down from Ulrik Laursen over the line. At half-time, we felt confident. Hibs were playing well and were clearly the better team. We could only throw it away now. Hibs, as we know, are very capable of snatching defeat from the jaws of victory but this was not to be one of our exercises in self-destruction.

Quite the reverse in fact. In the second half, Hibs were irresistible. It was clear that, unlike some of us supporters, the likes of Sauzée, Latapy, Zitelli and Paatelainen had no apprehension where our greatest rivals were concerned. They indulged in feints and flicks and darts and dribbles and laid the Hearts defence to waste. The goals just kept coming. Latapy released Zitelli and David beat Niemi. Paatelainen completed a sweet move to notch a historic hat-trick and celebrated by turning a massive somersault. Never has sixteen stone of Scandinavian muscle moved with quite such agility and grace. O'Neil then scored the goal which his outstanding play had merited. He lashed an unsaveable shot high into the Hearts net from a Zitelli corner. Then came the goal of the game. All night, Russell Latapy had tormented the men in maroon. He had always reserved his best for derbies but on this occasion he had surpassed himself. He had run the game and run his opponents ragged. Now he played a sumptuous one-two with Paatelainen before firing a raging volley past Niemi from the tightest of angles. Two minutes from the end, Hibs switched off and Colin Cameron scored a second goal for Hearts. The fans had been calling for seven but they had to settle for 6–2. Nine years on, this score has a real ring to it and the match, which produced this remarkable result, has gone down in the annals of Easter Road folklore.

Latapy had declared before the match that he loved Hibs and their fans. He was becoming so immersed in the club, he said, that he was reading up on their history. On this particular evening, he had contributed his own chapter to that illustrious history. It was a night full of images. I can close my eyes and see them now. Mixu's supersonic somersault, Franck Sauzée carrying John O'Neil on his back after the little man's goal, the arrogance and insouciance of the Hibs players as they teased and tantalised their opponents and, most of all, the huge happiness written over every Hibee face as we fans left the ground on a cloud of euphoria and headed into the night to drink a toast to the men who had won 6–2.

My own celebrations were restrained but no less joyous for that. We headed for home, savoured a couple of malt whiskies and took some photographs to mark a momentous occasion. My favourite picture shows me with my scarf wrapped round my neck holding up five fingers of one hand and a solitary digit of the other. My hand signal displays the requisite numerical information but the look of pure pleasure on my face says it all.

When Hibs went to Tynecastle for the festive derby, we all feared the worst. Jim Jefferies had described the 6–2 defeat as 'the biggest disappointment of my managerial career.' We were sure that Hearts would be totally fired up for revenge and that Hibs would have to cope with a major backlash. It didn't happen that way. Hearts were ultra-motivated all right but Hibs, at that time, were simply a better football team. A fine goal from Stuart Lovell, who was now playing in an attacking right full back role, put Hibs ahead. Hearts fought back to gain a draw but Hibs should really have made their superiority count and won the match. Russell Latapy once again provided a master class in the art of the playmaker. He came close to scoring on a number of occasions and was generally too hot for Hearts to handle. What we didn't know at that time was that this would be Russell's last derby match.

By the time that the final Hearts game of the season came round, Hibs were in the Scottish Cup Final. We had been blessed with a series of favourable draws against lower league opposition. The only scare which we had experienced was at Forthbank against Stirling Albion. Driving through, the weather had been clear and pleasant until we had reached Grangemouth Oil Refinery. At this point a thick mist descended. By the time we reached Stirling, the fog was extremely dense. Surprisingly, referee John Rowbotham allowed the game to go ahead. Visibility was poor and so were Hibs. Albion by contrast were in full cup-underdog mode, scrapping for every ball and playing well above themselves. At 2–2 with twenty minutes left, the tie was finely balanced but at that point Hibs substitute Tam McManus, who was making a name for himself as a young player of promise, slipped home the winner from a narrow angle. We knew then that we had the winning of the game but we wouldn't have put it past the referee, who had proved himself to be no friend of Hibs in the past, to abandon the game and make us go through it all again. Fortunately he didn't. McManus scored again as Hibs next beat Kilmarnock to progress to the semi-final.

By Hibs standards, the semi-final against Livingston was a comfortable and stress-free occasion. A friend of mine had given me a parking permit for the main Hampden car park for this match and it was a major luxury to be able to park right outside the ground and avoid the usual traffic chaos which accompanied a trip to the national stadium. In the ground before the match, I met up with my old friend from fanzine days Sean Allan. Sean had clearly prepared for the game by ensuring that his thirst was well and truly slaked. He was in ebullient mood and in great voice. He had composed a song of tribute to Russell Latapy and insisted on letting us hear it on several occasions before the teams came out.

In goal for Livingston was Ian McAldon who had played with Dominic at juvenile level. We were hoping that Ian wouldn't choose this match as his game of a lifetime and destroy Hibs' Scottish Cup dreams. We needn't have worried. In the first minute, Latapy set up John O'Neil to score with a fine shot. Without playing particularly well, Hibs did enough to win and second half strikes from O'Neil and Zitelli confirmed our place in the final. Prior to the final, there was one more derby to play and before it, we Hibs fans received bad news. The Hearts game was scheduled for a Sunday evening and, on the Friday before it, Russell Latapy had a night on the town with his friend Dwight Yorke of Manchester United fame. The tabloid newspapers got wind of the Trinidadian duo's high jinks and splashed photographs of their behaviour all over the next day's front pages. Alex McLeish was naturally incensed that one of his top players should behave so irresponsibly just forty-eight hours before a crucial match. He disciplined Latapy and announced that he would not play in either the derby game or the forth-coming Cup Final. In fact, Russell would never play for Hibs again.

McLeish's reaction was understandable but, in truth, it was an overreaction. Our manager was penalising the team, himself and the fans by his draconian response to Latapy's misbehaviour and Hibs were to pay a heavy price for his actions.

Hibs dominated the derby but were held to a goalless draw. We missed chances galore and Mixu Paatelainen, who had scored three times when he had last met Hearts at Easter Road, missed a penalty. Mixu tried to be too clever and attempted to dink the ball into the top of the net after the goalkeeper had dived. He got too much elevation on his shot and the ball hit the crossbar. Ironically, if Latapy had been playing, he would have taken the spot kick and would, I am sure, have scored. Once again though, Alex McLeish had had the better of a derby match, and had gone through the season without losing to his local rivals. All thoughts now turned to Hampden and the Scottish Cup Final clash with Celtic. 'The Hoops' under Martin O'Neill were enjoying an all-conquering season but we Hibs fans were not short of optimism as we looked ahead to the great day.

As well as my Quarry Park football on a Saturday morning, I was now playing regular five-a-side games with a great group of friends every Thursday evening. One of my Thursday footballer pals, Mark Fallon, had organised a coach for the final. He had planned events in style. The day would kick off with a full cooked breakfast and a couple of glasses of champagne in a city-centre hotel. From there we would board our coach and head for Hampden and, we hoped, Scottish Cup glory. The Brack family was delighted to accept Mark's invitation to join his travelling party. The day got off to a fine start. Breakfast was tasty and the bubbly slid down smoothly. In no time we were heading west on a bus full of banter, boozy breath and bonhomie. The singing was tremendous. One large gentleman, resplendent in a Hibs top hat, had prepared a song especially for the occasion and he aired it unceasingly until we reached Glasgow. The chorus of his masterpiece, sung to the tune of the old Lonnie Donegan hit 'My Old Man's a Dustman' went as follows: 'Frankie Sauzée's magic, he wears a magic hat and when he sees the Scottish Cup, he says I'm having that.'

We disembarked in high spirits and fortified by champagne and the company of thousands of fellow Hibees sung our way to the ground. Alex McLeish sprung a surprise by leaving out Stuart Lovell who had been a regular starter all season and replacing him at right back with young Ian Murray. Our inspirational captain Franck Sauzée, who had been injured against Rangers the previous week, was passed fit to take his place in defence. Hibs held their own for thirty-five minutes at which point Jackie McNamara, son of the former Hibs skipper of the same name, broke the deadlock. When my son Dominic had trained with Hibs as a schoolboy, McNamara had been part of that same training group. Alex Miller had chosen to release him while retaining his own two sons Greg and Graeme, neither of whom came close to being in McNamara's class. Jackie had punished Hibs for Miller's poor judgement on a number of previous occasions and he did so again on this Cup Final day.

McNamara's goal finished the final as a contest. Sauzée was not fully fit and was unable to exert his usual significant influence. The absent Latapy was sorely missed as we had all known he would be. Two second-half goals from the talismanic Henrik Larsson sealed Celtic's victory and we left Hampden in a dark mood, which contrasted starkly with the exuberant fashion in which we had entered the ground. Forty-three years after my dad had taken me to that anti-climactic 1958 Scottish Cup Final against Clyde and promised me that Hibs 'would win it soon', I led my family home with despair in our hearts. It seemed like Hibs were never going to lift the Scottish Cup in my lifetime. When we arrived back in Edinburgh, we didn't know what to do with ourselves. We decided to head down to Easter Road and gathered outside the stadium to greet the team on its return. When the players stepped down from their coach they looked as broken-hearted as we felt. Each and every one of them was visibly crestfallen. However, they made time to console the supporters who were there to meet them. No one was more gracious in offering us consolation than the great Franck Sauzée.

Alex McLeish indulged in his now traditional summer

spending spree prior to season 2001–2002. In came goalkeeper Tony Caig from Newcastle, full back Alen Orman from the Belgian League, utility player Derek Townsley from Motherwell, Spanish centre forward Paco Luna, former Dundee United front man Craig Brewster and, most significantly of all, Ecuadorian international Ulises de la Cruz. De la Cruz was an attacking right back whom McLeish had spotted starring against Brazil in a South American World Cup qualifying match. He had splashed out £750,000, which was comfortably a record fee for Hibs, to purchase the flying full back and as we took our seats in the newly opened West Stand for the first match of the season, like all those who sing Gerry Marsden's Liverpudlian anthem 'You'll Never Walk Alone', we had hope in our hearts. This hope was to prove misplaced. None of the new signings was a consistent success although most of them showed signs of why our manager had brought them to Easter Road. De la Cruz was superb going forward but less impressive in the conduct of his defensive duties. His playing style was of the languid variety and the early signs were that Hibs had paid too much for him.

Hibs had qualified for the UEFA Cup and were handed a tough task in the first round when they were drawn against the Greek team AEK Athens. AEK had an impressive European pedigree and were certain to prove formidable opponents for us. A huge army of Hibees travelled to Greece for the first leg. Sadly, just as they were arriving in the Greek capital, the news broke that the Twin Towers in New York had been attacked and destroyed by terrorists with a consequent major loss of life. The game was postponed and the Hibs contingent had to turn round and come back home. When the game did take place, AEK won 2–0 and looked to have booked their place in the next round.

The return leg at Easter Road was to be one of these memorable Hibernian nights. All 17,500 seats in our newly reconstructed stadium had been sold. Alex McLeish had asked Hibs fans to 'raise the roof.' They didn't let him down. The small group of Greek fans present weren't exactly lacking in the noise department either. In this amazing atmosphere, Hibs, led by the marauding De la Cruz, who was having by far his best game to date, laid siege to the Athens goal. The interval arrived goalless and was the occasion for Hibs fans to give the most incredible rendition of 'Sunshine on Leith' I have ever heard. The stadium united in filling the half-time air with an awe-inspiring version of the Proclaimers' haunting melody. The inspirational singing seemed to galvanise the team even further and Paco Luna scored two fine goals to level the match and the tie as Hibs poured down the slope. In the last minute, Luna rose unchallenged at the back post for a header which should have put Hibs through in a blaze of glory. Sadly he missed, heading the ball inches the wrong side of the post when it looked much easier to score.

As the match entered extra time, Luna's miss seemed to hand the momentum back to AEK. With the assistance of some weak goalkeeping from Nick Colgan, the Greeks scored twice. A wonderful twenty-five-yard rocket from David Zitelli ensured that Hibs won on the night but we had lost a tie which we could and should have won. After the game, our manager proclaimed, 'Only Lady Luck prevented Hibernian being in the next round in Europe.' He was partly right. AEK had indeed had the luck but Hibs could also point to profligate finishing and poor goalkeeping as reasons for their undeserved European exit.

The first derby of the season at Easter Road was to be Alex McLeish's last as Manager of Hibs. We won 2–1 with both goals coming from the enigmatic De la Cruz. The first was a left-footed wonder strike from distance and the second, in contrast, was a tap in from two yards out. Hibs won 2–1 so McLeish maintained his magnificent record in matches against the old enemy. The manager now signed De la Cruz' compatriot, Eduardo Hurtado. Hurtado was allegedly an international centre forward and he rejoiced in the soubriquet 'The Tank.' He was the least dangerous tank that I have ever seen. Surprisingly, and unfairly, given his previous success, murmurings about Alex McLeish's management were starting to surface round about this time.

Little did we know what fate had in store. During his on-field address to the supporters on the day in which the First Division Trophy was presented after victory over Falkirk, McLeish had told the fans that he intended to stay with Hibs. He was about to go back on those words. Late in 2001, when for the first time he was starting to struggle as Hibs manager, he was offered and accepted the opportunity to manage Rangers. A lot of Hibs supporters have never forgiven Alex McLeish for this. During his time at Ibrox, he was known by Hibs fans as the 'Ginger Judas.' Personally, I thought that he had been great for Hibs and like any one of us, when offered the opportunity to move on in our career, he had taken a job offer which had come his way. I don't blame him for that nor do I hold it against him. In my view, Alex McLeish was a fine manager who gave Hibs back their pride.

In the eyes of Hibs supporters, there was only one man who could possibly replace McLeish. That man was of course Franck Sauzée. As sweeper, Franck surveyed and commanded all before him. He read the game well, played with huge intelligence and insight and seemed to have the total respect of his team mates. He certainly had the respect of the fans. In fact, he was revered by them.

The club board obviously agreed with us supporters because in double quick time, Franck Sauzée was installed as the successor to Alex McLeish. His first match in charge was at Dunfermline next day. I remember vividly standing in a vast crowd of Hibs fans behind the goal at East End Park acclaiming Franck as he made his way down the track to the technical area before the game. He, in return, applauded the crowd and it felt like being present at the start of a new and exciting era.

Unfortunately the Sauzée era was to be tragically short. Franck struggled to win matches and the players who had responded so readily to his on-field promptings were less responsive to his managerial guidance. Ironically the team's best performances under Franck were two impressive draws against Celtic and Hearts. Games against lesser teams were lost. Most disappointing among these were a League Cup semi-final reverse to Ayr United and a 4–0 drubbing from a fairly ordinary Motherwell side.

After a few short weeks, Chairman Malcolm McPherson pulled the plug on Franck Sauzée's brief reign as manager of Hibs. We were all sorry to see him go but McPherson's pragmatic decision was probably correct. Under Franck, Hibs were in free fall and relegation was a real and frightening possibility. The players he had signed such as Jarkko Wiss, Lilian Martin and Freddie Dacquin were simply not good enough and something had to be done. In appointing Sauzée, Malcolm McPherson let his heart rule his head. In sacking him, he ensured that his head was in the ascendancy.

It was truly heartbreaking to see this great player who had nailed his colours so magnificently and with such total commitment to the Hibernian mast, leave in such unfortunate circumstances. Franck took his dismissal with typical dignity proclaiming, 'That's life. That's football.' The fans welcomed him back for a presentation a few weeks later to mark his great service to the club. At the end of that function he was kind enough to pose for a photograph with some of our family. I will treasure that photograph forever. Perhaps some day, Rod Petrie will invite Franck back to Easter Road so that he can take a bow before a home match and be given a proper send-off by the fans who hold him in such high esteem. Franck Sauzée will always have a place in the pantheon of Hibernian greats.

15

BORING, BORING BOBBY

The summary removal of Franck Sauzée from his managerial position was an act of pragmatism. Hibs could not afford to be relegated again so our chairman acted swiftly and decisively. His decision was not well received by a large section of the club's support. Many others regretted the need for Franck's dismissal but saw the wisdom in it. The misjudgement which had been made was the appointment of 'Le Grand Homme' not the termination of his employment. Much though we all loved Franck Sauzée, and still do, it was very clear, very quickly that, magnificent player that he was, he was not cut out to be a successful football manager. The same pragmatic approach, which had been adopted in relieving Sauzée of his duties, was applied to the appointment of his successor. The new incumbent of the managerial hot seat at Easter Road was the ultimate in hard-nosed managers, Kilmarnock's Bobby Williamson. Williamson had been extremely successful at Rugby Park by playing a pressing game and developing a counter-attacking style based on ball retention and acceptance of a high ratio of the small number of chances which were created. No one could quibble with his appointment. Perhaps he would make Hibs harder to beat while retaining the style of football which Hibs fans had come to expect as their right.

Williamson's first match was at home against St Johnstone

and a Hibs win was essential to ward off any lingering thoughts of dropping back into the First Division. A large crowd gave the new manager a rousing reception. This least sentimental of men seemed visibly moved by the warmth of his welcome. He started his reign in positive fashion with a 3–0 victory, which was climaxed by a thunderbolt of a third goal by the barn-storming young centre forward Garry O'Connor. In his short time in charge, Franck Sauzée's most significant act had been to blood promising youngsters like O'Connor and his fellow striker Derek Riordan. He had also, very wisely, tied them to long-term contracts. Regrettably Williamson's flying start proved to be a false dawn. We were no harder to beat than before and our free-flowing football was replaced by a dour, defensive brand of play which disillusioned fans and reduced crowds.

In Williamson's defence, he had taken over at a time of financial frugality at Hibs. The big spending of the McLeish era, which had been funded mainly through a Sky Television contract that no longer existed, had come to an end and parsimony was the order of the day. This lack of funds prohibited Williamson from strengthening his team, although it has to be said that he spent any money which he was given very poorly indeed. He brought in defenders like the Frenchman Yannick Zambernardy and the Hungarian Janus Matteus who were accidents waiting to happen. As a fan, you just couldn't relax when you watched these players defend. They alternated recklessness with lack of concentration and were an open invitation to score for opposing forwards.

Williamson recognised their inadequacies and brought in yet another defensive player. He signed centre half Colin Murdock from Preston North End. Murdock was recommended by then Preston manager Craig Brown. Brown was talking up a player whom he had just released, which didn't make total sense. Murdock, a Northern Ireland international, had begun his career at Manchester United and was also a qualified lawyer. In his early days at Easter Road, however, his defending bordered on the criminal. He was painfully slow and prone to poor decision-making. It has to be said that he improved and had some good games as his career with Hibs progressed but even when he was playing well, he was never far away from a costly aberration. He had a big heart but the supporters' hearts were usually in their mouths when big Murdock was around.

Williamson's other signings were not great successes either. Stephen Glass was bought from Watford. We remembered him as a cultured left-sided midfielder in his Aberdeen days. The version which Hibs acquired was much diminished. The Glass we got was lightweight, peripheral and often injured. From time to time, he would show a flash of what he was capable of with a fine pass or a good strike but, in the main, he failed to deliver. A new centre forward came in in the shape of Stephen Dobbie who had been freed by Rangers. Dobbie's shape was, in fact, small and stocky but he was skilful and nippy and a useful fringe player. He was, though, no more than that.

Williamson's best signing happened by chance. When Hibs were running in Holyrood Park, Bobby met Mixu Paatelainen who had been released by the French club which he had joined on leaving Hibs. Mixu was jogging to maintain his fitness and was happy to stop for a chat. He was happier still when Hibs' new boss offered him a one-year contract. Although now in his mid-thirties and not quite the player he had been, Mixu went on to have a good season during which he was easily one of Hibs' best players. He also managed to score his fair share of goals. This, in itself, illustrated the paucity of Hibs' resources in the Williamson years.

During Bobby Williamson's reign, I didn't buy a season ticket for the first time in years. The boring, negative play which his team was producing totally depressed me. I wasn't prepared to pay a substantial sum of money to watch players as poor as most of those he had brought in. In Williamson's first full season, we had seats in the lower part of the new West Stand very close to the manager's dugouts. Our manager, resplendent in a tracksuit top zipped up over a shirt and tie, would turn to the crowd and snarl comments in response to their criticism. At one game, a supporter shouted, 'Williamson, this is absolute rubbish.' Leaving his dignity behind, the manager, with a contorted expression on his face, roared back, 'You try doing something with this load of sh***.' Leaving aside the inadvisability of indulging in public arguments with your supporters, our leader had completely omitted to mention that he had signed, selected and coached the group of players which he was denigrating.

I didn't like this type of behaviour, but I liked one of Williamson's public pronouncements even less. Asked by a reporter to respond to complaints from fans that his team was playing boring football, he had answered by saying that those fans who were looking for entertainment should go to the cinema. That comment sickened me. As a family, we Bracks had been brought up in the tradition of Hibs as a team which embraced the philosophy of attacking, cultured football. Having heard our manager's opinion on this approach to the game, we took a family decision not to renew our season tickets. In truth, this was more of a principled gesture than a genuine commitment to non-attendance as we still went along to most matches and paid at the gate. We didn't like the current state of affairs but we knew that Hibs would be with us long after Bobby Williamson had gone.

Williamson's standing in the popularity stakes was not

helped by a fairly dismal derby record. If a Hibs manager wants to win over the fans, he has to beat Hearts on a regular basis. Williamson had two particular derby nightmares. At Easter Road, we led 1–0 for most of the match and then threw the game away by conceding two goals in the last five minutes. Phil Stamp scored Hearts' winner and his nauseating celebrations compounded our agony. Referee Willie Young sent him off for his over-the-top communion with the Hearts fans behind the South Stand goal but that was little consolation to us Hibees, who had watched our team turn certain victory into abysmal defeat. Worse was to follow. In the New Year derby at Tynecastle, Hibs led 2–0. Hearts pulled level but Hibs regained the lead. In added time at the end of the match, we got a penalty. Mixu kept up his 100 per cent unsuccessful penalty record in derby games by having his shot saved. Thankfully Grant Brebner followed up to ram home the rebound. In the Brack household, unrestrained celebrations were the order of the day. We punched the air, slapped hands and planned a night to remember.

We were listening to the game on the radio as we were maintaining our post-Mercer takeover stance of never putting a penny in Hearts' pocket. Two minutes into stoppage time, Hibs were now 4–2 up and, surely, out of sight. Incredibly and incomprehensibly, we allowed Hearts' substitute Graham Weir to score twice in the two minutes which remained. Our defending was shambolic and the surrendering of a victory for a draw, which felt like a defeat, was shameful and unforgivable. As a mature and normally civilised man, I should have known better but my fury and disappointment was such that on the final whistle, I picked up the radio and threw it against the wall in anger. I have not been allowed to forget this ultimate gesture of despair and frustration. I am not proud of my action but it demonstrates my strength of feeling at this nadir in Hibs' derby fortunes.

By choice or more probably by necessity, Bobby Williamson began to introduce talented young players into the first team set up. Scott Brown, Derek Riordan, Garry O'Connor, Kevin Thomson and Stephen Whittaker all began to feature regularly. We have to give Williamson credit for this but before we give him too much credit, we shouldn't forget that he allegedly tried to swap Derek Riordan and Stephen Whittaker for the Inverness Caledonian Thistle centre half, Bobby Mann.

These young players displayed real promise but were not helped by the fact that the team was playing in a sterile fashion. They were also being asked to take too much responsibility too soon owing to the inadequacies of some of their team mates. However, the 2003–2004 CIS League Cup was to provide a suitable showcase for their precocious talents. Exactly one week before Christmas, we met Celtic in the quarter-final at Easter Road. Colin Murdock was suspended for the game so Williamson was forced to blood yet another youngster. Eighteen-year-old Jonathan Baillie came in at centre half and played like a veteran. Baillie seemed to have many successful years ahead of him. Sadly injury was to cut short his career.

On this night though, it was good news all the way. Scott Brown ran at the Celtic defence time and again, Riordan was classy wide on the left, O'Connor was rumbustiousness personified and Thomson controlled the midfield area with a maturity way beyond his years. Celtic took the lead in fifty-five minutes when the towering Stanislaw Varga headed home a corner. Hibs, though, were not to be denied. First Grant Brebner coolly slotted home a penalty-kick equaliser and then with just nine minutes left, Kevin Thomson scored the winning goal with what the next day's *Daily Record* described as 'a quite sensational strike.' He drove an unstoppable left foot shot past Rab Douglas' left hand into the corner of the Celtic net. This was a great victory for Hibs coming, as it did, against Martin O'Neill's all-conquering side of Sutton, Larsson and company. It took us into a semi-final clash with Rangers and lifted the gloom of what had been, to that point, a very ordinary season. Typically, at this time of inconsistency and under-achievement, we followed this fine win with a disappointing home defeat to Dunfermline only three days later.

Leading up to the semi-final in February, Hibs' form continued to be patchy. No one expected our team to trouble Alex McLeish's expensively assembled outfit. Normally 15,000 or more Hibs supporters would travel to Hampden for a semi-final but on this occasion only 7,000 made the trip. This was indicative of our lack of confidence going into this match. I wasn't one of those who travelled along the M8 on what was a particularly inclement Thursday evening. In fact, I almost didn't see the match on television. Alan Mackie, the janitor at my school, was a Hibs fanatic, who travelled to every match, home and away. He asked me if he could leave a little earlier than usual to ensure that he arrived at Hampden in time for kick-off. I told him that this would be fine as long as he made certain that all doors and windows were closed. This would leave me simply to switch on the burglar alarm and close the front door when I left the school. Alan promised me faithfully that he would do this.

Just before 6p.m. as Linda McGee, my depute head, and I left the school the weather was cataclysmic. Torrential rain, whipped by strong winds, bounced off the ground. I told Linda that I would give her a lift home. First though, I insisted that we walk round the playground and confirm that all the doors and windows were indeed closed. Everything went swimmingly, which is an apt adverb given the intensity of the rain as we made our tour of duty, until we reached the nursery building. To our horror, we discovered that a window at ground level had been left unlocked by Alan in his haste to hit the road to Hampden. We weren't sure what to do. Should we just leave things and go home on the basis that nobody would be prowling round the playground on a night such as this, or should we reopen the school, switch off the alarm, collect the nursery keys, lock the main building again, go back across to nursery and stand in the dark in the downpour trying each of the many keys on the nursery ring until we eventually found one which opened the door? Although the former choice was a tempting option, our sense of responsibility told us that the latter course of action was the correct one. Then inspiration struck. I phoned the nursery teacher and told her of our plight. To my delight, she informed me that she knew of a way to secure the window in question from the outside. Even better, she would jump into her car and come and perform this task immediately. With the complete school building made safe and our consciences clear, Linda and I headed for home. After dropping her off, I raced up the road to my own house in time for a speedy snack and seat in front of the television to watch Channel 5's semi-final coverage.

Once again, Bobby Williamson's mixture of novices and nearly men rose to the occasion. Top man on the night was Swedish goalkeeper Daniel Andersson. He brilliantly saved a Mikel Arteta first-half penalty and followed this great stop with a string of saves to keep Rangers at bay. He was beaten once by Michael Mols but Hibs were always in the match. Tam McManus came on to play wide right in the second half and was outstanding. This talented but temperamental player often fell short on the big occasion but on this night, he was tremendous. Tam's foraging on the right was complemented by Derek Riordan's silky play on the left and eventually the equaliser came. It was supplied by a former Rangers player, Stephen Dobbie. The chunky little striker, also on as a substitute, crashed home an unstoppable close-range shot to take the game into extra time.

By this time, our living room was riven with tension. Was a famous victory on the horizon or were we heading for glorious failure? Extra time was engrossing with play raging from end to end, but the deadlock could not be broken. And so to that nerve-end-stretching experience which is a penalty shoot-out. Twice Andersson made great saves but Hibs also contrived to miss two kicks. At 3–3, with the breath in the Brack household being firmly held, Colin Murdock stepped forward. Many epithets could be applied to the big Northern Irishman but reliable is not one of them. We clenched our hands made clammy with tension, 'Why is he taking one? He's bound to miss.' We were wrong. Murdock held his nerve better than we were holding ours and despatched a perfect penalty into the corner of the net. The pressure was back on Rangers and in particular on Frank de Boer. This Dutch international star had a well-deserved reputation as a top player but he was not renowned for his expertise from twelve yards, having missed a vital kick in a World Cup match penalty decider. As de Boer stepped forward, Alex McLeish's heart must have been in his mouth. The Dutchman was in the position of becoming a hero or a villain. He missed and entered the latter category. McLeish now had his head in his hands. As de Boer's shot clipped the outside of the post on its way to safety, the Hibs players raced to their fans. The supporters, saturated but euphoric, cheered them to the hilt. The Brack family slumped in elated exhaustion on the living room sofas feeling the warm glow which comes from a great achievement, and the prospect of a Cup Final to look forward to. The next morning at school, Alan the janny bounced into my office, quite obviously still on a major high from the night before. I didn't have the heart to puncture his pleasure by telling him about the previous evening's open window so I contented myself with listening to his tales of triumph and anticipating with him what would surely be a Cup Final victory over lowly, cash-strapped Livingston.

Although his overall work at Hibs had been less than impressive, Bobby Williamson had done a great job in taking the club to the League Cup Final. Regrettably the goodwill he had won for himself by overcoming both members of the Old Firm en route to Hampden, was eroded by capitulation to Livingston in the final. Hibs fans must have outnumbered Livingston supporters by almost ten to one that day. We also had a much better team than they did yet still we managed to lose. Before the match, the atmosphere was upbeat. During the game, the massive Hibs support was eerily quiet as it watched its team perform ineffectually and began to fear the worst. In due course the worst arrived in the shape of two Livingston goals to which Hibs could not reply. The prevailing mood in the stadium was now suicidal. There was something surreal, at the end of the game, about watching the Livingston players cavorting with the cup in front of a small pocket of fans, while the massed ranks of Hibees stood in stunned disbelief.

I have seldom felt so downcast after a Hibs defeat (and I have had plenty of practice) as I did when I trudged out of Hampden on that depressing March Sunday afternoon. The next day, the Primary 7 pupils at my school were going off to school camp. They were gathering at 8a.m. I was at the school early as ever to exchange pleasantries with the parents and send the children safely on their way. This was an occasion which I always enjoyed. My enjoyment was tempered that morning by the feeling of gloom which persisted from the night before.

There was little chance of Williamson's career at Hibs recovering from that setback. The fans, while never completely turning against him, never fully warmed to him either. First, Rod Petrie renegotiated his contract in a downwards direction. Then the chairman made it clear that he had no intention of standing in Williamson's way when Plymouth Argyle approached Hibs for permission to speak to our boss about filling their manager's post, which had just been vacated by Paul Sturrock. Williamson knew that Plymouth desired his services but he couldn't have felt wanted at Hibs. He bowed to the inevitable and headed for Devon. I don't think that too many Hibs supporters mourned his departure.

Rod Petrie deliberated long and hard about who should succeed Bobby Williamson. A host of names was bandied about by the media. A newspaper poll of Hibs fans threw up an even wider range of candidates but none of those named in this survey was actually the man whom Petrie had selected to take charge of Hibs future. The appointment of Tony Mowbray came right out of left field, leaving the media and supporters equally taken aback.

I was hard at work in my office when the janitor came in to tell me who Hibs' new manager was. To say that I was surprised by our chairman's choice would be an under-statement. I had hoped for a big name appointment and was disappointed at the decision which Rod Petrie had made. Alan, ever an optimist in matters Hibernian, urged me to give the new man a chance and told me that Mowbray's selection might just turn out to be inspired. I doubted his judgement but I shouldn't have done.

I knew that 'Mogga' Mowbray had been an abrasive and effective centre half for Middlesbrough, Celtic and Ipswich. I also knew that he had become first-team coach at Portman Road. I had no idea what kind of manager he would make.

We Hibs fans were, in fact, in for a very pleasant surprise. Mowbray may have been a rugged player but he was a quietly-spoken and dignified manager who brought stylish, classy football back to Easter Road. In his early interviews, he promised the supporters that he would ensure that Hibs, under his control, played in their traditional manner. Pure football would be the order of the day and entertainment would be back on the Easter Road agenda. The fans' reaction to this was initially sceptical. We were of the opinion that it is easy to make promises but much more difficult to deliver them. We needn't have worried. Our new manager was as good as his word and exciting times lay ahead.

16

TEENAGE KICKS

Tony Mowbray walked into his introductory press conference as an unknown quantity in managerial terms. He left the room as a new and interesting presence on the Scottish football scene. When Mowbray spoke, people listened. He had something to say and he said it in a quietly charismatic way. His original declaration of intent, that Hibs would play football in the proper way, was music to the ears of a support which had been anaesthetised into apathy by the pragmatic approach of his predecessor.

Mowbray was fortunate to inherit a squad replete with youthful potential. In Ian Murray he had a determined multi-purpose player who performed well in a number of areas on the field and who allied total commitment with his commendable versatility. Garry O'Connor was a battering ram of a centre forward, who more than compensated for any lack of finesse by harnessing his natural strength and speed to a straightforward approach to scoring goals, which was both refreshing and successful. Stephen Whittaker offered skill in abundance and a flair for launching attacks from defensive positions. In Kevin Thomson, our new manager had inherited a cultured left-sided midfield player who could win tackles, retain possession and thread passes with equal facility. Then there was Scott Brown, a feisty teenage tornado who combined running power and talent with an unquenchable will to win, which occasionally led to a loss of control and trouble with referees. Brown may have collected more than his fair share of yellow and red cards but this was only because he cared so much about winning and refused to accept any cause as being lost. The jewel in the crown of this collection of youthful gold, which had been mined by the club's Head of Youth Development John Park, was Derek Riordan. Slight of frame and not overinterested in back-tracking or tackling, Riordan had a tremendous football brain, unlimited natural talent and the ability to score lots of goals with either foot. He notched his fair share of typical striker's goals but he also regularly contributed wonder goals to Hibs' cause.

Tony Mowbray moved swiftly to make signings which would complement his nucleus of novices. He brought in Guillaume Beuzelin, a classy French midfield playmaker, and David Murphy, a solid left back with a silky first touch and a penchant for overlapping. He also acquired Dean Shiels from the Arsenal youth set-up and signed Gary Caldwell, who had had previous successful loan spells from Newcastle with the club on a two-year deal. These were all excellent acquisitions and none of them cost a penny. Mowbray also brought goal-keeper Simon Brown from Colchester and centre forward Sam Morrow from Ipswich. These two players were to be less successful additions to the Hibs squad.

Hibs started the season by losing at home to Kilmarnock. The score flattered Jim Jefferies' team as they scored with their only real attack and even then with the aid of an error from Hibs' new goalkeeper. There was much to be pleased about in the way Hibs played if not in the result. In the next home game, there was even more reason for optimism, even if the final score was again disappointing. Hibs ran Dundee ragged and early in the second half led 4–1. At this point, Riordan, who had already converted an exquisite curling free kick, scored with a sublime left-foot volley. The linesman flagged him offside even though he wasn't and the game turned. Hibs eased off and Dundee came back to achieve an unlikely and undeserved 4–4 draw. Our team's late capitulation had been disappointing, but some of the football which they had played had been positively exhilarating.

In September 2004, I moved from my Head Teacher's post to a position in the Education Department. I received many generous gifts and kind messages among which I am delighted to say was a letter from Tony Mowbray marking my contribution to primary school education and inviting me to be his guest at the forthcoming Hibs home match against Dundee United. This had thoughtfully been arranged by Alan my janitor.

I very much appreciated this gesture and enjoyed a memorable day out meeting players, having a drink in the board room and watching an excellent 2–0 victory from a seat in the directors' box, which featured the first Hibs goal from another example of embryonic excellence, Steven Fletcher. From this point on, Hibs' results began to match their performances and we were soon in third place in the league, a position which we did not relinquish for the rest of the season.

As autumn gave way to winter, Hibs headed for Parkhead. Once again I was there with my Celtic-supporting friends. I still had not witnessed a Hibs victory in my many visits to that impressive and intimidating stadium in the East End of Glasgow. I didn't see one this day either but I did see the young Hibs team totally outplay the league champions. By virtue of clinical finishing, Celtic won 2–1 with a late goal but even their manager, Martin O'Neill, conceded that Hibs had passed his team off the park. The Celtic supporters around me raved about the quality of Hibs' play and the exciting wealth of young talent in the team's ranks.

We enjoyed an excellent festive season, winning every game but one and doing so in style. The exception was the New Year derby at Easter Road which ended 1–1. Hibs were magnificent in every department except finishing. In the final fifteen minutes alone, Garry O'Connor and Sam Morrow contrived to miss five clear-cut chances between them. This excellent form was carried into the Scottish Cup campaign and Hibs' hopes of ending their 103-year-long hoodoo in this competition were boosted by the return from long-term injury of Scott Brown and Kevin Thomson. Brown returned to the starting line-up in time for the quarter-final against a rugged and determined St Mirren. He marked his return by breaking the deadlock just before half-time. A second-half O'Connor strike ensured Hibs' passage to Hampden for the semi-final.

Our opponents were Dundee United who were involved in a desperate fight for SPL survival. Indeed at the time of the semi-final, they were sitting at the very bottom of the league. Hibs' trip west was depressingly familiar. We dominated the game and eventually took the lead through a second-half Riordan penalty. At that point, we should have pressed on and sealed a place in the final. Instead, we sat back and conceded two late goals. There were 22,000 Hibs fans at the match and at the end we filed out of the ground in saddened silence as the 5,000 Dundee United fans celebrated their triumph over a vastly superior team which had handed them victory through a lack of focus and belief. Once again Hampden had proved to be a graveyard for Hibernian hopes. The match took place on the day on which Prince Charles married Camilla Parker Bowles. In Scottish Cup terms, Hibs were once again the bridesmaids and as far as ever away from being the blushing bride.

The depression lifted the following Wednesday as we bounced back in style. We went to Tynecastle and beat Hearts

2–1. It was our first win at the unholy ground in six years. Gary O'Connor and Dean Shiels supplied the vital second-half goals after an absolute howler by Simon Brown had given Hearts a half-time lead. Both O'Connor and Shiels celebrated their goals with gusto and a marvellous photograph in the next day's newspapers showed them sliding jubilantly in tandem in front of the massed ranks of the Hibs support. At the end, the team ran to the fans. O'Connor threw his shirt into the crowd and players and supporters savoured Tony Mowbray's first derby win. It was great but I couldn't help reflecting that it would have been even better if we hadn't capitulated at Hampden four days earlier.

The SPL split came into action three days later and the fixture computer threw up another derby. Rarely, over the years, had Hibs and Hearts met twice in the league within a space of a few days. This time the teams finished level at 2–2. Again, it was a game which Hibs should have won but a late and avoidable equaliser by Andy Webster allowed Hearts to escape with a point. The highlight of the game was a sensational strike by Derek Riordan who raced past Robbie Neilson and drove a diagonal twenty-yard left-foot rocket past Craig Gordon from a difficult angle. It is one of the best Hibs goals I have ever seen.

Riordan's collector's piece of a goal was so good that Tony Mowbray was moved to say, 'If you only looked at the goals which Derek scores, you would think that he was going to be the new Pelé.' This was a compliment of the backhanded variety. Mowbray rated his striker's talent very highly indeed but he considered that he fell short in the work rate department. More and more, he substituted Riordan and this caused increasing tension between the two of them. Riordan thought that his high quality play and portfolio of top-class goals should be enough. Mowbray wanted all of this plus industry.

As a fan, I was on the player's side. I don't recall Jimmy Greaves running miles in every game but I do remember him scoring more than thirty goals a season. In a footballing context, I have always preferred class and talent to graft and toil. It seemed to me, that where Derek Riordan was concerned, Tony Mowbray wanted to have his cake and eat it.

Hibs more or less sealed third place and a passport into Europe when they went to Celtic Park and won 3–1 in the last few weeks of the season. I had been attending these matches for some years now and had never managed to see a Hibs victory. I had enjoyed the odd nerve-wracking draw but I had never come away with a win. As luck would have it, I wasn't able to go along on this occasion. Patrick and Dominic were now proud fathers. Their wives had given birth within two days of each other. Patrick and Sharon had a lovely little boy called Daniel and Dominic and Angie had a beautiful daughter named Roisin. Roisin's baptism was fixed for the day after Hibs met Celtic and we agreed that the Saturday would need to be given over to preparations for the next day's celebration, so I couldn't make the trip to Parkhead. I came out of John Lewis at around 3.40p.m. having been dispatched there on a shopping mission. I put on the car radio and to my delight and surprise, Hibs were 1–0 up. Garry O'Connor's goal had, in fact, been a thing of beauty. Riordan had started the move in his own half with a cheeky backheel. Scott Brown had fastened on to this and run fifty yards holding off a series of challenges as he did so. He then set up O'Connor, who turned the centre half expertly and side footed home a precision strike.

By the time I got home, Celtic had equalised. I now feared the worst but Tony Mowbray produced a masterstroke. Once again he substituted Riordan and once again I complained. This time he was right and I was wrong. On came Ivan Sproule.

Mowbray had plucked Sproule from the obscurity of part-time football with Institute in Northern Ireland and had paid the princely sum of £5,000 to secure his services. The winger was small, intense, fiery and possessed of supersonic speed. He also possessed a talent for trickery and if his finishing was inconsistent, it could be lethal when he got it right. On this occasion, he very definitely got things right. He raced away from the Celtic defence and fired the ball into the net from a tight angle. Scott Brown followed this by using his strength and determination to resist the attentions of two Celtic defenders and bang in a third and decisive goal. I was back to the old kitchen radio syndrome. I liked to attend as many games as possible so that I could support my team. Being at the game also saved me having to listen to radio commentaries which created enough stress in me to shorten my life expectancy significantly. This day, however, had offered no alternative to listening to the radio and the tale which emanated from the airwaves was a happy one indeed. Margaret and I were not only proud grandparents but Hibs had just beaten Celtic at Parkhead. I had a lot to be thankful for and little to complain about, but I have to admit that I was just a little disappointed not to have been at Parkhead with my friends when Hibs actually managed to win there.

Hibs ultimately stumbled over the line in third place. Our young legs tired in the last few weeks of the season but we hung on in there and qualified for Europe above Aberdeen on goal difference. Our last game was at home against Rangers. Nacho Novo's goal gave the light blues victory, Scott McDonald's brace at Fir Park gave Motherwell three points and Alex McLeish and Rangers the league title. Six years earlier, McLeish had celebrated winning the First Division Championship at Easter Road and now he was celebrating winning the SPL crown. We Hibees were celebrating too. It had been a great season and Europe beckoned. Tony Mowbray had transformed Hibs and the feel-good factor was back in town.

Season 2005–2006 held out tremendous promise for Hibs. The nucleus of the previous campaign's successful squad had been retained. Only Ian Murray had departed. A genuine, lifelong Hibee, Murray, like many before him and others to come, took the big money on offer from the Old Firm and headed west, in his case for Ibrox, on freedom of contract. Mowbray had persuaded most of his other young guns to commit themselves to long-term contracts. He had led by example by extending his own deal. His assistant, Mark Venus, had followed suit. Mowbray and Venus formed the perfect partnership. The manager was serious by disposition but warm of personality. He rarely displayed emotion. His players clearly liked him and responded to his promptings. Venus, a former Ipswich Town centre half like his boss, was all energy and exuberance and cut an animated figure on the touchline.

There were only two major additions to the first team pool. Simon Brown, the goalkeeper, who had been Mowbray's first signing, had proved to be depressingly fallible so a replacement had been procured in the shape of the big Pole, Zibi Malkowski. Malkowski looked the part and started well but all too soon turned out to be even less reliable than Brown. The other significant signing was Michael Stewart who joined players like Willie Hamilton and Alan Gordon in crossing the capital divide from Hearts to Hibs. Stewart, who had never quite lived up to the early promise which he had displayed with Manchester United, was welcomed with his own song, 'Oh Mikey, Mikey, you used to be a Jambo but you're all right now.' He enhanced the team's play as his dynamic, all-action style in the middle of the park complemented Scott Brown's directness and Kevin Thomson's more studied approach.

To say that the season did not start well would be an under-statement. One of our first league games was at Tynecastle and we lost 4–0. Hearts had a new manager in George Burley and he was having a major impact. Bankrolled by the club's eccentric millionaire owner Vladimir Romanov, Burley had speedily assembled a combination of top players and his team looked like being authentic challengers to the Old Firm's dominance of Scottish football. On this day, they were far too good for Hibs.

We bounced back though in the best possible way. On the last Saturday of August, Hibs went to Ibrox and achieved a famous victory. Rangers, including a certain I. Murray Esquire, were put to the sword to the tune of 3–0. The hero of the hour was Ivan Sproule. The little Irish speed merchant, for whom words like 'enigmatic' and 'mercurial' could have been invented, came on as a substitute for Garry O'Connor with half an hour to go and proceeded to write himself indelibly into Hibs' history. He had only been on the field for five minutes when he raced clear onto a long pass from David Murphy and expertly lobbed the ball over the advancing Rangers goalkeeper Ronald Wattereus. Rangers now laid siege to Hibs' goal and this commitment to all out attack proved to be their undoing. With four minutes left, a Rangers offensive broke down. Scott Brown collected the loose ball and, displaying his trademark stamina and skill, ran from one end of the field to the other before teeing up Sproule who drilled home a right-foot strike from a difficult angle. The winger wasn't finished either. He completed his once in a lifetime performance by robbing Fernando Ricksen and dribbling round Wattereus to record an unforgettable hat-trick and seal a truly memorable win.

Tony Mowbray revealed after the game that Garry O'Connor had not taken kindly to his substitution. He had asked angrily why he had been taken off and had been told by his manager that he hadn't managed a single shot at goal. O'Connor had raged back, 'How many shots is he likely to have?' Mowbray told O'Connor after the game that the answer to his question was 'three, at least.' Sproule confirmed in his post-match interview that his colleague had displayed sportsmanship and team spirit when he had calmed down. He said, 'Garry was the first to shake my hand and congratulate me at the final whistle. He was genuinely pleased for me.'

By this time our grandchildren were six months old and a new family ritual had been established. When Hibs were at home and we were going to the match, the grandchildren visited on a Sunday. If it was an away match weekend, they came on Saturday. After lunch, we would all go out for a long walk and arrive back in time to catch the full-time results. The jubilation on this day of Sproule's tremendous treble was totally unconfined. The little ones looked on in wonder as the adults danced around the kitchen in response to the glad tidings issuing forth from the radio. They didn't know it yet but they were becoming Hibees by osmosis.

In the UEFA Cup, Hibs had drawn the Ukranian side Dnipro. Dnipro had a growing European reputation and a squad full of big money players and this was clearly not going to be an easy tie. We drew 0–0 at home and would have won if we hadn't given our opponents more respect than they probably deserved. The usual excellent Hibs European away-support travelled to the Ukraine almost exactly half a century after the great Hibs team of the 1950s had headed for Essen to begin their campaign in the inaugural European Cup. Ironically, we played better football in this second leg than we had in the first but managed to lose heavily. The referee's impartiality was less than obvious and Dnipro benefited from a number of debatable decisions, not least the award of a dubious penalty and the chalking off of a perfectly legitimate goal by Steven Fletcher. In the end we lost 5–1 but the score was hugely flattering to our Ukranian opponents. A final twist to our Eastern European saga was that Dnipro were reported to have offered Hibs seven-figure sums for Ivan Sproule and Derek Riordan after the match. Both players had caused them problems over the two legs and both players very quickly turned down the opportunity to leave Easter Road for pastures new.

Over at Tynecastle, Vladimir Romanov was making his mark. He had responded to George Burley's achievement in providing Hearts with their best start to a season in many years by sacking the successful manager. It was a mind-blowingly illogical decision but hadn't to this point derailed Hearts' SPL challenge. They were still undefeated in the league when they came to Leith for the second derby of the season. In charge of Hearts that day was John McGlynn. John had played for Bolton and Berwick Rangers before retiring and setting up his own plumbing business. He had also taken his first steps in coaching by building up a juvenile team from scratch with his brother Charlie, a man blessed with entre-preneurial flair. In no time Charlie had recruited some excellent players, my own son Dominic among them, and John set forth to coach these lads to success. Within four years, the team, Lothian United, had won the Scottish Cup at under-sixteen level, which was an amazing achievement, and John's coaching prowess was recognised by Jim Jefferies, who had put him in charge of youth development at Tynecastle. He had progressed from this position to first-team coach by the time Burley joined Hearts. During Lothian's Scottish Cup winning campaign, Dominic had scored three goals to see them through a very difficult quarter-final tie in Fife. After this match, John McGlynn had signed Paul Sheerin, later to be a cup hero with Inverness, and relegated Dominic to the bench for the semi-final and final. But we didn't hold this against John who was a good man and an excellent football manager. We generally wished him well but on this autumn day at Easter Road, we wished him nothing but defeat and despair.

That is exactly what he got. Hearts were strong and resolute. Hibs were fast, full of flair and ultimately irresistible. In the second half, we attacked the Famous Five Stand end and unleashed wave after wave of attacks on the Hearts' goal. Something had to give and it did. With Sproule at his speedy, scintillating best, Hibs notched goals from Beuzelin and O'Connor to end Hearts' winning run and provide their supporters with some measure of consolation for the drubbing which we had received from our age-old rivals in August. By this time, we had changed our season-ticket seats to the back of the lower tier of the new West Stand. This part of the ground was usually fairly sedate but on this day of derby dominance, it rocked like never before. The atmosphere was fantastic as was the result and indeed our celebrations on that happy Saturday night.

Tony Mowbray's second season in charge was proving to be particularly eventful on the Hearts and Rangers front. Hibs don't beat Rangers too often. We defeat them even less frequently at Ibrox. It is even rarer for us to overcome the light blues by three clear goals on their own ground. To embarrass them by that margin on their own turf twice in the same season is almost unheard of but that is exactly what happened in this second season of exciting, Mowbray-inspired, attacking football. The Scottish Cup draw sent us to Ibrox on Saturday, 4 February 2006. We all thought that surely lightning couldn't strike twice. Well, it could and it did. Hibs again won 3–0 with goals from O'Connor, Ivan Sproule, the man who loved scoring against Rangers, and newly-signed centre forward Chris Killen. Killen had been signed in the January transfer window from Oldham and had arrived at Easter Road with a reputation for goalscoring and being injury-prone. This was his debut and his goal was created by an exquisite pass from Derek Riordan. Both Riordan and Killen had come on as substitutes. Derek was not fully in his manager's favour because he had refused to sign a new contract.

We watched this lunchtime game on television as we were celebrating our grandchildren's first birthdays that afternoon and were therefore not able to travel to Glasgow. To say that the birthday celebrations went with a swing would be a major understatement. The quarter-final draw paired Hibs with Falkirk and this away tie would clearly be difficult. Something else which wouldn't be easy would be holding on to our manager who was starting to attract the attention of other clubs. The day after the victory over Rangers, the *Sunday Mail* summed the situation up when it reported, 'Mowbray is intelligent and aware and a brave decision maker. It won't be long before Hibs are beating off serious suitors.'

On the Wednesday after the cup tie at Ibrox, Hibs entertained Livingston. They continued their impressive form by playing brilliantly, scoring freely and recording their favourite score of 7–0. Ivan Sproule was unstoppable, Riordan was restored and responded with two goals and the ever-improving teenager Steven Fletcher came on as a late substitute and notched a fine brace. Hibs were even awarded a penalty in this game by Charlie Richmond, a referee who seemed to be allocated Hibs' matches on a disproportionately frequent basis and who rarely did the club any favours. Mowbray was having great success against the Old Firm but his results against Hearts were more mixed. We conceded four goals at Tynecastle for the second time in the season shortly before the Scottish Cup quarter-final, but we did manage to see off Falkirk by the comfortable margin of 5–1. The semi-final draw threw up an Edinburgh derby and the SFA ignored requests for the tie to be held at Murrayfield, insisting that the game should be played at Hampden, thus condemning 50,000 Edinburgh football fans to unnecessary expense, travel and inconvenience.

Riordan and Garry O'Connor had both been on target against Falkirk but neither was able to play against Hearts in the semi-final. Riordan received a booking which ruled him out and O'Connor was sold to CSKA Moscow for £1.6 million. This was an excellent price for our blockbuster of a centre forward but there were serious question marks about the timing of the club's acceptance of it. By the time the semi-final came round, things had gone from bad to worse for Hibs. The list of top-level absentees was augmented by Scott Brown, Chris Killen and Michael Stewart all being unavailable through injury. The patched-up Hibs side, which took the field, initially did well and at 1–0 down early in the second half was still in the game. At this point, the hapless Zibi Malkowski took a hand by conceding two very saveable goals. Malkowski was never reliable but he seemed to be doubly error-prone when he came up against Hearts.

At 3–0, referee Stuart Dougal sent off Ivan Sproule. He then dismissed Gary Smith for a foul, which took place outside the penalty area, and compounded matters by pointing to the penalty spot. Paul Hartley scored with the kick to complete his own hat-trick and a day of misery for his former team. We had conceded four goals to Hearts for the third time in one season and had once again failed to overcome our Scottish Cup hoodoo.

The long journey home from Hampden was even more abject than usual on this occasion. There was little to cheer us up but one redeeming feature had been the debut of a young Moroccan centre forward called Abdessalam Benjelloun. The fans had already christened the young man 'Benji' and he demonstrated in this match that he was a player of no little skill. He also proclaimed in the local press that he 'loved Leith.' The denizens of the port were learning to love Benji too. In the final derby of the season, he scored an excellent late goal to give Hibs a 2–1 win. This meant that we had won two out of five derbies that season. It didn't, though, obscure the fact that we had lost the other three and conceded twelve goals in the process. When Benji scored his winning goal, he raced the full length of the field to celebrate in front of the Hearts support. This undeniably provocative act greatly amused the Hibs support but earned the striker an unsurprising booking. He claimed afterwards that it was a Moroccan tradition to run to the opposing support if you scored in a derby game.

Having had the good fortune to meet a seriously under-strength Hibs team in the semi-final, Hearts had further luck when their final opponents turned out to be lowly Gretna. The small club from a town better known for wedding ceremonies than football gave the Jambos the fright of their lives and only lost on penalties. Nevertheless, Vladimir Romanov, after sacking two managers in one season, was able to reflect on a major trophy won. We Hibs fans were just happy that we still had our manager as we entered the new season. Tony Mowbray had already declined the opportunity to manage his old club Ipswich Town and it seemed only a matter of time before another job offer came his way.

Hibs started off in the Intertoto Cup. It was an early opening to the campaign with our first match against Dinaburg from Latvia taking place on Sunday, 2 July. It was a day of spectacular, electric storms and the skies were so leaden that the floodlights had to be switched on. There was nothing dull about Hibs' play though. The team's attacking pyrotechnics matched the weather and we scored five excellent goals without reply. Margaret and I were flying to Ireland next day. My wife has a deep-rooted fear of flying and will only take to the air under extreme protest. On this occasion, I had persuaded her to put her anxieties aside on the basis that the weather in early July would be perfect for travelling by plane. The following morning provided more weather of the thunder and lightning variety and presented me with a wife who was in high dudgeon and extreme panic in equal measure. I was informed that the plane would definitely crash and that it was all my fault for taking the decision to cross the Irish Sea by air. My ears took more punishment than the Dinaburg defence had done the previous day. Fortunately the weather eased, the flight was trouble-free and we had a great week's break in Derry, the city immortalised in song by Phil Coulter as 'The Town I Love So Well'. While there we visited Brandywell, the ground of Derry City, a club in the north of Ireland, which played its football in the league in the south of the country. Derry were managed by Stephen Kenny who had led them to success. We weren't to know it at the time but Kenny was poised to play a major part in Hibs season in the months ahead.

We returned in time for the next Intertoto match against Odense, a well organised Danish team, which was managed by Bruce Rioch who had captained Ally McLeod's Scotland team in its ill fated 1978 World Cup campaign in Argentina, and which featured in its ranks ex-Hibs stalwart Ulrik Laursen, who had reurned home after a spell with Celtic. One down from the first leg, we won 2–1 thanks to goals from recently signed centre half Rob Jones who, at six foot seven, was a towering snip at £150,000 and striker Paul Dalglish, son of Kenny, who had been recruited in the January transfer window.

This led to our exit on away goals but there had definitely been encouraging signs. There was more to be pleased about when Rangers, under the command of their newly-appointed French manager, came to town in September. Derek Riordan had joined Celtic in the summer, attracted by the significantly higher wage packet on offer at Parkhead. He hadn't really been missed though. He wasn't missed this day either.

Ivan Sproule was at his coruscating best and Chris Killen scored two excellent goals. The 2–1 final score seriously flattered the men from Govan. The next day's *Daily Record* was totally accurate in recording, 'It is no exaggeration to say that Hibs could have been five up inside the first twenty-six minutes so fast and furious was their assault on Paul Le Guen's side.' After this win, Hibs' league form was patchy. There were, though, two excellent home wins in the League Cup, with both Peterhead and Gretna being seen off and a total of ten goals being scored. Then came news which disappointed but did not entirely surprise Hibs fans.

West Bromwich Albion had been struggling to make an impact in the English Championship following their relegation the previous season. The board at the Hawthorns decided to dispense with the services of their manager Bryan Robson and replace him with a young manager of potential. They didn't have to look far to identify their man and it was no shock when they decided to go for Tony Mowbray. Rod Petrie did not stand in Mowbray's way and after just over two eventful, exciting and aesthetically pleasing seasons, big Mogga was on his way back South.

In the main, Tony Mowbray had proved to be an inspired piece of recruitment by our chairman. He brought the crowds and the good times back to Easter Road and signed most of our best young players on long-term contracts. Although he didn't always get it right in the transfer market; signings such as David Murphy, Guillaume Beuzelin and Ivan Sproule, who had cost £5,000 in total, were out of the top drawer. Mowbray was too quick, however, to make the point that both he and our best young players would move on if the opportunity arose. He seemed to regard Hibs as a feeder team for the Old Firm and England, and did not appear to fully appreciate just how big a club Hibs is. He also fell short in the most important games. In his first two seasons at the club, he took us to two Scottish Cup semi-finals. We threw away the first to a struggling Dundee United team after being ahead and comfortable with two-thirds of the match gone. The following season we met Hearts at Hampden with an injury and suspension hit line-up. This was a reason for concern but it wasn't an excuse to concede defeat before we took the field. In my opinion, Mowbray did not believe that he could win that match with the shadow squad which he had available to him. I am sure too that that message got though to his players which contributed to the ignominious 4–0 defeat which we suffered.

I never felt that Tony Mowbray's stay at Hibs would be long-term. He had made it clear from the outset that he saw Hibs as a stepping stone to bigger and better things. The abiding image of his reign is his team of talented young footballers running on to the pitch to the strains of the Undertones 'Teenage Kicks' and bringing with them the promise of fast, free-flowing football to set the pulse racing. Mowbray deservedly left with the good wishes of all Hibs fans and has continued to demonstrate his managerial prowess by leading West Brom back to the Premiership in only his second season in charge of the club. He was followed south by his assistant Mark Venus. Venus took charge of Hibs one last time before he and Mowbray renewed their partnership in the Midlands. The effervescent Venus led Hibs into the derby match at Easter

Road. A supreme piece of skilled finishing from little Moroccan playmaker Merouane Zemmama, who had been Mowbray's last signing for Hibs, and a Chris Killen header put us two goals up and seemingly on easy street. Yet again though, Malkowski plumbed the goalkeeping depths against our greatest rivals and two howlers by the big Pole handed Hearts a point which their play did not merit. This game symbolised the Mowbray era in many ways. Hibs had played superb attacking football but had failed to secure an important victory due to weak defending and, in particular, poor goalkeeping.

In his usual methodical manner, Rod Petrie took his time in deciding who should succeed Mowbray at the Easter Road helm. The man he appointed was John Collins, a former Hibs player and Scottish internationalist of distinction. Collins was a popular choice. His reign was to be short-lived but eventful in the extreme.

17

THE SECOND COMING OF J. C.

I had first seen John Collins play for Hibs when he had made his debut as a sixteen-year-old in a pre-season friendly match against Manchester City during the managerial term of Pat Stanton. My brother, who had played for Scotland Schoolboys, Falkirk and Meadowbank Thistle, was home on holiday from America for this match. He had taken up a soccer scholarship at a university near New York, leaving home on the day of Elvis Presley's death and had now settled in the States. When he made a trip back to his native heath, he always made sure that he would take in a Hibs game. Because of his playing prowess, he considered himself an authority on the beautiful game and was never slow to pronounce on the players he watched. His verdict on Collins' first step into the big time was, 'He'll never make it. He just passes the ball sideways.' It was true that the young playmaker had not attempted anything ambitious but this was one fraternal prediction which was to be seriously flawed. Collins developed into a modern midfielder of the highest quality. Small and compact, but as fit as any player could be, he won tackles, scored goals and was masterly in ensuring that his team retained possession at all times.

In his 163 matches for Hibs, John Collins had scored sixteen goals. After moving to Celtic in 1990 for £1 million, he increased his scoring rate and notched fifty-four goals in 273 matches for the Hoops. He then moved on to Monaco before finishing his career in the English Premiership with Everton and Fulham respectively. It was a distinguished CV by anyone's standards. After retiring, Collins had gained his coaching qualifications, studied developments in the game and waited patiently in his South of France base for the telephone to ring. In October 2006, his telephone did indeed ring and on the other end of the line was none other than Roderick Petrie Esquire, Chairman and Chief Executive of Hibernian FC.

The ever-cautious Rod had weighed all his options carefully but had ultimately decided to go for the former Hibee from Galashiels to carry on the excellent work which his successor had initiated. Collins' first match was at home to Kilmarnock. As he walked out to take his place in the technical area, he was accorded a warm, but not rapturous, welcome. With his compact, muscular frame encased in a designer suit, sporting a well established suntan and a raven black quiffed hairstyle, which looked like it had come straight from a Hollywood film, our new manager certainly looked the part. He had also spoken extremely well in his early interviews, displaying intensity and articulacy in equal measure. He had definitely talked the talk. Could he now walk the walk? His opening game was a microcosm of the Tony Mowbray reign with Hibs completely dominating inferior opponents, but failing to convert their superiority into victory and having to settle for a 2–2 draw.

Next up was a CIS League Cup quarter-final tie against Hearts. Hearts had won the Scottish Cup at the end of the previous season under the management of Valdas Ivanauskas. The Lithuanian had been Vladimir Romanov's third managerial appointment of the season. Now he was on sick leave and Hearts had yet another new man in charge in the shape of Eduard Malofeev who had played for the USSR in the 1966 World Cup. Malofeev had a talented squad at his disposal. A group of well-paid foreign players was under-pinned by the Scottish core of the team, which was composed of goalkeeper Craig Gordon, centre half Steven Pressley and midfield dynamo Paul Hartley. On this evening, Hibs were just too good for this strong Gorgie outfit. Gordon had defied Rob Jones three weeks previously in the league match at Easter Road when he had dived and twisted in mid-air to turn a powerful header to safety and prevent Hibs from winning. This time he was beaten by the big centre half, who was proving to be an excellent signing by our former manager. Half an hour into the match, Jones, whose goals normally came from his head, left footed a close range drive into the roof of Gordon's net. Hibs never loked like losing this lead and should, in fact, have increased it on a number of occasions.

It was a great start for the new man in charge and Collins was jubilant in his post-match press conference. Pointing out that both Rangers and Celtic had already been eliminated from the competition, he stated that Hibs now had a great chance of going on to lift the trophy. He also displayed, for the first time, an egotistical streak which was to resurface throughout his tenure. He informed the media that his team had played fantastic stuff and had won through, 'sticking to the game plan we worked on in training.' Apart from himself, Collins was referring to Tommy Craig who made up the other half of the managerial 'we.' Craig, who had left Hibs twenty years earlier after failing as a caretaker manager, was now back at Easter Road after long spells coaching Celtic and Newcastle United. Collins had apparently always valued Craig's coaching abilities and had brought him in to act as his assistant and mentor in this, his first managerial post.

The new managerial duo's excellent start continued when they won their first away match by no less than 6–1. Motherwell were the unfortunate recipients of this drubbing which combined speed, silky soccer and superlative finishing. It was Hibs' biggest away win in the league for a long time and it provided a very clear indication that Collins and Craig had inherited a strong squad of players, which was capable of going on to achieve great things if it was allowed to stay together. The team had a strong centre half in Jones who was also an infectiously enthusiastic presence. Steven Whittaker and David Murphy at full back exuded class and were just as effective in attack as they were in carrying out their basic defensive duties. Whittaker, in fact, was probably more expert in driving forward than he was in defending. The midfield was replete with top players. The spiky, super-skilled Scott Brown, tireless Michael Stewart, composed Kevin Thomson and cultured Guillaume Beuzelin had now been joined by the Moroccan box of tricks which was Merouane Zemmama. Waiting in the wings was the dynamic Dean Shiels and there was no shortage of forward firepower either. Chris Killen had seamlessly replaced Garry O'Connor. Although he lacked O'Connor's pace, the big New Zealander was a more natural finisher and held the ball up really well. The talented, tricky and tempestuous Ivan Sproule excited and infuriated in equal measure but was, without doubt, a player who was feared by every defence in the country. On his day, he could destroy any team. These two were backed up by the ever-improving Steven Fletcher and Zemmama's equally talented, but frustratingly inconsistent, compatriot Abdessallam Benjelloun. All we lacked was a reliable goalkeeper and a dependable central defensive partner for Jones. The current incumbents Zibi Malkowski and Shelton Martis were simply not good enough. Two of Tony Mowbray's less successful signings, they conceded avoidable goals on an almost weekly basis.

As we all know, when thing are going well for Hibs, there is always a problem just round the corner. The early days of the Collins/Craig axis were to be no exception. Scott Brown and Kevin Thomson had signed long-term contracts under Tony Mowbray. Now they acquired a new agent in Willie McKay and wasted no time in seeking to renegotiate deals which they had agreed to only a short time before. Predictably, Rod Petrie stood firm and said that he had no intention of making either player a new offer. Brown then handed in a transfer request, which he later withdrew. Thomson was relieved of the captaincy by Collins and the armband was given to Rob Jones. We could have done without this off-field wrangling and the media, of course, indulged in a feeding frenzy of speculation, trading quotes and counter quotes from the principal players in this unwanted drama and ensuring that Hibs' on-field momentum was temporarily derailed.

We fans were divided. We thought that Brown and Thomson's timing stank. We also felt that having signed contracts of their own free will, they should be prepared to honour these contracts. On the other hand, we suspected that Hibs were probably paying them less than they were worth and hoped that a compromise could be reached which enabled the players to stay within the confines of Hibs' wage structure while receiving an increase in earnings. When we met St Mirren at Easter Road two days before Christmas, injury and suspension prevented Brown and Thomson from taking the field.

This match provided conclusive proof that Hibs were not a two-man team. The Paisleyites were dispatched 5–1 with the commanding Beuzelin, inevitable Killen and effervescent Dean Shiels on target. Hibs' other two goals were made in

Morocco. First of all, Benji acted as provider for Zemmama, then his countryman returned the compliment to allow the centre forward to complete the scoring. Not for the first time, the goal which Hibs conceded was the result of a mix up between Malkowski and Martis. There was little time for festive frivolity for the players as a derby match at Tynecastle was scheduled for Boxing Day.

The Brack family stuck to their principles where Tynecastle was concerned. We had never attended a Hibs-Hearts match in Gorgie since Wallace Mercer's ill-conceived and insensitive takeover attempt had met the fate which it deserved, and this post-Christmas encounter was no exception. My daughter Lisa had by this time become engaged to a young man called Derrick Williams. Derrick had many fine qualities. He was also a Hearts supporter but a gentleman among that breed. He was kind enough to invite us to his flat to watch the derby on television. Hearts went two goals up with the help of yet another embarrassing blunder by the hapless Malkowski but Hibs fought back brilliantly to draw level through a Chris Killen header and a Dean Shiels penalty. Unfortunately, in scoring from the spot, Shiels got a little carried away and in his haste to get the game restarted and maintain Hibs' momentum, raced towards the net to collect the ball. He collided with Craig Gordon and the Hearts goalkeeper went down as if he had been struck by an Exocet missile. The result was predictable. Referee Mike McCurry produced his red card and, having regained parity in terms of goals, Hibs were now at a disadvantage in terms of personnel. During all of this, all Brack inhibitions had been cast to the wind and much shouting and screaming had ensued in Derrick's living room. He had accepted this mayhem without demur, proving himself to be a man of exceptional equanimity. When Hearts scored their inevitable winning goal, our prospective son-in-law allowed himself only the faintest of smiles and completed his seasonal display of impeccable manners and commitment to family harmony by joining us later in the evening for a dinner, which not surprisingly turned into a catalogue of complaints about Malkowski, McCurry and the theatrical custodian of the Hearts' net.

Measured examination of television evidence next day suggested that McCurry was probably right to send off Dean Shiels. John Collins didn't think so and launched an appeal which, not surprisingly, was doomed to failure. He was also, inadvisedly if amusingly, overheard after the match describing Hearts as 'a pub team.' Hibs had little time to reflect on a derby which had been lost when it should have been won because the Scottish Cup was on the horizon. Could we at last win this venerable trophy and end a separation from it which now stood at one hundred and five years? With the team we had, we would never have a better opportunity. With the transfer window open, all Hibs fans hoped that our manager would sign a new goalkeeper. He didn't but dropped Malkowski and replaced him with the youthful reserve goal-keeper, a local boy from Leith, Andy McNeil. He also decided that it was time to leave out Martis. Again he did not move into the transfer market. He contented himself with restoring the young centre half Chris Hogg who had been signed from Ipswich by Mowbray two years earlier.

An extremely difficult opening draw sent Hibs to Pittodrie. A magnificent Chris Killen goal put Hibs ahead late in the second half, but we conceded a last minute equaliser and lost Killen with a serious Achilles tendon injury. We didn't know it then but the big striker had kicked his last ball for Hibs. The replay at Easter Road was won 4–1, a scoreline which, in truth, flattered Hibs on the night. It was an important victory though and featured goals from Fletcher and Benji who were trying to fill the void created by Killen's injury. Hibs' other goal was scored by Michael Stewart who, on the stroke of half-time, met a Dean Shiels corner on the volley on the edge of the penalty area, and sent an unstoppable rocket of a shot into the roof of the Aberdeen net. Stewart did not appear after the interval and we all wondered if he had decided to retire on the spot because he knew that he would never surpass his goal for quality, no matter how long he played football. He had, in fact, been taken ill at half-time.

Hibs drew St Johnstone in the semi-final of the League Cup. Common sense prevailed and the game was allocated to Tynecastle. This signalled a return to the Hearts ground for the Brack family. It may seem petty now that Wallace Mercer is no longer with us and his family has no official connection with Heart of Midlothian Football Club that, as a family, we upheld a point of principle which was established in 1990. However, it was very important to us. Mercer's attempt to take over Hibs may have been dressed up in grandiose language about the formation of a united Edinburgh team which would be able to challenge the Old Firm. In reality, his intention, or so it seemed to us and many other Hibs supporters at the time, was to take our beloved team away from us and, as a consequence, remove something precious from our lives. In essence he was placing business and profit before humanity and community and that can never be right. That was our reason for making a vow never again to enter Tynecastle to watch Hibs play Hearts in a derby match. For us to have done so would have been to put money into the coffers of an institution which had tried to remove from existence the football club which meant so much to us. This we were not prepared to do. However, this was different. It was the semi-final of a national competition which was being held at a neutral venue so we decided that we would once more set foot inside Tynecastle Park.

The St Johnstone semi-final was played on the last day of January which was also, of course, the last day of the transfer window. A few days earlier, Hibs had sold Kevin Thomson to Rangers for £2 million. John Collins had stated repeatedly that neither Thomson nor Scott Brown would be transferred. Now, in complete contradiction of what had been previously said, our former captain had been allowed to move. Brown, in contrast, had pledged his future to the club, at least in the short-term. This was just as well, as Hibs made extremely heavy weather of seeing off First Division opposition and the driving midfield play of the little dynamo was probably the main reason that we managed to win.

Everything had started well once we had got ourselves into the stadium. Despite arriving well before kick-off, we had been forced to park well away from the ground. It had also been a struggle to find our seats in Hearts' new ultra-steep stands. Confusion abounded among supporters and stewards as to who should sit where. Tynecastle was thronged with Hibs fans and it seemed like most of us were in the wrong seats. We had barely settled down in our proper place to watch the game when Hibs were ahead. Ivan Sproule sprinted to the goal line and Steven Fletcher expertly converted his pin-point cutback. Shortly afterwards, a Scott Brown shot hit the bar. We sat back to enjoy the rout but it did not materialise. St Johnstone played splendidly and if they had been able to add a cutting edge to their excellent lead-up work, Hibs would have been in serious trouble. Rob Jones at the back was magnificent and time and again he and his fellow defenders repelled raids on the Hibs goal where young Andy McNeil also stood firm. This was not the way we had expected this game to go and the night was developing into one of tension as Hibs continually surrendered possession and survived through a combination of good fortune and strong defence.

The inevitable happened in the second half and Jason Scotland headed the equalising goal, which his team richly deserved. We all feared the worst. Capitulation and disappointment, as so often before, seemed to be on the horizon. Collins threw on substitutes in youngsters Lewis Stevenson and Kevin McCann as well as the skilled but unpredictable Benji. This made the difference. The ship was steadied and we made it into extra time. St Johnstone, at last, showed signs of tiredness. David Murphy scored with a free kick and Benji rounded things off with a superbly taken solo goal. He left three defenders including goalkeeper Kevin Cuthbert in his wake and rolled the ball into the empty net to send Hibs to Hampden. We were there but as a famous British general once said about a historic battle victory, it had been 'a damned close-run thing.' We headed home, elated but emotionally drained. We wondered why this team of ours never made things easy for its supporters and prepared ourselves for another roller coaster ride in the final. Our opponents would be Kilmarnock who had disposed of Falkirk in the other semi-final.

Before then, there was Scottish Cup business to be done. Gretna at that point were the form team in Britain and there was not even the remotest sign of the troubles which lay in wait for them further down the line. Bankrolled by the millionaire businessman Brookes Mileson, now sadly no longer with us, the little team from Raydale Park had achieved successive promotions and were on course to move into the top flight at the end of the current campaign. They had also reached the Scottish Cup Final where they had taken Hearts all the way before losing in the lottery of a penalty shoot-out. Now they were our next opponents in the trophy which had eluded Hibs for over a century. We worried that Gretna would once again perform a giant killing act and were anxious that the extra time played in the semi-final only three days earlier would have sapped our team's strength. Our concern was unnecessary. Perhaps because Hibs had beaten them 6–0 in the League Cup earlier in the season, Gretna gave us too much respect. Hibs weren't at their best but recorded a comfortable 3–1 victory. Benji, who was on fire, chipped in with two top drawer goals.

The quarter-final draw provided Hibs with First Division opposition once more. This time, we were heading for Dumfries to play Ian McCall's Queen of the South. I could recall trips to Queens' compact but atmospheric Palmerston Park ground in the early '60s. In those days, the men from South-West Scotland were in the top league and always provided stubborn opposition. We used to stay on in the town after the game, visit the local pubs and attend the Dumfries dancing before heading back home at around midnight on our supporters' bus. Whether there would be drinking and dancing this time depended on the outcome of what was a crucial match for Hibs in their quest for the holiest of grails which the Scottish Cup had become for our club. We were assured of a warm welcome and a competitive match and it was essential that Hibs turned up in focused rather than careless mode.

In the event, we needn't have worried. David Murphy fired home a fine shot from thirty yards just before half-time but Queen of the South equalised not long after the break. Hibs responded immediately with a goal from substitute Thomas Swunme who had been John Collins' only signing in the January transfer window. This turned out to be Swunme's only contribution in a Hibs jersey. He was limited to say the least and the judgement which had resulted in our manager signing him was a portent of things to come later in the year when Collins made a much more significant entry into the transfer market. On this day, though, Swunme's strike was enough to see Hibs safely into the Scottish Cup semi-finals. It also meant that we could now turn our attention to the League Cup Final.

The final took place on Sunday, 18 March, twenty-four hours after St Patrick's Day which, given Hibs' Irish roots, was not inappropriate. Hibs and Kilmarnock were so well matched on paper at this time that they were level on points in the league. All the signs, then, were that we were in for an extremely close encounter. We travelled through to the game on a coach organised by David Igoe. David was a member of a large Hibs supporting family. Three years earlier, his dad, Jimmy, had run our bus to the League Cup Final with Livingston. I had spent a fair bit of the journey seated next to Jimmy sharing lifelong Hibee memories with a man who had supported our team for even longer than me. Sadly Jimmy had become seriously ill and was unable to attend this final. His son had stepped up to the plate to uphold family tradition. Not surprisingly, the atmosphere on our coach was poignant. There was little confidence around either. We had all been in this situation too many times before. We were certain that Jim Jefferies' Kilmarnock would make life difficult for Hibs and nothing was being taken for granted.

The weather leading up to the match had been pleasant and spring-like but on Cup Final day the skies were grey and flakes of snow swirled in the air. Walking up to the stadium, we shivered in the cold air. The shivering may not all have been due to meteorological factors though as we were very, very nervous indeed. We took our seats and found ourselves, by sheer chance, close to old friends on both sides. We shook hands and sat back to find out what fate had in store.

On this day, destiny was to deal Hibs the happiest of hands. There was only one goal in an even first half. Captain Rob

Jones leapt high into the snowy sky and bulleted a majestic header from a David Murphy corner past Alan Combe in the Kilmarnock goal. This symbolised Jones' contribution to the season. Always committed and usually inspirational, he was a towering and commanding presence at the heart of the Hibs defence. He chose Cup Final day to surpass even his previous, impressive performances. None of us felt relaxed at half-time but midway through the second half, the nerves began to recede. Steven Fletcher and Benji had scored two excellent goals and Hibs, inspired by a once in a lifetime performance in midfield from the little left-footed teenager Lewis Stevenson, appeared to be on easy street. We should have known better. Slack defending allowed Gordon Greer to pull a goal back for Killie and we all began to think, 'Oh no, here we go again.' This, though, was not to be a day for one of Hibs' infamous Hampden collapses. Benji and Fletcher both scored again and we were able to enjoy the euphoric emotion of savouring certain victory as the game approached completion.

The full time whistle was the signal for Hampden to become a Hibernian heaven. 30,000 fans in green and white sang 'Sunshine on Leith' with passion and pathos. Down on the pitch, Hibee heroes cavorted and celebrated in their own individual ways. The classy Guillaume Beuzelin sported a ridiculous top hat and the widest of grins. Benji and his little pal Zemmama wrapped themselves proudly in their national flag. Scott Brown, who had stayed and won a cup when his friend Kevin Thomson had left the club he claimed to support, carried the trophy with big Jonesy. Chris Hogg, who had had his career resurrected by John Collins, smiled quietly and took it all in. The consistently brilliant but refreshingly modest David Murphy also showed his pleasure in a typically undemonstrative manner. Ivan Sproule, irrepressible as ever, showed that it was possible to limp and jig joyfully at the same time. Ivan had been injured late in the game but he was determined not to have his ecstasy inhibited by his agony. Contrasting emotions were displayed by the Man of the Match Stevenson who had come from nowhere to star status and the experienced Michael Stewart who had been an unused substitute for the final. Lewis was all smiles while Stewart was sulkiness personified. Finally, John Collins and Steven Fletcher both reflected on the fathers whom they had sadly lost and dedicated their triumph to them.

During our happy homeward coach journey, we all felt for our bus convener David Igoe. David and his brothers joined in the celebratory songs but their thoughts must have been with their ill father back home. Jimmy, who never missed a Hibs match if he could help it, would no doubt be wishing he could have been at Hampden, but also glowing with pride and pleasure at what his beloved team had achieved. We had an unexpected passenger on our bus. Kevin Little, now a man in his mid-thirties but once a pupil of mine, had managed to miss his own coach so came back with us. Kevin had clearly done some serious drinking prior to the game and the effects of his alcoholic intake hadn't yet worn off. Kevin was loud but cheerful. He kept telling everyone on the coach what a fine head teacher I had been. When he found out that I was still playing football as I approached my sixtieth birthday, he insisted on referring to me as 'Beckenbauer.' Fortunately, he sobered up as we approached Edinburgh and by the time Princes Street came into view, he, like the rest of us, was fully focused on savouring the victory celebrations which lay ahead.

We took up a position on Leith Walk to watch the open-topped bus drive past. As the bus continued its progress towards the foot of the Walk, we headed for the stadium where the party would really begin – or so we thought. Our first surprise was seeing the immense volume of people at the junction of Albion Road and Easter Road. The police would not allow supporters to move through to the ground until the players had passed. There was genuine congestion and people found themselves being pressed dangerously against the metal barriers which had been unhelpfully and unnecessarily erected. Appeals to the police to provide some crowd control led to curt dismissal or helpless shrugs of the shoulders.

We raced along to the stadium to find that the gates were locked. Requests to the police and stewards to let us in were met with aggressive negativity. Eventually a gate was opened and we began to move in. Just as quickly, the gate was closed again and our party found itself fragmented. The group left outside, which included Margaret and Lisa, was disappointed to say the least. Those of us who had got in had the edge taken off our joy by the realisation that our loved ones wouldn't be able to share these memorable moments with us. Our disappointment and, by this time, anger mounted when we entered the South Stand to discover that the ground was little more than half full. Why on earth, on a day of rare Hibernian triumph, were large numbers of the club's faithful followers, who had displayed devotion to the cause over many years, often in the face of adversity, being denied the opportunity to take part in something special?

When the manager and players took to the field with the CIS League Cup, the situation deteriorated further. Some over-zealous youngsters ran on to the field to congratulate their heroes. Instead of treating this minor act of excessive enthusiasm as exactly what it was, the police over-reacted and brought events to a premature halt. Nothing could take away the pleasure and pride of a great day in our team's history, but what passed for the post-match celebrations certainly did their best to sour what should have been an unequivocally happy experience.

Next day Margaret telephoned Rod Petrie who, to his credit, spoke to her at length. Our chairman told Margaret that all the major decisions the previous evening had been taken by the police. He gave her the name and telephone number of the senior police officer who had acted as match commander. When we contacted him, this gentleman's response was predictable. He insisted that he had acted in the interests of public safety and had taken every decision in consultation with the club. The excuses were ineffectual and there is no doubt that a major Hibernian party had quite unnecessarily been well and truly pooped. Rod Petrie decided to make up for the unsatisfactory post-match celebrations by parading the cup after our next match, which was a derby against Hearts. When most of us heard this news, phrases like 'tempting fate' and 'hostage to fortune' came into our minds.

The Hearts game did indeed provide the predictable anti-climax which we had all feared. Hibs played well enough without hitting top form. Our local rivals lined up ten men behind the ball and defended as if their lives depended upon keeping their goal intact. Time and again, Hibs won free kicks and corners. On each occasion Hearts defender Marius Zaliukas physically man-handled Rob Jones to stop him challenging for the ball. It was a clear penalty kick each time but referee Kenny Clark chose to turn the proverbial blind eye to every offence and Hearts escaped punishment for their repeated foul play. The final irony was that in a rare Hearts attack near the end of the game, Hibs' young goalkeeper Andy McNeil made an error and Zaliukas, of all people, scored what proved to be the only goal of the match.

To state the obvious, no one really felt in the mood to acclaim the players as they brought round the cup, which had been won so gloriously seven days earlier, after a derby day defeat that had been undeserved and earned by unashamedly negative tactics. There was worse to come. The Hearts fans in the South Stand refused to leave the ground at the end of the match. They knew that the cup could not be paraded until they had departed and therefore wilfully decided to stay put. The police who had dealt, in the opinion of many people, in a heavy-handed manner with Hibs supporters in their time of triumph the previous Sunday, now adopted a softly, softly approach. The Hearts supporters were allowed to stay seated and deliberately spoil Hibs' moment of glory for a ludicrously long time. When the upholders of law and order eventually managed to disperse the visiting supporters, many Hibs fans had already grown tired of waiting and left the ground. Those of us who remained were too cold and too frustrated to take much pleasure from the parading of the trophy when it eventually took place.

The derby may have been a letdown but we had much bigger fish to fry before season 2006–07 came to an end. We were in the Scottish Cup semi-final against Dunfermline, managed by former Derry City boss Stephen Kenny, who were languishing at the bottom of the SPL. Surely we would never have a better chance to reclaim this most venerable of trophies? As every Hibs fan knew only too well, it hadn't been in our possession since 1902. The great team of the 1920s, the Famous Five side which had won three league championships, the team inspired by the young Joe Baker, Turnbull's Tornadoes and his late '70s squad, and Alex McLeish's combination led by Franck Sauzée had all reached finals and failed. Now, John Collins stood on the cusp of a unique cup-winning double in only his first season in charge of the club.

The week before the semi-final, a major story hit the sports pages of the Scottish newspapers. It involved Hibs and it wasn't good news. Apparently, many of the players were unhappy with their new manager's manner and methods.

They had taken the opportunity, while he was back in Monaco carrying out some family business, to approach the chairman and request a meeting to discuss this issue. Instead of telling them that he would discuss any relevant matters with club captain Rob Jones and Collins, Rod Petrie, in my opinion wrongly, invited the players to his home for a meeting in the manager's absence. If the reports in the tabloid press were to be believed, almost all the first team squad had attended the meeting. When the story broke, Rob Jones was interviewed on radio and television. I genuinely expected him to say that there was no problem and that the team's only concern was the Scottish Cup semi-final which was now only three days away. Jones was demonstrably uncomfortable in these interviews and only succeeded in making himself and the club look foolish as he repeated the mantra, 'What goes on in the dressing room, stays in the dressing room.' This patently loyal man did not want to be seen to be publicly criticising his manager but he also wanted to stand by his team mates. All he managed to do was to make himself appear evasive and uncommunicative.

John Collins also met the media. He brought his mentor Tommy Craig with him. The young manager was clearly shocked and hurt but his press conference did him few favours. Mentor Craig appeared more like a puppet master. He held an apple in his hand and every time Collins was asked a question, Craig raised the apple to his lips and muttered what he thought should be the answer. His protégé then repeated this to the assembled throng. The effect was faintly ridiculous and only added to the pantomime-style atmosphere which now surrounded the club at this most vital time in the season.

The fans were perplexed and furious in equal measure. Hibs have always had a self-destructive streak, but this latest episode took the art of shooting oneself in the foot to new levels. As always though, we turned out at Hampden in large numbers. The fans made it abundantly clear whose side they were on at the start of the match when they gave John Collins the most rousing of receptions. They also backed the team but, on the day, Hibs lacked their customary sparkle with only Scott Brown playing to form. The stalemate which followed meant that both teams would have to return for Glasgow for a replay. This match took place on a Tuesday evening and was screened live on television. These factors contributed to a low crowd and an unnatural atmosphere. Hibs played better than they had done in the first match but were still below their best. We had all the pressure but couldn't score. As full time approached, Chris Hogg, who had been immense since John Collins had restored him to the team, gave away a needless penalty. He unwisely laid his hand on the shoulder of little Adam Hamill, a tricky winger on loan from Liverpool, who went down in the box as though he had been hit by a sniper's bullet. The referee Craig Thomson, who had turned away a stronger Hibs claim when Dean Shiels was bundled over, couldn't point to the spot quickly enough. Jim McIntyre who, only two short years earlier, had punished Hibs at the same stage of the competition as a Dundee United player, converted the penalty in insouciant fashion. Once again Hibs had failed to deliver at Hampden.

Hogg's foul had been ill-advised and unnecessary. What had preceded the semi-final had been extreme folly. A season which had promised so much, and to be fair had delivered the club's first major trophy for sixteen years, now drifted to its conclusion. The last match was at home to Celtic. In the week before this game, Scott Brown agreed to join Celtic for £4.4 million. The fans were not bitter towards Brown. He was a great young player who had always given Hibs his all and was now at a stage of his career where he was able to command higher wages than our club was prepared to pay him. For once Celtic actually paid Hibs the market value for a player. They had taken Gary Caldwell for nothing and paid token fees for Didier Agathe and Derek Riordan as they approached the end of their contracts. Within weeks of the season ending, they would also deprive Hibs of Chris Killen, again under the Bosman ruling. In the case of Brown though, Hibs received full value, as did the fans when he played his last match against the club he was about to join. The little midfield power-house was at his cocky, combative best as he ran at his prospective employers time and time again. Riordan gave Celtic the lead when young Andy McNeil failed to cover his near post, but Brown equalised with a powerful header from twelve yards. This effort was, almost uniquely, applauded by both sets of supporters. Hibs introduced Ivan Sproule five minutes before the end and the little winger delivered the season's *coup de grâce* when he danced round the Celtic goalkeeper and defence to win the match with a stoppage-time solo goal.

There had been a great deal of speculation about which players may have been the ringleaders in the revolt against the manager. Some early summer departures gave fans a clue to the possible identities of these players. Simon Brown and Michael Stewart were not offered new contracts. Brown, whose performances had lacked consistency, had never been short of confidence. He left in a blaze of publicity as he revealed all in a tabloid article after his release. He claimed that Collins had displayed arrogance and inflexibility and told a story about the manager removing his shirt to impress the players with his six-pack physique. Stewart took his leave with rather more dignity and continues to deny that he had taken a leading role in the players' revolt. The red-headed midfielder had a reputation for being outspoken and it had been clear for all to see that he had been extremely unhappy with his omission from the League Cup Final team. This did not mean, of course, that he had fallen out with his manager, but it was difficult to accept Collins' assertion that Stewart was being allowed to leave for 'footballing reasons' since he was clearly an excellent player.

There was one final twist to the Michael Stewart affair. Having joined Hibs from Hearts, he now crossed the capital divide once more to link up again with the never-ending soap opera which constituted life at Tynecastle under the regime of Vladimir Romanov.

To the great disappointment of most Hibs supporters, Ivan Sproule was also transferred during the close season. Fiery and charming in equal measure, Sproule was a fans' favourite. His pace and trickery could unlock any defence. He more than made up for what he lacked in consistency with his ability to change the course of a match with one flash of brilliance. The sale of Sproule to Bristol City for a less than huge fee was unnecessary and unpopular. This move fuelled further speculation. We wondered if Ivan was also being shipped out for insubordination. He certainly couldn't have been moved out due to a lack of ability. He was an exciting and highly talented player who would be greatly missed.

Two further players left Easter Road behind. Shelton Martis, who had never looked the part, left to rejoin Tony Mowbray at West Brom and Stephen Whittaker signed for Rangers for £2 million. The likeable Whitty was a tremendous attacking full back who occasionally fell short in the execution of his defensive duties and he, like Sproule, was a vital member of the Hibs squad who would be difficult to replace. In the space of two years, Hibs had sold or lost, under freedom of contract, almost a whole team of gifted young footballers. Unsurprisingly, this had left a gaping hole in the club's playing resources.

The challenge facing John Collins, then, as he prepared for

season 2007–08 was to identify and sign new players. When he had won the League Cup, his detractors, unfairly in my opinion, had claimed that victory was achieved with Tony Mowbray's team. Mowbray may have signed the players but Collins prepared, selected and motivated the team. He deserved credit for that. Now he had the chance to place his own imprint on the first-team squad. He embraced this opportunity with gusto bringing in no fewer than nine new players. The highest profile acquisitions were Alan O'Brien, an Irish winger from Newcastle United, who was described as 'faster and better than Ivan Sproule,' and Yves Makalambay, a tall, gangling Belgian goalkeeper from Chelsea. In both cases, the manager paid significant compensation to the Premiership clubs to secure the services of their fringe players.

As the Brack family took its seats in the West Stand for the new season, our mood was realistic. We knew that no club could lose the amount of talent which Hibs had and stay as strong. We also hoped that Collins' signings might prove inspired and that our team could remain competitive. The season got off to the best possible start. One of the new signings, Brian Kerr, scored very early in the first league match against Hearts at Tynecastle and this goal proved decisive. J. C. had achieved his first away win over the 'pub team' at the third attempt. Lisa, Dominic and I watched this game on television at the home of a family friend. We didn't have Setanta and we still had no intention of seeing our hard-earned money flow in Hearts' direction. In truth, Hibs won the match comfortably but the usual derby tension caused me to shout a little too loudly at times. I think that the lady of the house, a demure non-footballing person, was somewhat taken aback that a normally calm, sane person should get so worked up over twenty-two men running around a football field. After the match, I explained to her how important matches between Hibs and Hearts were and how rare it was for our team to do what it had done that night and win at Tynecastle.

Things continued to go well. Celtic were beaten at Easter Road. Hibs played well but rode their luck. Our 3–2 victory owed as much to two uncharacteristic errors by the gifted but bombastic Celtic goalkeeper Artur Boruc than it did to any excellence on our own part. In October, almost exactly fifty years after I had attended my first Hibs match, Hibs beat Rangers 1–0 in Glasgow. I was playing on Portobello beach with my grandchildren as the drama in Govan unfolded. Around 4.30p.m. I met a work colleague. When I commented that Hibs were no doubt losing at Ibrox, to my surprise and delight he told me that, on the contrary, they were 1–0 ahead thanks to a goal from David Murphy. Murphy was one of the few top players who remained from the Tony Mowbray era. By the time we reached our street, thinking of nothing else but what was happening in the West of Scotland, there were only a few minutes left. One of our neighbours passed us and said, 'You'll be pleased. Hibs are beating Rangers 1–0.' We got back into the house in time to turn on the radio and have a magnificent result confirmed. The season was only two months old and Hibs had already beaten Hearts and both members of the Old Firm.

As fanatical Hibs fans, we should have been on a major high but we weren't. The defeat of Rangers, praiseworthy though it was, had been of the smash and grab variety. Our results to date had flattered us. Collins' signings had proved to be mediocre. Makalambay, while displaying natural talent, did not look like a technically accomplished goalkeeper and had already made a number of errors which placed him in the same camp as his less than illustrious predecessors Simon Brown, Zibi Malkowski and Andy McNeil. O'Brien could run like Alan Wells but his footballing prowess was less than obvious and he was shaping up to be a major misfit. Whatever he was, O'Brien was certainly no Ivan Sproule. The other new players were industrious and enthusiastic but lacking in class. The early indications were that J. C.'s eye for a player was less than perfect and he had gone for quantity rather than quality in the recruitment stakes. Despite the team's superficially impressive start to the season, we feared the worst. We were sure that our luck would run out and reality would kick in.

We hadn't, though, bargained on things going pear-shaped quite as quickly as they did. In Hibs' next nine matches, the team only managed one victory against bottom of the league stragglers Gretna. There were some disappointing defeats and impoverished performances. Worst of all was a home defeat to St Mirren where Hibs were abject and devoid of organisation, ideas or commitment. Concerns about John Collins' tactical acumen and team selections were beginning to surface. He was leaving out players like Merouane Zemmama and Dean Shiels and picking his own signings, who were clearly inferior. The team's formation changed from game to game, and sometimes during the course of the same game.

In December, Hibs opened their new state-of-the-art training ground in East Lothian. The club had raked in many millions of pounds by selling its best players. The money received had gone to reduce the club's debt, which was both necessary and commendable, and to furnish the building of the training ground, which had been a pet project of Tony Mowbray. This development had cost in the region of £5 million. Many fans, myself included, wondered if this sort of money could not have been better spent on putting quality players in Hibs jerseys. After all, we had unearthed the best crop of young talent in generations without having our own purpose-built training ground. Nevertheless, the money had been spent and time would tell whether it had been invested wisely. John Collins appeared at the official opening of the training centre and spoke with great enthusiasm about the new facility and how he considered it would enhance the club's future prospects. He was upbeat and positive and gave no indication of being a man with major things on his mind.

Having passed my sixtieth birthday, I was close to retirement from the Education Department. The day after the opening of the training centre, which was the day before I ended my forty-year career in education, I received an e-mail from a colleague which was entitled 'J. C. Bombshell.' For a moment, I thought that I was about to discover some startling news about the Son of God. On opening the message, however, I was almost equally shocked to discover that less than twenty-four hours after laughing and joking with the press and media and discussing his hopes for Hibs' future, John Collins had resigned. He cited lack of funding for dealing in the January transfer market as his reason. Having witnessed his singularly unsuccessful set of signings to date, most of us thought that the board had been wise to resist the manager's overtures for more money because it was more than likely that he would not spend it well. We also wondered if there was something more to Collins' departure. His recent record had been poor and a testing set of fixtures lay in wait. Had the ever astute J. C. decided that it would make sense to bail out while his stock was still high, knowing that his future prospects with the squad that he had assembled were less than rosy, in the hope that further job offers would come in time as distance added lustre to his record with Hibs?

It is not really possible to judge a manager on a tenure of just over twelve months. John Collins had brought home Hibs' first major trophy in sixteen years and he deserved great credit for doing so. He had, however, clearly presided over a dressing room which lacked unity. There had been rumours of arrogance and intransigence and he had dealt with talented but dissident players by shipping them out rather than managing them and winning them over. Many fans considered his transfer-market incursions to have been disastrous. They were of the opinion that he lacked that essential ingredient of a successful manager, an eye for a player.

I was sorry to see Collins go. I had always admired him as a player and thought he had presented an impressive image of the club as a manager. Time would have told whether he was up to the job. He had chosen to walk away and no one had forced him to do so. As I reflected on his decision, I wondered whether it was genuinely about a lack of support from the board, since he obviously knew the financial parameters within which the club operated and these hadn't changed over his time in charge. Perhaps the real reason for Collins leaving was that he had looked into the future and hadn't liked what he saw. He perceived himself as someone who succeeded and didn't want to see that image change. If that's the case, then in the final analysis he had acted in the best interests of John Collins.

I think you can always tell that someone has a large ego when they refer to themselves in the third person. This was something which John Collins did on a regular basis. There is a difference between confidence and arrogance. When Scotland played Brazil in the 1998 World Cup, Collins coolly and expertly slotted away a penalty kick. That was confidence. Before the game, as the national anthems were being sung, he winked cockily to the cameras. In my opinion that was arrogance. I am sure that John Collins wanted to succeed as manager of Hibs for the good of the club. I am absolutely certain that he wanted to do well most of all to promote himself as a high-class manager who was good enough to be offered a top job in football management. When he calculated that his poor signings and the lack of money at Easter Road were likely to prevent him from achieving his managerial ambitions he walked away.

Twenty-one years earlier, when John Blackley had similarly decided to resign as manager of Hibs, his assistant Tommy Craig had stepped into the breach with less than successful results, which had ensured that he was not offered the manager's post on a permanent basis. Once more Craig was on the scene. Yet again, he declared his desire to become manager. Like his protégé of a predecessor, Craig was small in stature but big in self-belief. When asked what reasons there were for Hibs appointing him to replace John Collins, his response was to tell his questioners to look at his CV over the past thirteen months. This was a strange answer because the only obvious impact he had made in that time was to perform his ventriloquist act behind an apple at the post player-revolt press conference, and recommend the signings of Brian Kerr and Alan O'Brien, both of whom were showing distinct signs of being substandard acquisitions.

Craig took charge for the first time when Hibs met Celtic in Glasgow just three days before Christmas. I had retired the previous day and had ended my working life with a warm glow after receiving a marvellous send-off from family, friends and colleagues. The amount of kindness and generosity which had been directed towards me made me feel really good. Celtic were unlikely to be quite so magnanimous when Hibs came calling and I didn't feel at all good about our prospects at Parkhead. As always, I travelled to the game with my Celtic supporting friends. It was our pre-match custom to meet at the Whisky Society in Leith the night before the game to discuss the forthcoming match. We usually ended the evening with a forecast of what the score might be. This time, I was in extremely pessimistic mode and predicted a heavy defeat for Hibs.

I was wrong. Hibs surprised me, their opponents and 60,000 Celtic supporters by playing really well and gaining an entirely unexpected 1–1 draw. David Murphy scored Hibs' goal before half-time. When this excellent left back limped off clutching his hamstring in the second half, we weren't to know that we would never again see him play for Hibs. This fighting draw got Craig's tenure off to a fine start. Unfortunately, it was all downhill from that point. He was in charge for three more games and they were all lost. At Kilmarnock, Hibs were disappointing. At Paisley, they were woeful. Lawrie Reilly described the performance against St Mirren as one of the worst Hibs displays in his association with the club, which ran to more than sixty years. The home match against Rangers was lost 2–1, which sounds close. It wasn't. Rangers completely outplayed us and if they had been less intent on playing the ball around and more interested in adding to their lead, we could have suffered a very embarrassing defeat. Craig's team selections were idiosyncratic and, at times, baffling. John Collins had puzzled fans with some of his player choices and it was now becoming clear that his assistant manager must have influenced him significantly in making some of his less explicable decisions in respect of personnel. Despite his overt confidence, the paucity of the team's performances under Craig ensured that once again his application to be manager of Hibs was destined to be unsuccessful.

As always, Rod Petrie was refusing to be drawn into appointing a new manager until he was good and ready to do so. There were two very strong candidates. Motherwell's Mark McGhee was having a magnificent season. The tragic death of Phil O'Donnell and McGhee's key role in holding his club together after this most sad event, combined with his candidacy for the Scotland Manager's job vacated by Alex McLeish, effectively ruled this highly impressive manager out of contention. John Hughes had done a tremendous job at Falkirk. With resources far more limited than those available to whoever took charge at Easter Road, Hughes had gained promotion with Falkirk and established his team in the SPL. They had survived not by dint of graft and defence, but through a neat passing game which was both effective and pleasing on the eye. Yogi's passion for Hibs was well documented but the word on the street was that he had got on the wrong side of Rod Petrie during his time as captain of our club. I think that most fans would have liked Hughes to be given his chance to manage Hibs, but it became clear very early in proceedings that this was not going to happen.

For a time it looked like Paul Simpson, formerly of Carlisle and Preston North End, was the favoured candidate. This did not sit well with most supporters, myself included, because Simpson lacked charisma and had taken Preston to the brink of relegation before being sacked. Eventually, two days before Hibs kicked off their Scottish Cup campaign against Inverness Caledonian Thistle, the identity of our new manager was revealed. The chosen one was none other than Mixu Paatelainen. Mixu, much loved by all followers of Hibernian, had served his apprenticeship at Cowdenbeath and in his Finnish home-land with FC Turku. Now he was back where he belonged with the hopes of what had become a disillusioned Hibs support resting fairly and squarely on his massive shoulders.

18

MIXU *IN SITU*

Mixu Paatelainen's appointment as manager of Hibs was well received by the majority of Hibs support. He may not have been everyone's first choice and still had much to prove in management but he was a Hibs man and a highly regarded one at that. As a player, Mixu had served our club nobly over two spells. In his first spell, he had of course, contrived to score a hat-trick in the 6–2 thrashing of Hearts, which Alex McLeish's team had achieved in the autumn of 2000. That in itself was sufficient to guarantee the new man in charge a generous measure of goodwill.

Mixu had no option but to hit the ground running. He took up his post on a Thursday and on the Saturday Hibs met Inverness Caledonian Thistle, a team which always caused us problems, at home in the Scottish Cup. It was my pleasure to mark my retirement by buying tickets for this match for all the family. The Bracks, then, were out in force for what was clearly a crucial contest. Hibs came into it having managed to win only one of their last thirteen matches, and that against the team at the foot of the league. Mixu's first team selection made much more sense than the choices made before him by Tommy Craig and John Collins. Creative players like Merouane Zemmama and Dean Shiels were restored to the side and Hibs, looking like a totally different team and certainly playing like one, produced by far their most convincing performance against the Highlanders since their advent to the top flight, winning 3–0. All three goals came from Dean Shiels, a slight but skilful player, who had been shamefully marginalised under Collins and Craig. That night on television, Collins in the role of media pundit, was asked why he had consistently failed to select a player as good as Shiels. He justified his actions by claiming that he perceived Shiels to be 'an impact player.' Watching the programme, I mused that it must be hard to make an impact when you are either sitting on the bench or in the stand.

Now, the new boss had to turn his attention to the league. Hibs were in ninth place. To Mixu's credit, results improved quickly. An early surge of victories, helped by a run of home matches against teams in the lower half of the league, enabled the club to rise quickly into the top six where they stayed for the rest of the season. During that time both results and performances varied. There was some very good play and some extremely disappointing displays. In the end though, the season ended on a low note with the team performing unimpressively and the fans growing restless.

The last of our top players, David Murphy, was sold to Birmingham City for £1.5 million in the 2008 January transfer window. Murphy's transfer did not just mean the loss of a classy, reliable, understated defender, but also also signalled the departure of a whole team of talented players within the space of less than three years. Such relentless selling of a football team's assets may improve the balance sheet in the short-term but can only be deleterious to a club in the long run. If the team you put on the park is mediocre then performances and results will suffer. In turn, this will lead to crowds falling and less money coming into the club, which defeat the purpose of the original selling policy.

Hibs find themselves in exactly this position at the moment. You cannot sell or lose, through freedom of contract, a list of quality players such as Whittaker, Murphy, Caldwell, Beuzelin, Brown, Thomson, Sproule, Riordan, Killen and O'Connor without suffering the impact of such a policy. Due to their selling policy and the fortunate incidence of an exceptional crop of young players who all represented realisable assets, Hibs have significantly reduced their debts. They have also built and paid for a state-of-the-art training complex. There is now a need to build a new East Stand to complete the redevelopment of the stadium. This will not be cheap and the club's debt will rise again with the result that expenditure on players will continue to be restricted.

All of this leaves Hibernian Football Club at a crossroads. They will soon be a capital city club with an excellent stadium and a first-class training ground. They will be in debt but that debt will not be excessive or unmanageable. They will, however, find it difficult to achieve success on the field. If your wage ceiling is such that top rate players will only accept it for a short time, then you will consistently lose these players and the continuity, which is a prerequisite of successful team building, will not exist. Rod Petrie and Sir Tom Farmer need to realise that football clubs ultimately stand or fall by what their team does on the pitch. Football is played on grass not in the boardroom or the bank manager's office.

Sir Tom has made it clear that, for all his huge wealth, he has no intention of bankrolling Hibs. That is fine. A one-off splurge of big money signings wouldn't work. It would make for an uneven wage structure and dissension in the dressing room. Any short-term success achieved would not be sustainable. What would help greatly though would be for Sir Tom to pay for the new stand and to clear what is left of the club's overdraft. This is something which most people would assume he could easily afford and would make a huge positive difference to Hibs. The majority of Hibs supporters already think highly of our owner. A gesture like this would ensure him immortality in the Hibernian community.

Mr Petrie has often been the object of unfair criticism. The supporters' major complaint is that he sells all our best players and this prevents a team, worthy of winning honours, from fully developing and staying together. There is some validity in this viewpoint. We could have held on to players who were well within contract for longer than we did. There has, at times, been almost indecent haste in the apparent rush to cash in on some our top performers. In the end though, given our limited crowd potential, Rod Petrie has had to sell players. By doing so he has placed the club in a strong financial position. Despite the perception that he is miserly in providing his managers with transfer funds, Rod Petrie has actually been generous in the budgets, which he allocated to both John Collins and Mixu Paatelainen. Unfortunately, J. C. and Mixu have both made poor use of the funds they have been given. Collins signed a large number of ordinary players. Paatelainen has already exceeded double figures in terms of acquisitions and very few of the players he has brought in have been of genuine Hibs class. Rod Petrie is now at a stage where he has to indulge in some carefully controlled speculation in the transfer market. He must monitor his manager's signing plans extremely carefully and ensure that the emphasis in future is on bringing in what Alex Miller would have described as 'quality players' rather than flooding the club with large numbers of journeymen.

As Manager, Mixu Paatelainen is clearly committed to the Hibernian cause. His passion for our club is there for all to see and no one can doubt the enthusiasm which he brings to his work. What is in doubt though is both his ability to identify and sign players of pedigree and his tactical expertise. He changes his team selections frequently, and often illogically, and does not seem able to settle upon an effective playing formation suited to the talent which he has at his disposal.

Under Mixu, performances and results have been inconsistent. A major clear-out of the mediocre players he has brought to Hibs is called for and the manager must ensure that future recruitment is more successful. He simply cannot afford any further mistakes in the transfer market.

Thankfully, not all of Paatelainen's signings have been failures. Colin Nish may look awkward but he is a good centre forward. He is also a lifelong Hibs supporter. The two returning prodigal sons, Ian Murray and Derek Riordan, have never hidden their allegiance to our club either, and having them both back at Easter Road is the most positive outcome of Mixu's managerial spell to date.

Murray exudes fighting spirit and his crunching tackles and driving runs have galvanised the team in every match in which he has played. He has been superb at left back, steady in central defence and inspiring in midfield. To receive the best return on his talents, Mixu should deploy Ian Murray consistently in a midfield holding role.

Rod Petrie should be congratulated on recapturing Derek Riordan from Celtic. Riordan is no angel but his footballing skills are undeniable. His control, vision, passing and ability to score both simple and spectacular goals, mark him out as a player of the utmost class. It's wonderful to have him back at Easter Road. At the time of writing, Derek has not recaptured the impressive form of his first spell with our club. Given time and enhanced fitness, I am sure that the true quality of this fine player will shine through once more.

As I reach the end of this book, Mixu Paatelainen's Hibs are a team in transition. We have the nucleus of a successful side but lack quality in certain positions. No doubt our best young players will continue to move on. We must reluctantly accept that fact. If, however, some of the money acquired from transfer sales is invested wisely in players of the quality of Murray and Riordan, then Hibs can continue to progress on the field as well as off it.

At the moment, however, periodic good performances are offset by regular let-downs. To date season 2008–09 has been one of disappointment. We have departed the Intertoto Cup, the CIS Insurance League Cup and the Scottish Cup at the first time of asking. The capitulation to Hearts in the premier Cup competition was abject and embarrassing. Our manager needs to make a lasting, positive impact soon or his job will be in jeopardy. This would be a shame since Hibs supporters like Mixu Paatelainen and respect his playing contribution to our club. In the final analysis though, success in football management is judged on performance and, in particular, results. To date, Mixu has come up short in both departments. As this book goes to press, Hibs are fighting to qualify for the top six in the SPL. The team and our manager should be achieving more. We have to hope that season 2009–10 will see them doing exactly that.

I have followed Hibs for over fifty years. I will always support and love this most romantic and enigmatic of clubs. For most of every year, each Saturday and many Wednesdays will continue to be tension-ridden occasions which can raise me to the heights of happiness or plunge me into the depths of despair. I know that disappointments will continue to outnumber triumphs. I am aware, too, that Hibs will always be inconsistent and frustrating. Despite that, we will retain our support, which is faithful beyond reasonable expectation, because Hibs fans are not hitched up to a bandwagon of success. We follow our team because we love it and it means everything to us. We know that we won't win trophies very often, we're resigned to losing our best players and we accept that referees will rarely do us favours. Despite that we always come back for more. I do not know how many more years of supporting my club are left to me but I do know that I will never desert the 'colour of the grass.' I will continue to pay up, watch and hope.

My biggest hope is that I will live long enough to see Hibs lift the Scottish Cup. Like Martin Luther King, I have a dream. My dream is that in the not-too-distant future, the whole Brack family (grandchildren included) will sit in the stand at Hampden and watch Hibs win a Scottish Cup Final by playing our traditional free-flowing football. Such an occasion – and the celebrations which would follow it – would make me the happiest man alive. I have been blessed in all aspects of my life. I have enjoyed good health and career success and have been privileged to be surrounded by a loving family. There has only ever been one thing missing. That thing, of course, is the Holy Grail of the Scottish Cup which has eluded Hibernian FC since 1902. Great Hibs teams and not so great Hibs teams have tried to win this trophy. They have all failed. Surely we will win the Scottish Cup again at some time in the future. I hope and pray that when this eventually happens, I will be around to witness it and savour it. In the meantime, I will continue to support my beloved, but infuriating, team through thick and thin. Once a Hibee, always a Hibee!